DICKER

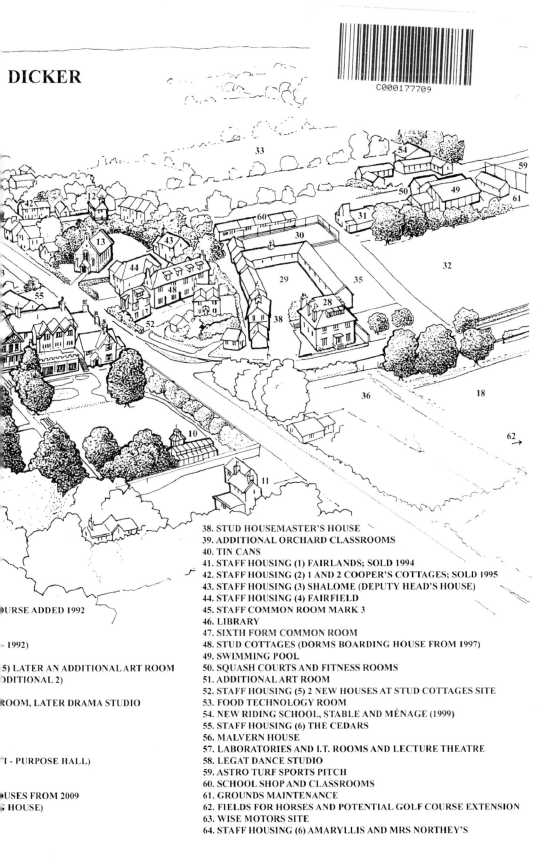

C000177709

URSE ADDED 1992

- 1992)

5) LATER AN ADDITIONAL ART ROOM
DDITIONAL 2)

ROOM, LATER DRAMA STUDIO

I - PURPOSE HALL)

USES FROM 2009
HOUSE)

38. STUD HOUSEMASTER'S HOUSE
39. ADDITIONAL ORCHARD CLASSROOMS
40. TIN CANS
41. STAFF HOUSING (1) FAIRLANDS; SOLD 1994
42. STAFF HOUSING (2) 1 AND 2 COOPER'S COTTAGES; SOLD 1995
43. STAFF HOUSING (3) SHALOME (DEPUTY HEAD'S HOUSE)
44. STAFF HOUSING (4) FAIRFIELD
45. STAFF COMMON ROOM MARK 3
46. LIBRARY
47. SIXTH FORM COMMON ROOM
48. STUD COTTAGES (DORMS BOARDING HOUSE FROM 1997)
49. SWIMMING POOL
50. SQUASH COURTS AND FITNESS ROOMS
51. ADDITIONAL ART ROOM
52. STAFF HOUSING (5) 2 NEW HOUSES AT STUD COTTAGES SITE
53. FOOD TECHNOLOGY ROOM
54. NEW RIDING SCHOOL, STABLE AND MÉNAGE (1999)
55. STAFF HOUSING (6) THE CEDARS
56. MALVERN HOUSE
57. LABORATORIES AND I.T. ROOMS AND LECTURE THEATRE
58. LEGAT DANCE STUDIO
59. ASTRO TURF SPORTS PITCH
60. SCHOOL SHOP AND CLASSROOMS
61. GROUNDS MAINTENANCE
62. FIELDS FOR HORSES AND POTENTIAL GOLF COURSE EXTENSION
63. WISE MOTORS SITE
64. STAFF HOUSING (6) AMARYLLIS AND MRS NORTHEY'S

WHY DOES ANYONE WANT TO GO TO YOUR SCHOOL?

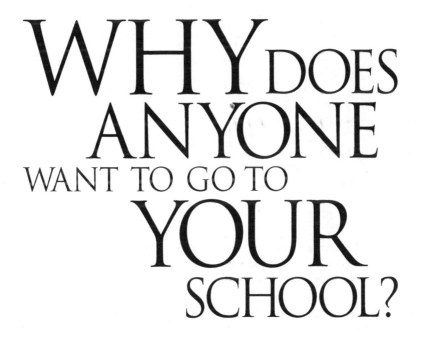

THE STORY OF ST BEDE'S AT THE DICKER 1978-2001

ROGER PERRIN

Lennard Publishing

Published in 2013 by
Lennard Publishing
a division of
Lennard Associates Ltd
Mackerye End, Harpenden
Herts AL5 5DR

© Roger Perrin 2013

The right of Roger Perrin to be identified as the author
of this work has been asserted in accordance with the
Copyright Designs and Patents Act 1988.

All rights reserved. No part of this publication may be reproduced, stored in a
retrieval system, or transmitted, in any form or by any means, without the prior
permission in writing of the publisher, nor be otherwise circulated in any form of
binding or cover other than that in which it is published without similar
condition including this condition being imposed on the subsequent purchaser.

A catalogue entry is available from the British Library.

ISBN 978 1 85291 154 6

Production editor: Kirsty Ennever
Designer: Paul Cooper
Front cover photograph: Angela Perrin
Endpapers: David and Alastair Graham

Printed and bound in the UK by Biddles
part of the MPG Books Group
Bodmin and King's Lynn

CONTENTS

DEDICATION

Why does anyone want to go to your school? is dedicated to three people: first to my father, Alan Perrin, who fortunately lived long enough to see the school solidly established, secondly to Angela, my wife, and thirdly to David Baker, sadly deceased.

My father, a leading Christian Scientist, taught my brother and me many valuable lessons; he played a central role in our early childhood as our mother had died when I was only three. Two particular principles, taught by word but mainly by example, were always invaluable. Firstly he showed us the importance of raising people up, something to which he devoted his own life: in business and in life in general he always looked for the best in everyone he met socially or who worked for him. That example profoundly influenced the way St Bede's School developed, as I hope will become apparent.

He also showed us that if things were done in the right way then the only problem that could frustrate success was fear. He would rise to any challenge fearlessly but this fearlessness was a quiet, internal, gentle characteristic – there was nothing belligerent or bombastic about it.

Without my wife Angie we would never even have got St Bede's off the starting-blocks. Her constant encouragement and support have been matched in value only by her wise counsel, her tireless and self-effacing work and her unobtrusive leadership.

Nothing over the years has ever been able to match the excitement and the feeling of good fortune and safety of arriving home, knowing that she would be there. These were two people not to let down.

David Baker was a governor of the school from the beginning and chairman from 1981 until 1999. He gave Angela and me unconditional friendship and support throughout; when things got tough David was a wonderfully calm and reassuring presence and supper in his kitchen with his wife Margaret always brought perspective. When things went well they were greeted modestly and with the generosity of spirit that marked him out. Thinking of David always brings to mind the wonderful description of charity in 1 Corinthians chapter 13 and in particular the section 'vaunteth not itself, is not puffed up....'. It is hard to imagine a more unimportant important man and equally hard to imagine how things would have gone without his steadfast presence.

ACKNOWLEDGEMENTS

It was good of my governors at the school to encourage me to write this account and I hope they will not regret having done so.

I have had much help, generously given, from many people in assembling this book. Derek Newton has always been at hand to aid my memory of facts and events and was kind enough to read through my manuscript and verify its truth. Tony Meier, the current chairman of the school's governors, and Rosemary Newton, a governor of very long standing, were gracious and long suffering enough to proof read too and it was a good thing they did for their skill in detecting grammatical flaws and inconsistencies was of the very highest order.

Others, too numerous to mention, contributed photographs and besides them there were those who said that they were looking forward to reading a copy, even buying one, and that was very helpful indeed.

I am indebted to David Graham and his talented son Alastair for the mapping which adorns the endpapers of the book.

Kirsty Ennever, the most tactful and skilful editor, pulled things into shape with great patience and no little self-sacrifice. She pointed out literary clumsiness, ill-advised statements and factual inaccuracies so politely and with such diplomatic nicety that it made chidings a pleasure to receive.

It was so kind of Griff Rhys Jones to write a foreword and beyond the call of duty to add in an afterword too. I am honoured that such an excellent writer should risk associating his fine prose with my offerings and hope it will do him no harm. He gave me an invaluable tutorial at the beginning so that I was able to start writing and he probably sensed that Angela would keep me working when the excuses started; I am grateful that indeed she did.

My greatest debt though is undoubtedly to Adrian Stephenson for agreeing to publish this book. He is a great friend of long standing but he did not have to put the name of Lennard Associates at risk by undertaking the task. It has been a real pleasure to discover at first-hand what he has been doing so professionally all these years when I thought he spent his entire time playing hockey.

FOREWORD

I remember we were delighted with Mr Perrin when we first encountered him in 1970, or whenever it was. We were new to Medieval History. This was an arcane choice as an A-level subject, and attracted some of the more (hem hem) romantically inclined of the fifth form – Holloway, Deakin and me – and others I can't now remember and remain too lazy to look up. Mr Perrin was not really much more deeply informed than the rest of us. He was quite a new schoolmaster. He seemed rather amused to be discovering the whole subject, indeed, teaching it for the first time, simultaneously.

I remember, vividly, his characteristic slight uncontrolled curl of the lip and a glittering eye which seemed to imply that he was going to 'have a go', come what may, that it didn't really matter a whole lot, and that there was something wickedly amusing about the whole enterprise and the gall of it. All rather winningly juvenile, really. And we were bolshie six-formers at the end of the sixties the bolshie decade, absolutely and unequivocally convinced in our bolshie way that cleverness, our cleverness, a cleverness for which we had been primed and selected in our Essex direct grant school, was the only worthwhile value in the universe. It was a school of opportunists. It believed in itself. There was no deference to class or money, or equality. Smart-arse was king. Our Oxbridge set was about swagger, balls and knowing laughter. Our teachers were there to prick our bubbles with amused condescension, but a thinly disguised hint of approval. I rather liked the way that Mr Perrin liked to launch himself on a discourse on, say, the Knights Templar, knowing full well that he was awarding himself points for ingenuity as much as acuity, or even research. He freely admitted he was still reading the stuff. It was fresh to him and fresh to us. We got along just fine.

After leaving, I kept in touch intermittently. I hardly know why. Admiration really. I was lucky with my teachers in the sixth form – I rather liked them all. They were all men of principle and dedication. Exemplars. Enthusiasts. How did they remain so with a different set of boys tramping out in front of them every year? It makes them even more exemplary. But I corresponded with Roger and he told me stories about Yick and Spiv and HB and all the other stars of the theatre that is the staff. We caught up and filled in.

Now I have a chance to know what it was he was doing himself the rest of the time, by reading this book. This is the story of his life, his achievement and his fun. All headmasters have an act. They take centre stage and in front of the quizzical gaze of a lot of other teachers and hundreds of surprisingly suspicious children they have to give the impression that all is going to plan. They have to, even if they don't have a plan. The inmates must never be allowed to guess that anything other than the proper maintenance of discipline and the demands of the institution are in order and not only that but preordained by some ancient tradition. How marvelous to read that in reality all is chaos. That far from conjugation or subjugation the headmaster is worried about the wiring or the plumbing, or the accounts. It brings a great blast of Ealing Comedy to the affair and one half expects to see Margaret Rutherford striding out of the nearest bramble bush. She doesn't, but the adherents of Gurdjieff, Messrs Gabbitas and Thring, Horatio Bottomley MP and other captains of industry come marching through the shrubbery.

On the one hand, this account is totally separate from my experience of Roger Perrin. I am selfish enough to focus the whole of Mr Perrin into two years in that long classroom next to the careers office behind the school shop. For him that was a fraction of the story. On the other hand, it was the person that we met then, that I meet now when he rings me up to ask me to write this, that person who made this subsequent story happen. He is still so much exactly the same bloke. So did what I liked and rather admired get passed on to others? Thanks to this marvellously readable account, I know that it did.

AFTERWORD

I really should write the afterword too. I made my entrance and departed before this story began and then rolled up at the very end, when Roger was retiring. Derek Newton invited me to what he called 'a little dinner party'. Could I, perhaps, say a few words about what Roger was like in the old days? This was understatement of an overstated mien. 'Little dinner party'? It was a huge event. There were thousands there. I goggled. I should have realised. Thousands had been affected by his slightly *dégagé* presence over the interceding 40 years. Only those who could squeeze into a tent the size of Wembley were able to come to pay tribute.

I had prepared just those 'few words', as asked. They were hardly adequate for a stadium crowd. I spent the meal quaking, grim, and as usual abysmal company for my neighbour. (In this case, Angela. Sorry Angela) Two other headmasters spoke before it was my turn. Real professional speakists, they swaggered up and transfixed the audience. In my misery, I noticed that they were orating slowly and deliberately. As headmasters will. So I decided to emulate them. I only had five or six sentences. 'Ladies ...' I began, and waited. For about a minute. The throng began laughing; possibly with embarrassment. Good. '... and gentlemen.' A nice warm cackle. Off we went, like a praying mantis on valium.

I learned a valuable lesson from those teachers that night. About timing. Like all lessons from all teachers it was one that I have never been able to apply, ever again, in real life. I came to observe and stayed to marvel. This was like Mr Chips. There were the usual beaming faces, ranks of them, the usual crazy evening dresses and over-prepared haircuts, and an almost palpable wave of good feeling. Respect and affection, I suppose. For Roger. I just had to pay tribute. So I did, concluding with a salutation in dog Latin.

'No Latin,' was Roger's only instruction for this bit of puff. So, no Latin. I'll leave it out. I can't remember it anyway. Except to say *Salute Rogerus*. A-plus.

Griff Rhys Jones
November, 2012

9

This book is a history of the first 23 years of St Bede's School at The Dicker, now a leading independent school known as Bede's Senior School. It is still happily situated at The Dicker, in the village of Upper Dicker in East Sussex. In combination with its junior school, St Bede's educated more than a thousand children and young people in 2001, a huge contrast to the 23 on the roll in the first term of its existence in 1978. The names of those founding pupils are to be found in an appendix at the end of the book.

'I DON'T KNOW WHY ANYONE WANTS TO GO TO YOUR SCHOOL'

Some time in 1999, I can't be certain about the exact date, I received a phone call which began with the words just quoted. The caller was that well-known commentator on educational matters, Dr Anthony Seldon, who was then head of Brighton College, a long-established independent school in East Sussex. A number of students had left Brighton College in the late 1990s and transferred to the school that I was then running, St Bede's School at The Dicker. This fact clearly perplexed the competitive and ambitious doctor, who was in the process of revitalising Brighton College and endeavouring to turn it into what was on its notice boards – 'The Leading School in Sussex' – whatever that meant. 'If you would like to come over to see how we do things,' I replied, 'you would be most welcome. But really it is very simple – we look after each of our students.'

That may seem a quite ridiculously simple philosophy, but if 'looking after' is carried through with a detailed thoroughness that is not subject to any educational prejudice, enslavement to received wisdom or a compulsion to follow current educational fashions then, believe it or not, people *will* want to come to your school.

St Bede's School at The Dicker had been in existence for just over 20 years in early 1999. Its students were boys and girls aged between 13 and 19 (years 9 to 13 in educational language) and there were between 500 and 550 of them, of whom about 300 were boarders. St Bede's had started up as a school in 1978 with 23 boys and girls who were 13 years old or thereabouts. My name is Roger Perrin and I was appointed head of this school before it opened. When I completed my contract in 2001, bequeathed to my successor were over 600 students at The Dicker; and, as I write this in 2009, there are about 900 (nearly1400 if one includes the preparatory school of the same name, situated in Eastbourne, with which it merged in 1999). This is the story of how St Bede's by 2001 had become the largest independent school in Sussex, having been almost certainly the smallest just over 20 years before: the story, I dare to suggest, of the UK's leading independent foundation of its type of this generation.

Those who have encouraged me to write this history have two quite separate agendas. Firstly there are those who realise that unless someone records what actually happened at the beginning, then there is a very fair chance that when, at some future date (the centenary of the institution for example), a history is commissioned, there will be a shortage of genuine authoritative documentation of the earliest days. Thus, with no one alive to consult, the future author's imagination (an essential tool for any really good historian) can suffer an adrenaline rush so to speak – and the result can be an enjoyable form of historical fiction. Thus there is some desire, understandably, for an accurate chronicle of events.

Secondly, there are others who want to know why this little project succeeded, against mighty odds, where others that perhaps appeared more glamorous fell by the wayside. Possibly this history will satisfy this second requirement to a greater extent, for the first can mostly be answered by carefully detailed appendices that list the progress of finances, student numbers, the development of and acquisition of the school's buildings and properties, and the details and dates of office holders and other key members of the school's establishment. In any case, miraculous as some of the events in this history might seem, who from St Bede's would dare take on the Venerable One at his own game...?

WANTED: HEAD FOR NEW SCHOOL
Apply PO Box 305, *Times Educational Supplement*

In the late 1970s we were living in a school boarding house beside the Ingrave Road in Brentwood, Essex, the very house that, by chance, features in Jack Straw's recent autobiography. With the assistance of Angela, my wife, I as housemaster looked after 50 or so boys who were boarders at Brentwood School. I taught medieval history in which the school had a long and rather distinguished record. I also spent hours coaching football (the 'on the carpet' sort played by West Ham) and cricket (after the style of Gooch and Lever). The chairman of the governors was Sir Hubert Ashton, a former captain of Essex CCC, the head was Richard Sale, formerly an opening batsman for Derbyshire and a Football Association Councillor, while the school shop was run by one Ken Preston, a legendary opening bowler for Essex.

I was a keen games player who had by now been entirely won over from a career in the law (I had taken up teaching to provide some funds in a difficult interim period, whilst changing from solicitor to barrister): hence desiring the opportunity to play and coach sport, or rather games, for a large part of every day I found myself under a distinctly sympathetic regime and thoroughly enjoying myself. In addition, through running the school's library, another side-line, I gained much valuable insight into how to counter despair and how to resist the temptation to generalise about the unsatisfactory nature of humanity.

I had also by this time earned my only claim to fame – unbeknown to me at the time, I had become Griff Rhys Jones's favourite teacher! (The comedian, actor and author revealed this, with pleasing reasons, many years later in *The Guardian*, in an article I have chosen to take seriously!)

As housemaster of one of the school's boarding houses, my days were long and full, there were seven of them in every week and school holidays were deserved and relished. What I have failed to tell you is that, with three young children aged four and under, Angela, whose grasp of reality and sound judgement I was accustomed to rely on, had understandably had enough of sharing our living space with 50 or so charming boys and the superb staff that came with them. Simultaneously she was required to look after our own family, as well as control a team of cleaners, listen to all their tales of domestic ups and downs, providing sympathy and guidance as required, cook meals for our resident staff, in addition to managing all the health and welfare issues that concerned the boys and of course their parents.

In a rare moment, when Sally did not need feeding, Lucy was not exercising her lungs or a two-year-old's initiative and Giles was not being taken to or collected from Mrs Potter's nursery school, Angie advised me that the time was right to look for another job. Hard to believe I know, but there you are! This was early in 1978.

I found the *TES* (*Times Educational Supplement*) in the staff common room. Much thumbed it was, as usual, by those who liked to demonstrate in public that they were ripe for advancement. I secretly smuggled the paper back home for an hour or so. Quite genuinely, this was the only time I had ever surveyed the lists of appointments vacant. That very day, though, I obediently produced a CV and applied for the headships of two ancient schools up north which I knew I had no chance of getting and didn't want to go to anyhow.

Out of a sense of adventure, lured by the 'cloak and dagger' approach, and to further demonstrate my commitment to the family plan, I wrote to PO Box 305: Wanted Headmaster to Start New School, it read. It turned out that the contents of PO Box 305 were sent to Eastbourne, to be opened by one Peter Pyemont. As I set off for an exploratory interview my head of department, Joe Hodgson, renowned for producing succinct and utterly memorable remarks ('anyone can write a long essay – it takes a good man to write a short one') asked me where I was going. 'Oh! Eastbourne', he said. 'Well, you won't have anywhere else to go then!'

A CONVERTED GARAGE

If you analyse the qualities of truly excellent teachers, it seems to me that there are three traits that they all exhibit. First, the ability to be a really good salesman or woman, with an enthusiastic belief in their product; second, good acting skills; and third, they tend to hate losing.

Peter Pyemont had all three of these attributes. He was well known on the county hockey scene as someone who, whilst skilful, did not take prisoners; he enjoyed acting and producing plays; and he was a first-class salesman. It was this last quality that he needed most when interviewing any potential head of the proposed new school.

The background was this: Peter was currently head of the preparatory school he had attended as a boy. He had bought it at the age of 25 when his enthusiasm for stockbroking had waned. The school was called St Bede's and it occupied a very tall, imposing building with views directly out over the English Channel. Under Peter's management, the school had, by 1978, grown from one with a roll of 70 boys to one that educated both boys and girls, numbering well over 300. Indeed, St Bede's was one of the first co-educational preparatory schools in the country and, by leading the way, it had become hugely popular.

The school had by now become a charitable educational trust, overseen by a board of governors selected by Peter Pyemont himself. Quite rightly, they agreed with his views on education and in general let him get on with his job unhindered. He had won their confidence with a mighty successful operation and now he and the board members wished to provide the advantages of their collective vision and methods to boys and girls after they left the preparatory school at thirteen.

It was as well that their confidence in the head was already well established, for the reality of this proposed new school was a little less clear. Before me, on my arrival, displayed upon an impressive board was a collection of architect's drawings, which were clear if you knew what they represented. Peter Pyemont's commentary on them was certainly very clear, of the … platoon <u>will</u> advance at 0500 hours and <u>will</u> capture the enemies' … variety. He informed me that '… the new school will start in these buildings which <u>will</u> be ready by September'. (It was now April 1978.) '... and in the course of the first year of operation we <u>will</u> acquire new premises outside Eastbourne where the school <u>will</u> have its permanent home ...' he continued firmly.

There was absolutely no mention of where the boarders would sleep or where a head and his family would live – but so what? Isn't it amazing what power can exist in an architect's drawings, even these drawings which showed the conversion of the headmaster's garage into a new school? It was obvious to Peter – and so to me – that the plans would work. Such are the powers of the gifted salesman!

Most of the rest of the interview was taken up with exchanging anecdotes about various teams and individuals to be found in the upper echelons of the south-east's hockey-playing fraternity. As I had entered the room where the interview was to take place, which was adorned with pictures of vibrant activity, showing victorious boys and girls all supremely happy, the most amazing thing for me was to be confronted with a face that was surprisingly familiar, from Oxfordshire v Sussex hockey matches.

MEET THE GOVERNORS

'If you are still interested in the job I think you ought to come and meet the governors as they would like to speak to all the short listed candidates.' Peter Pyemont phoned back the next day and another outing to Eastbourne was arranged.

Although the new school was to be called St Bede's, it was to be a newly formed and separate Charitable Trust and to have a quite separate board of governors from that of the prep school. It was not immediately apparent to me why this had to be the case but the reasoning soon became clear. The governors of the new school had been (still were at this stage) governors of the prep school, but they were only the ones who wholeheartedly supported the setting up of a senior school.

It later transpired that some of the other prep school governors felt that the establishment of a new senior school would upset other local schools that had long dominated the market for the over-13 age group and would thus put the relationship with, say, Eastbourne College, at risk. They also thought that such a project would distract both the head and the preparatory school staff from their primary tasks. Further, some felt that the presence of a group of adolescents would lower the tone of the place and put the reputation of St Bede's at risk (in fact for at least ten years there remained among some of the prep school governors and certain staff a feeling that association with the 'other' St Bede's, even by name, was a bit of an embarrassment.) Some also felt that the preparatory school should not waste its money on risky ventures; it was, in the words of one of the governors, the most profitable preparatory school in the country, so why put that at risk?

Thus the governors I met were those who went along with Peter Pyemont's plan. He regarded these people primarily as friends; thoroughly useful sources of expertise they may have been, but largely they were there, in his view, to formalise his decisions. After all, he had selected them all himself in the first place. As Peter had decided to offer me the job and the governors seemed happy enough, following a surprisingly short interview including a brief discussion of salary; during this I said that I would be happy as long as we were not any worse off than we were at Brentwood and that was agreed, although Jack Hawkins, of whom more later, did suggest that, as an incentive, part of the salary might be ten per cent of any profits; if only one could have read the future! A letter came the next day, offering me the post. Incidentally, I had also met the prep school's bursar, Colonel Mitchell, who was sadly to die within a few months of our meeting. He was replaced by Lieutenant Colonel Oliver Keef, who was additionally to act as bursar to the new senior school for its first two years. Of great significance, I also met the preparatory school trust's secretary and clerk to the governors, Sidney Penhallow – 'Pen'. Here was someone of whom Peter Pyemont certainly took notice, and who was to be an immense help and support to me too during our school's early years; more about him later.

The founding board of governors of the new school consisted of: Denis Martin-Jenkins, the chairman (he ran Ellerman Lines, a famous shipping company); Jack Hawkins (chairman of Hawkins and Tipson, a medium-sized industrial conglomerate and a major local employer); Tim Foord (a local solicitor); Professor Michael Thompson (Professor of Physics and later Vice-Chancellor of Sussex University); David Baker (a local farmer); Anthony Hawkins (a local accountant); and Peter Pyemont himself. As we shall see two of these governors in particular, David Baker and Peter Pyemont, were to become critical to the success of the new school. Jack Hawkins was also vitally important in the first year or two and would have remained so I am sure but for his untimely death.

Once the firm job offer arrived, a serious family discussion ensued back in Brentwood. With much sadness, but enthusiasm too, on my part, and rather less sadness on Angela's, it was decided that this was too good an opportunity to pass up. If the venture succeeded it would be really exciting. If it were to fail it would almost certainly do so within a year or two and at the age of 37 it would be possible for me to resume my career almost as if nothing had ever happened. It was, in snooker terms, 'a shot to nothing'.

It was difficult telling Richard Sale that we were leaving – he had become a good friend and had been really generous in the opportunities he had given me in a most distinguished school. He had taken me on in 1970 as a not-very-experienced prep school teacher with no teaching qualification and a lowly degree in law, to teach a timetable that was largely at sixth and seventh form (Oxbridge entry) level.

Richard asked me whether I was really certain about my decision; in his view it was a risky venture. Also, as it was May, he pointed out that he could not release me until December 1978. Peter Pyemont said that was all right and that he would be the acting head of the new school, which was to open in September, for its first term.

WHY HAVE A NEW SCHOOL ANYWAY?

So was this new school a good idea or was Peter Pyemont just hyperactive? Was there any discernible need for an additional school to serve this age group? After all, the boys could leave St Bede's prep school and go on to Eton, Winchester, or the Sussex schools – Lancing, Ardingly, Hurstpierpoint, Brighton, Worth Abbey, Eastbourne College (day or boarding) – or indeed anywhere in the UK. The girls could choose from at least six local independent schools (day or boarding) or they could choose Roedean, Benenden or any other girls' school they wished.

Despite these considerations, though, a logical case could still be made for the development of a new school. When local school politics were added in there were other incentives that the competitive Mr Pyemont would have had in mind. One thing obviously missing from the existing short-list of schools was that not one of them was co-educational. The new school would be the first co-educational senior independent school in Sussex, apart from the Rudolf Steiner schools, which were lovely but not to everyone's taste. Given that most preparatory schools and all the state schools were co-educational, what was there about the eight weeks of the summer holidays that turned boys and girls from happily co-existing to being in need of segregation?

I can't carry on with the narrative without a deviation at this point, for I can hear the well-rehearsed apologists for single sex senior schooling warming up in the background: boys and girls, they say, get better results if they are segregated.

I suppose to some extent it depends what you mean by 'results'. But it is worth considering that, whilst all the earnest learning of academic subjects is going on, the protagonists, i.e. the students, who inevitably are of a different generation from most of their teachers, are actually growing up. In my view they have a right to do so in an environment that acknowledges that the other half of the world exists and that they can learn to cope with it successfully.

Let's put it this way: the sooner one is 'dumped' in a relationship and learns that life goes on and that there are better opportunities round the corner, the better; for the later this situation occurs – and for most of us it will occur, sooner or later – the more injurious to health and prospects it becomes.

All I do know, as someone who was educated in a male-only environment from the age of 9 to 21, and whose teaching experience before 1979 had been in single sex establishments, is that after just a few months in a co-educational school I would never have gone back to teaching in a single sex model. The atmosphere in a co-ed school was just superior in everyway. It was more varied and exciting, more instructive, just more reasonable. The girls had no time for stupidly 'macho' boys, or teachers who shouted. Both of these types in turn wanted to be respected by the girls or colleagues and so they 'grew up'. The boys, meanwhile, had no time for those who whispered behind others' backs or teachers who were fussily 'schoolmarmy'. Both of these types, too, had a wish to be respected by the boys and similarly they 'grew up' as well, or left. There were far less petty explosions in the staff common room from either the male or the female teachers, none of whom would wish to look ridiculous in the others' eyes.

Those who claim the superiority of the single sex school speak for a very small minority. Sometimes they have no experience of co-ed schools themselves, having often come from highly selective schools where the results are bound to be excellent but would actually be no better than those of a similarly selective co-ed school. Supporters of single sex schools also tend to ignore the fact that there are some well-balanced and highly successful Americans, and even top-performing Europeans, few of whom are likely to have been educated at such a school.

A few years on, when St Bede's girls were invited to local boys' schools for dances, I would often ask them how they got on. They would tell me what form the evening had taken and usually said that they had enjoyed themselves. On one occasion I asked what the girls from Roedean were like. Oh, the reply came, they were really nice but they were so young for their age, and at the end of the evening they had to be rounded up for they were off in the bushes with the boys! These were all sixth-formers too, as the St Bede's girls were. Maybe this was just a one-off occasion – I am sure the Roedean girls are not like that now – but small wonder if they were then, having been so segregated. Boys were not a 'big deal' to our lot!

Of the schools mentioned by name in the first paragraph of this section, all except one of the boys' schools are now fully co-educational while most of the girls' schools have closed, although a small number who indeed do a good job remain, prospering to a greater or lesser extent.

Now where was I? Yes, we were to be the county's first co-educational senior school, but there were other reasons why starting out at this particular time made sense. By 1978 every grammar school in Sussex had been done away with and, although parents could always move house to Kent, it seemed likely that there would be more candidates in our area for independent schools as sadly the comprehensives that the county offered were not thought to be performing that well. I say sadly, for the idea behind comprehensive schooling seems really good; but for various reasons these schools were badly mismanaged from government to local authority and then teacher level. This could lead to another digression, but I resist – maybe later!

There were other reasons too as to why a new co-ed senior school seemed so viable. The success of co-ed preparatory schools meant that many parents were asking where their children could go on to that followed the co-ed pattern. Also in the late 1970s the established independent schools were often over-subscribed, meaning that many were refusing to take those boys, and to a lesser extent girls, who could not score high marks in their entrance examinations (generally Common Entrance). In particular the increasing numbers of boys and girls from other countries, whose first language was not English, were difficult to place for they were 'known' to lower 'standards' wherever they went – or so the small-town, small-island versions of the English middle classes believed. Peter Pyemont also saw that a number of other local prep schools were starting senior schools and he did not wish St Bede's to be left behind. As it happens, all of these other foundations have either come to very little or in the majority of cases have failed and disappeared altogether.

THE GRAND OPENING

Angela and I drove down to Sussex from Brentwood on a Sunday in early September 1978 for the start of the new term. We were due in Eastbourne for a late tea at which we would meet the new boys and girls and their parents and also the staff of the new school. When we arrived they were all there in the smallish entrance hall outside Peter Pyemont's study; we all fitted in quite easily and chatted away in a very relaxed manner.

Eventually I climbed the staircase that led from the hall and, thus elevated, welcomed everyone, commiserating with the nervous newcomers who were about to experience, in several cases, their first night at boarding school, but assuring everyone that this would be a happy place. Then I introduced the staff to them, emphasised how lucky they were to be a part of such a successful school, and wished everyone luck.

Then we drove back to Brentwood and on the journey wondered whether they would all still be there when we returned properly in January. How would those in floods of tears when we left, saying goodbye for the first time to parents who lived halfway across the world, survive that night, we wondered? Would the delightful but inexperienced staff still be there with their initial enthusiasm still intact?

Whatever happened, the school now officially existed; it would have a history. The opening had been about as low-key as could possibly be imagined; there was a desire to go about things as quietly, almost secretly, as possible. Elspeth Pyemont, an accomplished publicist who kept the local press busy with accounts of the achievements and advances of St Bede's, remained silent on this occasion and sensibly so, for it was in our interests to get off to a quiet start without jeopardising the excellent relationships with other local schools with annoying fanfares.

THE NEWCOMERS

The true heroes of St Bede's senior school remain the parents whose faith – bravery? foresight? desperation? foolhardiness? – made them decide to entrust their children to this untried venture. Second on the 'honours board' were those who committed their careers to working for such an obviously fragile organisation. Perhaps this was not quite the case for the very first intake was part of, or at least they thought they were part of, a school that had been running since 1895.

The majority of the first 23 students (whose names are recorded in Appendix 1) were boys and girls who had been at St Bede's Preparatory School. These 13 had liked it so much that they wished to stay on in a co-educational environment. Their choice undoubtedly gave added confidence to the other ten, who were of nine different nationalities and had been recruited mainly through the well-established agencies of Gabbitas-Thring or Truman and Knightley. Of the 23, 15 were boarders and eight were day pupils. They were all aged 13 or 14 and were all, in everyday language, in year nine. They ranged from being academically very able to those with significant learning difficulties, from being literary high-fliers to those with an inability to speak any English at all.

Of this first intake, 17 were boys and six were girls. These proportions remained uncannily constant for the next two decades. These students and those who joined them in the second year determined the very nature of the new school, its ethos, its radical and pragmatic responses, the very way it was run. There is nothing very surprising about this for what is a school if it does not respond as precisely as is possible to the needs of its students? The fact that the boys outnumbered the girls by about two to one was not a disadvantage. Girls were happy to be in a minority whilst boys were relatively hopeless if the roles were reversed. It became apparent to me over the years that two or three girls in a class of, say, 15, would form a close bond and be a strong unit. Three boys in such a class would constantly try to outdo each other and would wind up with four 'mothers' each! Additionally, there was a wide gulf in maturity, particularly between the ages of 13 and 15; by the time they were 18, the boys had caught up.

The other newcomers were of course the staff, of which there were three full-time teachers. Mary Bide was one of these and this was her first post. Besides being academically gifted, Mary also possessed the warmth, good humour and positive spirit that won over her classes at once. She clearly liked the boys and girls and this was just as well as she taught all the maths and all the science in the school. Mary was to remain a marvellous contributor to the school for its first four years. It was no surprise that she later became one of the first women to be ordained into the Church of England. At one time she was Precentor at Oxford Cathedral and at the time of writing is the Rector of Wimbledon; friends of mine from SW19 speak very highly of her sermons.

Stephen Barnes was also starting his first teaching job. He was a likeable enthusiast and taught all the English, history and geography, or at least he did so until I arrived to help him out a bit in the second term. I was the other full-timer and when I eventually turned up I taught some English, some geography, some history, woodwork (a course based on the contents of my tool box), musical appreciation and coached all the boys' games.

The preparatory school provided various part-time assistants – Peggy Metcalfe of Swiss origin taught French, Mrs Boyle taught cooking (over the next 20 years this subject posed briefly as 'home economics' before it graduated to the grand title of 'food technology'), Mr Taylor taught art, while P.E. and games came under Mrs Miller and Mrs Cousins for girls, and Mr Smith, Mr Pyemont and myself for boys. There was a bursar, initially Colonel Mitchell, who, as mentioned earlier, died suddenly, being succeeded soon afterwards by Colonel Oliver Keef who, as has already been mentioned, remained bursar of both schools for the first two years of the senior school's existence.

EXISTING AND SURVIVING

The school's first year, spent in the converted garage (it was now two classrooms and a small common room for the boys and girls) whilst otherwise sharing all the prep school's facilities, was not a truly comfortable time in a number of ways. We existed with the enthusiastic support of Peter Pyemont but under the critical gaze of most of his staff. They were used to neatly dressed little people who, cheerfully on the whole, busied about their day with charm and innocence. They were very obviously unused to adolescents who wore no particular uniform, were far too large and had (in the case of the boys in any case) a secretive and faintly hostile culture, which involved a minimum (or so it seemed) of conventional good manners and not infrequently an unintentional boorishness. This stemmed from a mixture of acute self-consciousness, self-absorbedness and macho/hormonal development. These students were simply not good enough at queuing peacefully, they didn't eat up, they grunted and they developed essential skills such as spitting a long way.

The prep school's discipline (often petty in their eyes) highlighted why the natural break in schooling should come at the age of 13; up to about that age there are almost exclusively benign ways to control a school made up of mostly malleable innocents, or at least semi-innocents, who are on the whole cheerily good-natured. By contrast a school whose age-range starts at 13 will only contain adolescents; it will require a quite different regime, administered by those who find adolescents amusing or at least unpredictably exciting and who are practised at 'taking no notice' and appearing laid back, though firm in the face of objectionable behaviour.

The detailed fault-finding of those used to a junior school regime just makes matters worse. One of the reasons why so many schools in the state sector are not as successful as they could be is that 11- and 12-year-olds who are mainly not adolescent are obliged to look up to and copy their elders, who are just at the age when their examples are not helpful, to say the least. These 11- and 12-year-olds could have had the experience of being at the top of their junior school rather than at the bottom of a large school which rendered it essential for their own self-esteem and preservation to ape those in years 10 and 11. Further, spending three years perfecting adolescent behaviour without any really pressing academic goals such as GCSE to focus their minds, compounds the problem. As so often, don't blame the young, blame their unimaginative organisers.

Enough of that, though! At St Bede's Senior School lessons went on, games were played, pictures were painted, objects were made and the year was survived pretty successfully by most. On our arrival, during a snowstorm early in January 1979, we discovered that a delightful flat had been rented for us in Downs House, which was not at that time part of the prep school. Our children, beginning with our son Giles, went on to establish a 12-year-long, extremely happy association with St Bede's Prep.

The girl boarders in our new school lived in the prep school girls' boarding house, Meads End. The boy boarders, meanwhile, were housed at 21 Darley Road, Eastbourne, which was rented from a Mrs Marr for £108 per week. There were ten boys there, so it was lucky that the rules and fire regulations applicable to houses of multiple occupancy were blessedly backward at that time. The boys were 'supervised' by their housemaster, Stephen Barnes. (I have failed to say that they were under the control of their housemaster for that would not have been entirely true, nor indeed as events would show were they, in that first term, truly under even the remote control of that firm disciplinarian Peter Pyemont – let's call him PP from now onwards.)

Experience of boys' boarding school life and the suspicious and cynical outlook that such experience brings on were not part of Stephen Barnes's armoury. Those of us who know about these matters recognise at once that if it's all quiet and peaceful in the house, then something or things illegal are most certainly going on. It could even mean that the inmates are not actually there! The unpredictable bed check at one a.m. often pays off and, invaluably, also passes, valuably for the authorities, into the folklore of the house.

The consequences of this management 'innocence' came most unfortunately to my notice shortly after I had arrived in January 1979. Too much peace was, or should have been, the first sign of a problem. The third sign that all was not well was the appearance of a policeman, the second having been a phone call to let me know that four of our boys had been arrested for removing items from Boots the chemists without paying for them. The items taken were those essentials for the adolescent boy – deodorants, hair products and other items to enhance their sex appeal. The policeman wanted to search 21 Darley Road, an intelligent move, for there he discovered the results of many another raid on the good shopkeepers of Eastbourne. The whole story eventually wound up with charges, cautions and a headline in the *Eastbourne Herald* 'Police Discover An Aladdin's Cave' – as it happened, the culprits were almost exclusively from Middle Eastern parts and indeed to add to the quality of the news report one of them was actually called Aladdin!

Shortly after this incident, and of course at a time when we were trying to build a reputation that could be put before the heads of local preparatory schools, came another phone call. It appeared that not all of our boys stayed in at night – what a surprise! What was genuinely surprising though was that they went out armed! Apart from performing a little graffiti-spreading, so beloved of certain adolescents, they had entered the premises of a keen local rival preparatory school and had used the swimming-pool clock for target practice with an air gun whilst drying off after an illicit swim. Luckily, the head of the school involved was a reasonably laid-back character, who was later to become a good friend. At the time, profound apologies and some financial recompense smoothed things over almost unnoticed.

However, something had to be done to make it clear to everyone that we were not at all happy with such goings on and the culprits were asked to leave. Of course this was not good for business, in the short run at least. Cutting down the numbers in a school by about 25 per cent is poor for cash flow and unsettling to the parent 'investors'. It was a good demonstration though of the theory that a reputation grows if it is seen that strong discipline exists. The numbers in the school grew back to 23 by the beginning of our third term. Whether the newcomers would be any more law-abiding was a different matter!

There was another occasion when I believed that the total population of our little school had vanished entirely. Stephen Barnes was a keen cross-country runner and he had taken the whole school, all of them, on a run. Dusk became darkness and still there was no sign of them. Had he decamped to a rival organisation? Had they all vanished over a cliff? Eventually a phone call came through: they had been attacked and thrown into a panic by a large Alsatian dog and had fled, most of them, to a phone box. Somehow virtually the whole school was now cowering in this phone box, besieged by the slavering Alsatian; indeed I could hear it growling and barking in the background. We went up onto Beachy Head and rescued them. Who else, I mused, can say they have been head of a school that could be contained almost in its entirety in a phone box or rounded up by a dog?

FINDING MORE STUDENTS AND A PERMANENT HOME

I have to say that in the first few months of 1979 I myself sometimes wondered why anyone came to my school. Although by the beginning of March we had found a building from which the school could operate from the start of our second year in September, any parent or potential student had to commit to joining an establishment with no past record and with no building that could be viewed, either because we did not have one or because when we did have one to see it would without doubt have snuffed out any interest in all but the most compulsive of gamblers. I could only assure those I met that we had a wonderfully enthusiastic staff and that 'all would be well on the day'.

Despite my fears, by September 1979 an additional 42 students had signed on and indeed they all turned up. Where had they come from? Between January and June I had visited more than 80 preparatory schools in the south-east of England and had sent a modest little prospectus to hundreds of others. It was indicative of the very high standard of impeccable good manners that marked out these preparatory school heads that to a man they responded positively to me as a cold caller on the phone, asking if they would spare the time to see me so that I could tell them about a new school. And so I spent days rather like a brush salesman rushing from school to school, sitting in headmasters' studies having a genial chat, explaining what we were about and enquiring whether there might be one or two of their students, who were perhaps difficult to place, whose parents might like to contact me. In the vast majority of cases I was heard out politely but often it was clear that our school was not the sort of place that would be of interest to their clientele.

In some places I provided a good excuse for the head to have a drink at or near lunchtime; at others the bottle could be opened a little earlier in the evening than was usual; in other words I was a brief diversion from reality. At most schools there was plenty of reminiscence about mutual acquaintances; the fact that I had taught for five years at the Dragon School in Oxford usually sparked interest and brought forth a good tale or two.

However a few of these meetings produced some new boys and girls to join us in September 1979. They were almost all introduced as young people who were unlikely for one reason or another to get many, if any, marks if they were to take Common Entrance – perhaps they had just arrived from Iran and spoke no English or they found maths almost impossible or they were rather behind in their reading. Perhaps they were immensely difficult characters teetering on the edge of expulsion, described as "well-meaning" but "something of a challenge"; being new to the game I had no doubts that we could turn things round. Of the total number, 13 came on from St Bede's Preparatory School.

Apart from two or three 'word of mouth' recruits, like our first intake the rest came through the agencies such as Gabbitas Thring, later to become Gabbitas, and Truman and Knightley, who did very well for us and out of us. Agencies charged the schools to which they sent students ten per cent of the first year's fees. (In fact most of the well-established and popular independents hardly used them as they had no need.) Most of the boys and girls that came via this method came from overseas; but a certain number were students who were difficult to place and whose parents turned to the agencies to sort things out for them. Those difficult to place in the late 1970s and early 1980s were often those who had been asked to leave their schools or those with particularly profound learning difficulties. Generally speaking those who came from overseas took the agencies at their word and never even saw the premises their children were to inhabit – a huge blessing to us in 1979!

Why were the agencies so good to us over the early years of the school? Well, it was productive to go and see them in person every year, for in that way they could obtain at first hand information about how the school was developing and reports could be given on those they had recommended to us. Most importantly, though, we figured in the forefront of their minds and not just in a filing cabinet. (I remember one such visit particularly well. It was a brilliant spring day. To pass the time between an appointment with Gabbitas and one with Truman and Knightley, PP and I went rowing on the Serpentine; two men in dark suits just about 'pulling their weight' – a rare sight!)

Understandably the agencies liked schools that could solve their problems rather than just trying to put obstacles, often of an academic nature, in their way. In addition they liked schools that were reported back on favourably by their clients and, although I did not know this at the time, I was told later that St Bede's did particularly well in this respect.

Throughout the years St Bede's has continued to use agencies most successfully, although after the first decade our network spread all over the world and the regular visits to keep the agencies up to date became more exciting for the marketing department that carried them out. Until 1992, I was the marketing department! After a few years, the majority of entrants came as a result of 'word of mouth' recommendations rather than through the agency route.

But we must get back to the narrative. The converted garage could not accommodate more than 20 or so, while St Bede's Preparatory School definitely could not countenance any more of these ever larger aliens destroying the atmosphere and appearance of sweet, smiling innocence. We were told that the search was on for a permanent home for our school and that it was being conducted by one Rosemary Ross, a born negotiator and deal-maker employed by the firm of estate agents known then as Stiles, Horton and Ledger.

Towards the end of February 1979 PP said that we ought to go and see a couple of possible houses that Mrs Ross had found. As it happened, both were in the village of Upper Dicker. As it had also happened, about a year before, and well before we had any knowledge of St Bede's, Angela and I had been granted four days leave from family commitments by generous grandparents; blindfolded I had stuck a pin in a map of the UK to determine where we would go, and it turned out that East Sussex was to be the destination for our short holiday. We had driven through Upper Dicker at the time, unaware that a 'dicker' referred to an area of land capable of supporting ten (*decem/dix*) families in Saxon times. Rather we had commented on the potential embarrassment of having such an address and wondered what it would be like to be the vicar of Dicker.

Now by some amazing fluke I was back there again. The first place PP, Angie and I looked at was called Camberlot Hall. Completely hidden by trees, this rather run-down building with its tower seemed both out of place and incredibly spooky. Fortunately it was also too small to allow for any significant development and therefore the fact that it wasn't selling because the structural surveys were so dire did not need to concern us.

The second property was called The Dicker. This grander but certainly not beautiful house had been developed in Edwardian times as the country retreat of one Horatio Bottomley MP. Bottomley's biography has been written by at least two different authors and is recommended reading – in short he was the illegitimate son of an East End seamstress and had turned out to be a bright spark. Rising from humble employment in a printer's workshop, he had become the Member of Parliament for Hackney in 1906 when there was a Liberal (i.e. as left-wing as it got in those days) landslide. Between then and 1920 he was bankrupted out of Parliament on at least two occasions but returned with larger majorities each time; acted as the government's official recruiting speaker to raise troops for the First World War; founded the Hansard Printing Company; founded and became proprietor of the first tabloid newspaper, *John Bull*; and was heralded as possibly the next Prime Minister, having been recognised as the best orator in the House of Commons.

As the self-appointed scourge of the aristocracy and the upper classes through his often scurrilous but highly popular newspaper, Bottomley was hated by the establishment. He was truly regarded as 'the people's friend'. He also successfully defended himself in over two thousand law-suits brought against him by those dissatisfied with his business dealings or by the utterances of his newspaper. The great KCs of the day, including such stars as Marshall Hall and F.E. Smith, suffered defeats in court by Horatio, who was held in awe by them or so it was said. It did not, however, come as a total surprise to the nation when Horatio, having encouraged the many readers of *John Bull* to invest in Victory Bonds (after an exciting year or two these proved to be a 'Ponzi' scheme, paying out interest owed from the money of new investors but keeping the capital for Horatio's personal use), was found guilty of fraud at the Old Bailey in 1922. His great defensive skills and obfuscations on this one and only occasion failed to sway the jury. He was sentenced to seven years, initially spent at Wormwood Scrubs and latterly in the gaol at Maidstone.

His lavish spending at Upper Dicker was much appreciated by the village locals. As his star rose, so he employed many of the inhabitants and the architecture of the village makes it clear that the main period of development was Bottomley's. He was generous to them all; and even caused the train to stop at the nearest point on the main line at The Dicker Halt (named after Bottomley's house). This is now Berwick Station.

In addition Bottomley set up a stud farm in the village. He kept his racehorses in Alfriston with the trainer Jimmy Hare (one of them called, I believe, Hawfinch, won the Cesarewitch at Newmarket in 1897) and created a private racecourse on his land in Upper Dicker; a part of the grandstand can still be seen in a field now owned by the school's neighbours at Clifton Farm. Great were the numbers of famous people who came to Bottomley's race meetings and to stylish parties at The Dicker, which contributed mightily to the local economy. Equally extravagant was the party held to welcome the great man back from his stay in Maidstone: the Hailsham Silver Band played him back to The Dicker over the three miles from The Dicker Halt with tunes such as 'Here the Conquering Hero Comes' and at five o'clock the next morning villagers were seen carrying home pails of ale. I know this because back in 1980 I spoke to two people who had been at the party; both had worked for Horatio and had also witnessed the sad break-up of the estate in the 1930s at a sale instigated by Bottomley's son-in-law, Major Cohn.

In the future the school would put together once again much of Bottomley's estate and it is fair to say its pride would to some extent be restored. In his heyday Horatio Bottomley drank champagne for breakfast every day and was cheered onto the racecourses of Belgium and France by the bookmakers! In the end he died penniless and in receipt of the state pension (a means-tested benefit in those days) that his Liberal Party had introduced after the 1906 election. However he was still accompanied by his faithful mistress, a musical artiste – the one and only Peggy Primrose. Browsing at a bric-a-brac stall in Frome one day, I found a leather bound volume into which had been pasted all the many obituaries of Horatio, cut from newspapers from all over the world and annotated by Peggy Primrose herself: what a fluke! This marvellous book is still in the school's possession.

Despite being such a rogue, Horatio Bottomley was described by the vicar of Soho, who conducted his funeral service, as 'a man after God's own heart'. Indeed, regardless of his many fallibilities and capability for recklessly and optimistically distorting the truth, this man of great energy, generosity and kindness was probably rightly so described.

As you will realise by now, I never have been able to resist a good deviation! But back to the matter in hand: The Dicker, plus 14 acres and one or two eccentric outbuildings, was purchased by St Bede's School Trust (Sussex) Ltd in March 1979 at a cost of £140,000. Now the fun truly began.

FINANCING THE NEW SCHOOL

I should have said that the fun had actually begun a little earlier. Just as contracts for the purchase of our new home were about to be signed, PP and I went along to the National Westminster Bank in Eastbourne to confirm that a loan 'agreed' in person by Peter with the then manager, the tall, amiable Bunny Thomas, was still in order. We were met by Bunny's newly appointed successor, a short and distinctly *not* amiable person, who told us that there was no chance that he would agree to such a loan, and that in any case he was opposed to independent schools. The new man was doing what we were to discover was almost standard practice at the time, which was to demonstrate quickly on appointment how much tougher he was than his predecessor: this change in attitude was prompted by too many friendly relationships having led to deals that, in the language of 2009, could turn 'toxic'. Frankly this man did not like our prospects and, in a way, who could blame him. What a piece of luck! Strange as it may seem, this is exactly what it turned out to be.

When he heard about our setback, one of the governors, David Baker (who was to become our chairman in 1980 and remain so until 1999), suggested that we visit his bank, Barclays in Sloane Square, instead. So in February 1979, armed with a business plan put together by our admirable accountant, Marcus Page-Wood, which demonstrated with surprisingly persuasive clarity our path to a profitable future we, David, PP and I, arrived in Sloane Square to meet someone who was to become one of the more important people in the school's history. Manager John Huxley counted David Baker amongst his top clients and it took him little time to agree to fund us. Consequently we were able to go ahead with the deal to buy The Dicker.

John Huxley really did us proud. It was an advantage that he was enjoyable and humorous company; he liked a day out, and particularly one spent at the races, so by nature was inclined to take a bit of a risk. Apart from that he was genuinely interested in our project. Additionally, and perhaps crucially, he was able to communicate his enthusiasm to his superiors, who resided in awe-inspiring offices in Pall Mall.

Thus it was that from 1979 to 1983, years in which the school was to grow from 23 students to just about 250, when so much capital investment was needed to house and provide for the students' growing educational requirements, we had John's constant support. We also had the enthusiastic backing of Christopher Martin-Butler, a main board director of Barclays. He and his Labrador dog occupied one of the luxurious offices in Pall Mall and it was said that if a tricky decision had to be made, Christopher would consult the dog, and if it barked then that meant yes, go ahead!

On at least two occasions Mr Martin-Butler came to visit The Dicker and really liked what he saw; and thus it was that, amazingly, Barclays at one time loaned us one and a half times the value of all our assets. Without that help and, dare I say, the foresight of two courageous bankers, there is a very strong chance that the school would have ceased to exist. So thank you, David Baker, for a very timely intervention.

The school's first ten years were desperately difficult financially. As I have said, it was obvious that as the numbers grew, so too would the demand for capital, and people often used to quiz me about the school's endowment. The founding of schools in the UK had in the past been the work of benefactors. Very often the Church, in the guise of a bishop and chapter or a Holy Order such as the Jesuits, had provided all the funding in exchange for a greater or lesser control of the curriculum. For example, in the second half of the nineteenth century, Canon Woodard had raised funds from the devout rich or from repentant sinners to fund his group of schools. The Quakers set up numerous foundations, as did the Methodists. Wealthy men or Corporations sometimes decided to improve or further enhance their public image by setting up schools – The Drapers, The Mercers, The Haberdashers, The Corporation of The City of London, Sir Antony Browne at Brentwood (profiting from the dissolution of the monasteries, he got Battle Abbey and its estates), Sir Roger Manwood – the endowments just rolled in. But who was behind St Bede's at The Dicker? It was Barclays Bank and others of that ilk, plus the business plans of Page-Wood and Co and the willpower of the management, allied to the willingness and ability of most of the trusting parents to pay their fees on time.

Finance raised by loans from banks or overdraft facilities was not always as sure as it might appear, for although the school was always able to service the interest and repay the instalments throughout its first decade, it could not predict that it would suddenly grow by a further 60 or 70 students when these often signed on only a few weeks in advance of a new school year. For obvious reasons none could be turned away. Thus there were sudden calls for capital – for example, to buy a new boarding house in July and have it ready for September – and this immediate need to spend money put unbearable pressure on our cash flow.

New bank managers, under pressure from head office in times of economic uncertainty (the late 1970s and early 1980s was one such period, when at one stage interest rates reached 17 per cent or even more) wanted to sweep their stables clear of risk and had a weak sense of the particular history of accounts which might at first sight have appeared doubtful.

In 1984 John Huxley moved on and Christopher Martin-Butler retired. Their successors, whilst charming, were not prepared to lend us any additional capital funding and we had to have more, or else those who were about to arrive in the school would have had nowhere to sleep or study. Thus within our first ten years we moved, cap in hand, from the National Westminster to Barclays and then most surprisingly to 3i (Investors in Industry plc) and then to the Alliance & Leicester and via them to their offshoot Girobank. One or two building societies (the names of Southdown and Leeds come to mind) were also involved for minor deals too I recall.

John Huxley's charming successor at Barclays in Sloane Square, now the Knightsbridge Business Centre, smiled and said that he could not help us but he did have a favour to call in from 3i. Down to Upper Dicker came a young man (later the longstanding chief executive of Capita Services, one of the UK's largest and most successful companies) called Paul Pindar. Paul was immediately likeable, really positive and wanted to help and so 3i took over all Barclays' loans (except our overdraft) and gave us some more capital too. In exchange for this the company required monthly financial reports and a more controlling influence on the school's affairs, as is the style of venture capitalists.

By 1987 Paul Pindar had left 3i and the company also had a new chief executive, a tough uncompromising Scot. I did not enjoy meeting him. Hemmed into a corner in an office in Waterloo, surrounded by said Scot and three of his henchmen, I was told that their business was about holding equity in a business and exercising management control, not financing charities, and that therefore they wished to stop supporting us.

Once again, a surprising refusal by a trusted partner led to a much better result for the school in the long run, as someone who was to become a truly influential friend and who was also to become a first-class governor of St Bede's, now took his place in the narrative. Another important name could be added to the list of those whose significance in our development could never be overestimated, as Baker, Pyemont, and Hawkins J. were joined by Griffiths.

Mervyn Griffiths, a governor of the preparatory school, was at that time high up in the hierarchy of the Alliance & Leicester Building Society (later to become part of Santander). Back at home after the uncomfortable meeting with 3i, and in some desperation, I phoned Mervyn at his office in Hove. I told him our story and asked if it would be at all possible for Alliance & Leicester to help us.

His response was an extremely positive one. In no time at all, seemingly, he had arranged for valuations to be done, set up a 25-year mortgage charged on the school's property, and conducted the necessary negotiations with the Charity Commissioners. As a result, all the school's funding was now swept up into the hands of the Alliance & Leicester, which gave the school complete freedom from the sort of interference that we had endured under 3i. The long-term funding arrangements meant a lot less to pay out in cash each year too and from 1988 onwards the funding of the school was totally secure.

I cannot tell you what a difference it made, not having to suffer the permanent anxiety that a bank could, on the change of a manager, effectively finish the school. The previous lack of security had been all the more difficult to bear as St Bede's had made surpluses on its trading accounts every year from the financial year 1980-81 onwards.

In looking back to the days of financial uncertainty and anxiety in those early years, I recall one particularly low point when it seemed as though we faced extinction. PP, ever positive and optimistic, and I found ourselves cap in hand in what seemed to be a rather dingy flat in London. Two hours later the Nigerian prince, whose flat it was, had introduced us to seemingly countless children and had agreed to pay the school £80,000 in advance to cover their educational costs over the years ahead. Was it a good deal? In one way it was not, because the discount was enormous and we had to work really hard with the children. Looked at another way, it saved the school and £80,000 was quite a sum in 1981 or 1982. Phew! That's what we felt. We might even have said it as we left the flat and started home.

Throughout this period, as at many other times, our legal affairs were looked after with consummate skill by Nevill Barker of Dawson & Co of Lincoln's Inn Fields in London. Nevill even out-toughed the hard Scot from 3i, who, having kicked us out, wanted thousands of pounds in compensation for our loan agreement being terminated early! Yes, seriously! They got nothing.

THE DICKER

When she was asked years later to recall the day she first viewed The Dicker, for an edition of the St Bede's Yearbook, Angela wrote the following: 'On a bitterly cold day in February (1979) Roger, Peter Pyemont and I were on our way to The Dicker; a strange name for what was to turn out to be an even stranger building. Recently arrived in Sussex with three young children aged five and under, with Roger appointed head of a new school of 23 students situated in a converted garage, the journey to Upper Dicker was an adventure; down winding lanes we went, across a bridge and quite suddenly there it was in front of us – rather forbidding, sinister one might almost say. Right and first left and we were beside two wrought iron gates tethered by a large, rusty padlock. As the struggle began between key and lock, I peered through the bars to what lay beyond. To my right there were broken greenhouses everywhere and remains of old walls and posts intertwined with undergrowth all weather-beaten and sodden.

'Once inside, we bore left past a half-made indoor swimming pool (where finance offices are now) and down a path to the back door where another lock and key negotiation began. The smell was there as soon as the door opened. A rancid dampness familiar in shut neglected houses pervaded everywhere, for no one had lived there for two years. My goodness! It was so cold, so cheerless. Past small rooms (now the kitchen), along corridors, some tiled, some magnificently floored in wood, we apprehensively moved round the house. It was terribly quiet except for the occasional drip, drip of leaking radiators burst by the winter's frost and water pipes in similar condition. There were magnificently panelled rooms and wonderfully carved fireplaces under layers of dust, exquisite floors, just detectable under layers of filth and grime, cobwebs everywhere, broken windows and odd relics of former times were scattered here and there. We found amongst other things a desk that Roger's secretary was to use for the next 16 years, a safe that is still in service in the finance office and two portraits in the panelled library (stripped alas of its ivory inlays) presumed to be of relatives of Horatio and now in the salon.

'The warmer freshness of the air was a great tonic as we emerged from within and with relief looked out towards the grounds. Grass waist high was everywhere divided here and there and flattened by the passage of a goat, chickens or other intruders glad of the freedom of such uninterrupted space. Incidentally we came across the goat later, one of two as it happened, resting from its gardening duties in its home in the aviary (later, most appropriately, music rooms). We could not see the lake through all the wildness and so we made our passage across overgrown gravel paths, just visible beneath our feet. Through the grey mist I could detect the colourless silhouettes of magnificent trees huddled round the lake and grand flights of steps that seemed of no apparent purpose. At last my first glimpse of the lake with its island, strange huts and dilapidated bridge; as I looked back towards the house, less ugly on this side, I wondered at the former beauty of these mysterious grounds.

'As we turned to our right down some stone steps to the sunken garden (now science laboratories and ICT), rabbits startled by intruders scattered into the orchard beyond. The old aviary was on our left, neglected and sad like everything else here. We wandered left past the gnarled and twisted trees of the old orchard down to the woods beyond (O is for orchard in the O classrooms). On our return we passed the tack house (CDT to be) and the kennels (future ceramics). Ivy grew everywhere, broken windows and broken doors battered by the winds and weather hung damaged everywhere.

'We slowly went back up the drive, each of us silent. I was lost in my own thoughts. What do we do? Where do we live? What about Giles, Lucy and Sally, so very young? Were they, too, to be caught up in this madness? We paused by the gate and I glanced back at the old stable block (S rooms) at the bottom of the drive. PP's voice came from behind me, clearly and decisively, "And so, chaps, it's over to you". A shiver went down my spine and I turned to Roger and asked "So what do we do now?" and all he said was "We just start" and start we did.'

Nicely and atmospherically put but in truth, with the completion of the purchase not due until sometime in March 1979, the situation was in some ways worse than that. How on earth was this charming and to some extent inspiring shambles to be turned into a school within five months?

The inspiring side was that here were buildings and a small park that could be restored to provide a lovely place for young people. The whole set-up would defy any attempt to render it institutional, which would give the school the touch of eccentricity that any really good school deserves; at least I think it does. What it clearly would never be was the large 'mental asylum' model so favoured by the great Victorian school builders, the type possessed by many of our local competitors-to-be. It was so easy to imagine laughter and boys and girls enjoying happy lives here; the very name was a start, and there was a helpful informality about the place.

The immediate task was not, however, to dream. There were 28 burst radiators and a similar number of burst pipes, the roof was leaking, some of the buildings were near-derelict and the wiring was useless. There wasn't enough electric power anyway and the water supply was extraordinarily lacking in pressure, necessitating a complete overhaul. There were no kitchens and no classrooms or science laboratories. The gardens were a hideous mess and there was nowhere to play any games. In addition, a severely damaged if magnificent conservatory needed serious attention, as did a collapsing bridge across a dangerous looking lake. However there was a library and it had shelves, the dining-room was of truly superior size as befitted Horatio's pretensions, and there were plenty of bedrooms, in poor shape but full of character. There was a boudoir too – surely the place to teach French!

It should be mentioned at this stage that the property bought by the school in March 1979 was not the entire property known as The Dicker. Bottomley's son-in law, Major Cohn as has been mentioned, had sold up in the 1930s and one of the lots sold was 'the Country House known as The Dicker', which included 20 acres of land. This had been bought by a bachelor barrister called Peter Pickard (incidentally, for £4,000), who, when he sold it on in the 1960s to Admiral Oldham and his wife (for £12,000), kept back seven acres on which stood two gardeners' cottages, the tack house, the kennels, all the kitchen gardens where the derelict greenhouses now barely stood, the orchard and the woodland beyond it, and of course an access. Mr Pickard saw a potential development site and kept an eye on things from his home in Glasgow through a trusted agent, Bill Brooke.

I got to know Bill Brooke quite well over the next year or so and he was a great help for he knew, as a plumbing and heating engineer, all the details about water and boilers and radiators which he had personally installed. In a shed we found a large old Dennis lawnmower with a trailing seat which alas could not be made to work, but Bill Brooke told me that he had witnessed Peter Pickard's party trick whereby he would mow the lawn standing on his head on the mower's seat – tell that to the average jury!

The Admiral and his wife lived in The Dicker after they bought it and set up there The Downs and Weald Society which ran courses in the arts under the leadership of their resident artists Lewis Creed and his wife Louisa, who was one of the Nicholsons of artistic fame.

Also residing at The Dicker during the Admiral's time was Beryl Pogson, who was one of the 12 disciples of the philosopher George Ivanovitch Gurdjieff. Gurdjieff was the founder of 'The Work', a philosophy whereby all people could solve their problems by working together in communities in which all contributed daily work according to their talents.

Into this positive philosophy The Downs and Weald Society fitted most neatly and The Dicker, through The Work and Beryl Pogson, became known throughout the world as a centre for the followers of Gurdjieff. This commune sat mysteriously in the village throughout most of the 1960s and 1970s and their work influenced The Dicker greatly through the presence about the property of marvellous mosaics and patterned symbolic paving in the grounds, as well as window engravings and ceramic pieces. Bottomley's aviary was converted by them into a ceramics studio and their positive spirit was a real presence about the place.

I was fortunate enough to learn a lot more about The Work and its connection with The Dicker from Lewis Creed, with whom I have maintained correspondence, as has our son Giles. By chance Giles encountered in a literary sense both Gurdjieff and Beryl Pogson, and then in his further researches Lewis and Louisa and their connection with The Dicker, whilst studying for his degree in Religious Studies and Philosophy at Edinburgh. One of Lewis Creed's nieces came to the school as a student and a wonderful local potter, Jonathan Chiswell-Jones, who has his studio and shop in Hankham, learnt his skills from Lewis at The Dicker.

But back to the Admiral; he sold up and moved to the West Country in 1975, passing the house on to an Indian gentleman. This new purchaser had it in mind to turn the property into a country club, specialising in exotic massages; wealthy Arabs, who were a real presence in the 1970s, would be able to arrive in their helicopters to be suitably pampered. Money however was in insufficient supply and the 'owner', pursued in vain by his creditors, returned to India. The caretaker, who was supposedly in charge of the conversion, stripped out and sold the ivory inlays from Horatio's doors and panelling in lieu of his wages and abandoned ship, leaving the goats in charge.

There had been two periods of intensely positive activity at The Dicker – first Horatio's and then that of the followers of Gurdjieff – and now a third was about to begin.

PREPARING FOR ACTION

In March 1979 Stephen Barnes and I took the whole school on a 12-mile walk across the South Downs, from the preparatory school to The Dicker. We unlocked the front door, photographs being taken as we did so, and showed the boys and girls what was to become their new home in the coming September. They were mightily excited and thought it was going to be marvellous. Being children (almost all of them were still 13 years old), the practical problems didn't even occur to them; they just assumed that everything was bound to happen and made their own plans about where they wanted to sleep and how they could enjoy fishing in the lake.

I did not like to worry them but five months seemed an impossibly short time. Not knowing the area and its builders and tradesmen and not having any employees of our own to do any of the work was not exactly sleep-inducing. However, this is where the governors come in, and this time it was Jack Hawkins who rose to the occasion.

Jack was the chairman of Hawkins and Tipson, a medium-sized conglomerate that was the largest maker of ropes, be they hemp, synthetic fibre, or steel, in Britain. The company also made garden furniture of all sorts and a miscellany of other products such as bridge tables; indeed, Jack cleared out his factory's discarded stock of director's chairs and bridge tables and gave them to the school. On sunny days we still sit about on one or two of the former and many of the school's early lessons took place with the students sitting around the bridge tables.

Jack himself was a distinguished bridge player and during our first year at The Dicker ran a weekly bridge club at which he taught anyone who signed up how to play. He was also a man of immense drive and quick practical appreciation. He could see that if the school was to succeed, not least in its short-term goal of having usable premises within five months, it needed to achieve a great deal but was unable to spend much in the process – hence the small contribution of the bridge tables. Jack asked me to go to his office and meet his works engineer, a Mr Banks. He was neither a Gordon nor a Jeff, in fact he was never referred to as anything other than 'Mr Banks'. Jack told me that Mr B knew everything about, and everyone in, the local construction scene and that whoever was selected as our builder would do all in their power to keep in with him.

And so it was that if drawings were required Mr Banks or someone in his office would do them. The building inspectors were all familiar to and compliant with Mr Banks too. Through this great (though physically small), unassuming, unflappable man, we made the acquaintance of Suttons the builders. Mike Sutton at that time ran the firm and they were based in Berwick, three miles down the road from The Dicker. (Mike ran the local General Stores there too, and effectively Glynde Cricket Club as well.) From most of the houses in Berwick came forth, or so it seemed, a Reg or a Tony or a Fred, each of whom was either another Sutton or at least a close relative and each was supremely skilled in one or other of the trades.

Between them, these marvellous people sorted everything out for us. Reg, in particular, who was a plumber renowned for the apparent slowness but absolute accuracy of his work, was for a number of months almost 'a member of the family'. He emerged daily from his garden gate in Berwick at 7.28am, passing on the way his neat rows of onions, cabbages, potatoes and runner beans that mirrored the precision of his work, got on to the small lorry and was driven to The Dicker. He never missed a day, was never flustered or frustrated by the many inadequacies of building suppliers or men from offices, took exact breaks at precise times, and plumbed, even as he spoke to me, until he left again at 4.30pm. It was the work of outstanding men like this, urged on by their hard-driving but more explosive boss Mike and fine-tuned by Mr Banks, which meant we had habitable buildings in which to work and sleep in September 1979.

What was to go into these buildings was another matter. During the summer, I, armed with catalogues provided by Colonel Keef, organised the equipping of the school – tables, chairs, beds, stationery, cupboards, blackboards (those were the days), wastepaper baskets, ovens, a bain-marie (that was a new one on me), toasters and grills of truly impressive proportions, washing-up machines, saucepans and roasting tins, laboratory equipment and benching, telephones and telephone lines, copying machines, notice boards, polishers, mowers, rakes, spades, forks and, of course, people to work them.

Luckily two months of this time were the summer holidays, for in addition there was still recruiting of pupils to be done and the daily round of teaching and ministering to those already with us during the summer term. Luckily, too, Angela was there for she oversaw the 'domestic' organisation. Despite the demands of our three young children, she called up the suppliers she had used when running the house in Brentwood, set up and equipped a cleaning staff and programme, made all the curtains for the whole of The Dicker, ensured that there were dormitories for the boarders that were aesthetically pleasing by colour and design and ensured that the housekeeping and laundry arrangements were in place. She even had time to organise a medical room and appoint a school doctor; as a physiotherapist herself this was perhaps not too difficult.

I do remember an exciting journey to Emsworth in Hampshire when we bargained down a retiring doctor and came away with his examination couch, upon which hundreds of St Bedians were to be diagnosed and treated. For the next 22 years Angela provided expert 'physio' to all who needed it in the school, ensuring that many a vital player was fit for the next match; she also attended with the school doctor a daily surgery, held at 8.15 every morning except Sunday, to take care of the sick or injured or those with the need to avoid something that day.

Digressing slightly, we were extremely fortunate in our medical set-up, as for most of the period covered by this book our school doctor was Colin Tourle who came from a partnership in Hailsham. He arrived at the school without fail at 8.15am and held his surgery in what had been Horatio Bottomley's snug bar. He was, and still is, a marvellous doctor, careful and extremely astute in his diagnoses. It was an advantage that he had a great sense of humour and a most infectious laugh; he told some hilarious medical stories. Colin certainly needed his humour for he had to deal with some pretty rare diseases brought on by impending French tests and the like and quite a lot of rubbish. His wry smile, with not a word spoken, when, on checking a sore throat, he espied his first tongue piercing remains a favourite memory for Angela and indeed for Colin. It is impossible to say how fortunate we were to have such outstanding medical service.

As I said, Angie made every curtain that was needed for all the new 'houses', saving thousands of pounds, and she made every aesthetic decision that was required both inside and out. In the gardens, she and the gardeners she had chosen rescued the landscape from its desperately sad state and waged a successful battle against the forces that would have turned the gardens into a version of a town park or strimmed the whole lot for the sake of a misguided 'neatness' or, more accurately, to avoid work or the need to get off a ride-on machine.

Angela also managed all our cleaners and their supplies and oversaw with charm and tact the operations of the kitchens and at least one temperamental chef. She appointed the matrons who looked after the boarders and was always on hand with advice if they needed it.

That she did all this unpaid for most of the years we were running the school was a very important factor in our survival and subsequent prosperity, for at all stages we clearly spent far less on administrative overheads than other schools I came across – and, incidentally, more on paying the staff who worked directly with the students than most of the others too. There was a harmony and happiness about the areas in which Angela worked and this was an important atmospheric advantage for the school; she worked self-effacingly, often barely observably, but vitally, almost like Castrol in an engine.

Other important makers and doers joined our staff during these hectic months. There was our first maintenance man, Peter Howard, a carpenter and site foreman who could turn his hand to most things and had built his own house in Hailsham. He started the revival of the outbuildings and operated from various workshops – firstly in what is now the school prefects' room and later, when we had purchased them from Peter Pickard of whom more in due course, in both the Tack House and the Kennels.

From Upper Dicker came Peter Spiers, our first gardener and groundsman; he firstly tamed things and then he created a tolerable play area from the ruins of Bottomley's tennis court and croquet lawn beyond the lake. During this period we put in two more tennis courts, which acted as a hard play area for any game but in particular for tennis and netball. These remained as the main netball and 5-a-side football area, resurfaced with astro-turf and provided with floodlights in the 1980s, until 1999, when the present science laboratories and ICT department were built over them.

Peter Spiers also created an area for cricket nets and certain field sports in the space behind the lake. He dug out an impressive long-jump pit and when it was filled with sand I asked him to christen it. Despite his 50-odd years, and the fact that he was wearing wellington boots, down the cinder runway he galloped with an athletic bounding run; he hit the board and I measured, in feet naturally, a leap of approaching six metres!

He was a remarkably fit man, whose effervescent presence we missed when he decided to buy a guest-house in Eastbourne. When that was later sold he could – and still can – be seen, well into his eighties, managing the maintenance and sweeping up cheerfully (whistling characteristically of course), at the Enterprise Centre in Eastbourne.

It was uncertain how much the two Peters liked each other, but we admired their work and they were a pleasure to talk to; both really entered into the spirit of things at the school.

PICKARD

Whilst all the activity preparing for the arrival of, by the late summer, some 65 boys and girls was going on, no one had actually asked us where we were going to live when we moved to The Dicker. It soon became apparent, as nothing was said, that sorting this out was also one of my responsibilities. Clearly we had to be on the spot, for we were in charge of the boarders (for the first year I was their housemaster) and therefore we could not disappear either at the end of the day or at weekends. This meant we would have to look around, telling our children in the meantime that everything would be all right. As it happened our search lasted for just a day – the gardeners' cottages that Peter Pickard had held back when selling to Admiral Oldham, if you can remember that far back in this narrative, might be available, as no one was living in either of them.

Now at this stage, in June or July 1979, we actually had no idea about Pickard and therefore no idea as to who owned the pair of cottages. However a chance conversation in the village shop with Glen Carr, who ran this small general store and post office with his wife Phil, revealed that a distant relative of theirs who lived in Hailsham, called Bill Brooke, knew all about the cottages.

Through Bill we discovered the telephone number of Mr Pickard. I phoned him in Glasgow the same evening and told him who I was and what we were doing, and asked him if there was any chance of us living in either of the cottages. He told me that we were welcome to live in Number 2 Crossways Cottages but that he needed Number 1 so that, for tax purposes, he had an English domicile.

When I enquired about the rent, Mr Pickard replied that we need not bother about that, but that he would like us to pay the rates (the forerunner of council tax). We were told to keep the place in order and that, if we wanted to, we could also use the outbuildings he owned (Tack House and Kennels). Additionally we were welcome to remove all the broken down greenhouses that were on his land, situated just inside the gateway to the school!

All this seemed a remarkable piece of luck as well as a very generous response: above all it was a relief that we were to have a home. How much of the generosity resulted from the fact that during the course of our conversation we discovered that we had both been at the same very small college at Oxford, Corpus Christi, I will never know – but at least the revelation prompted Peter Pickard to say 'well in that case you must be a gentleman'!

Peter Howard prepared the cottage for us. It had two small bedrooms upstairs, two small rooms downstairs, a microscopic kitchen (unchanged since it had been built before the First World War) and a bathroom downstairs and 'out the back', which had been quickly and cheaply built on by the Canadians when their troops were billeted in The Dicker during the Second World War. They had used the cottages as the sergeants' mess. The foundations of a further military building, now demolished, dominated the garden.

The Canadian Army had been quite a presence in this part of Sussex and those soldiers billeted in Arlington and Upper Dicker were featured humorously, it goes without saying, in Spike Milligan's personal war memoirs. (I won't tell you any more, because you ought to read them!)

In the cottage's small space, the five of us were to spend a cosy eighteen months. I think poor Sally had to continue to sleep in a cot until she was nearly five!

MORE ABOUT GOVERNORS

You will have noticed that twice within the first eighteen months of our existence a governor stepped forward to play a critical role in our survival and development: first David Baker on the financial front and then Jack Hawkins with his invaluable assistance in converting The Dicker. The main role of a governor of a charitable educational trust is not a glamorous one; it is to act as a totally unpaid trustee, who can take no advantage, either personally or for any business with which they are connected, from their position on the board of governors (trustees).

Governors are there primarily to see that the trust is being run in accordance with its aims and in a lawful fashion. Is the trust's money safe or is the bursar siphoning it off? Is the head abusing his powers and turning a blind eye to the cannabis factory behind the biology lab or chastising those in his charge with undue and illegal enthusiasm? Are the accounts being audited properly and being sent in to Companies House and the Charity Commissioners at the right time? Governors also appoint the school head and receive a termly report from that person, whom they can question as much as they like. They should be familiar with the school's premises and get to know the school's staff who all, along with parents, have access to the governors. Usually such contact is facilitated through the chairman, if anyone feels that they cannot get a solution to a problem via the head.

The board of governors is also there to provide a sounding board for the head if he is uncertain about an important issue. They must do their best to show an interest in and support the school, usually through attendance at school events. In general, governors' meetings take place once a term and for most these represent the main occasion when they fulfil their duties. The trust's secretary summons the governors, and also manages the formalities of agendas and the taking and distribution of minutes, as well as advising on procedural matters.

Our first trust secretary led the governors firmly and knowledgeably; they did as Sidney Penhallow told them. Not surprisingly really, for Mr Penhallow, 'Pen' as he was known, had worked for many years as a managing clerk at Dawsons, the official solicitors to the IAPS (Incorporated Association of Preparatory Schools). He was at the time secretary to many preparatory school trusts, a considerable number of which, including St Bede's preparatory school, he had 'formed' in the legal sense.

I found Pen a great support and ally during the formative years of the school. He really knew how schools worked and it was a sad moment when he resigned through ill-health in his eighties, just before his death. When he left the trust it was 1985 and the school was up and running quite strongly and Pen had, through his wisdom, calmness in a crisis and good-humoured friendship, been an important part of the team. He knew many of the prep school heads whom I had brushed up against in my early career at The Dragon School and we often exchanged amusing anecdotes. He could quickly assess a less than satisfactory governor and he would give me a knowing nod if he liked the sound of one of my ideas. Pen was a major presence from the moment he arrived – chauffeur-driven, dark-suited, in a large and appropriately black limousine – until he departed, having chatted over the very large whisky that completed his lunch.

Our early governors' meetings took place at various venues and it was not until David Baker became chairman in 1980 that the meetings were held regularly in the school. Previously we had met at the head office of Ellerman Shipping in London, at Hawkins and Tipson's hospitality suite in Hailsham and in the public bar (converted for the occasion into a private room) of the Plough Inn in Upper Dicker. All these venues had one thing in common, which was that 'refreshment' was readily to hand and this suited not only the secretary but also one or two of the governors who preferred to be 'refreshed' as regularly as possible. Whether the quality of our meetings was enhanced or not by such considerations is difficult to assess, but certainly the meetings in the school's Salon, followed by being hosted by the students at school lunch, seemed to mark a point at which St Bede's became a reality rather than an exciting, somewhat eccentric experiment.

We were blessed with a governing body that possessed all the skills required; we had an accountant, a lawyer, businessmen and educationalists. In the first few years the board changed a lot and it was not until the late 1980s that a settled group of governors preside over an increasingly confident and indeed profitable school. Those who took fright at the enduring financial difficulties of the earliest years and did not want to be linked with a failure quickly departed; personal circumstances or issues of law took away others; while there was even one governor who acknowledged his appointment but never appeared at any meetings or events and never sent in any apologies for absence. So unworldly was he that he probably never opened his post and had only agreed to join us out of a sense of kindness and had, in any case, clearly forgotten all about us!

Those who were of a bureaucratic turn of mind, desiring to see five-year plans in which the school's needs were expressed in terms of cost per square metre of buildings, staffing needs, projected student numbers and fee levels and risk assessment tables were soon frustrated, made their excuses and left. We never knew how many students there were to be until the end of August each year, and even then that was not a reliable figure, rendering staffing partially guesswork; additionally we had to be opportunistic about the acquisition of buildings and provision of facilities.

The school was a reaction to circumstances; a reaction to its pupils, to opportunities that emerged locally, a reaction to its staff and their enthusiasms, even to interest rates that in 1979 reached 17.5 per cent. I could have spent hours producing five-year plans rather than teaching history, coaching games, negotiating for second-hand portable buildings and finding pupils, and then more hours tearing them up. In truth it has always seemed to me that planning is the easy bit and the temptation to sit and plan rather than develop a fast and decisive mode of reacting to circumstances can become a disease, and indeed lead to a feeling of failure. Certainly any detailed plan in the early days of St Bede's at The Dicker would have had to be rewritten at least every month or even every week.

Fortunately, as some governors left, others joined, others who were aware that the development had to be left to the man on the ground, i.e. me. I could be questioned when necessary and would be quick to act on a helpful suggestion but was best left to get on with things. That was the major blessing I received from our governors – they were real supporters of the school and not interferers. We *were* allowed to get on with it.

The governors even allowed me to appoint the bursar when, after they had had two goes and found two retired but relatively youthful colonels, neither of whom was particularly helpful, they told me to find one myself. The first of their colonels was a delightful man who although appointed, failed to turn up, while the second was used to sheltering under the Queen's Regulations when it came to man management and knew next to nothing about finance except what he had 'learnt' in a training programme in which businesses always went to plan. As for the concepts of negotiating on price, getting the best deal and tactfully paying bills as late as possible, these had been in their former careers the concerns of the Ministry of Defence which could always fall back on the taxpayer and was not always noted for its budgetary skills. When we appeared to be running out of money and the bank was kicking up a fuss, our colonel would send me gloom-filled notes. Luckily, after I had received one outstandingly pessimistic one, I asked him whose side he was on: he took offence at this and resigned.

When the governors said I could have a go at finding someone myself, I fortunately came upon the retired finance director of a company that had gone through both hard times and prosperous ones and who was an expert in finance – what a blessing he was. Dennis Butler knew about money and financial manipulation; he knew about contracts and employment and understood that a good bursar would, in the course of a year, save the school his own salary.

Dennis was a witty and likeable man who was additionally a supporter of Fulham FC – a distinct advantage in my judgement, and we even went to a match together on one occasion (v Portsmouth in the Cup. They were managed by Alan Ball at the time. Fulham won!). He kept our enemies (creditors and taxmen) at bay and luckily was with us long enough to see us prosper financially – his contribution, modestly given, should never be underestimated.

As for dealing with buildings and ordering supplies and managing the workforce, that was left mostly to me, though in certain areas to Angela and the heads of department on the academic side. It was an important step forward in school management to get away from the traditional concept of the bursar, often a jack-of-all-trades having no real mastery of even one essential part of his/her impossibly wide role. Our finance directors rightly had the respect of all working at the school, for they knew what they were talking about. And so did any of the others fulfilling various aspects of the bursar's role, for each was capable of saving the school much unnecessary expense.

FREEDOM!

From September 1979 then, the school had its own home at The Dicker; there were now 65 students. They were to be divided into two year groups, called First Year and Lower Fifth. The Lower Fifth were those who had survived the first year of operations in Eastbourne, plus a few additions; these students were to choose their subjects and start the two-year courses leading to GCE 'O' level – these examinations were still called that in 1979, although CSEs and then GCSEs were just around the corner. The First Year group comprised all new students aged 13.

I liked the silly arrangements in English schools whereby it was possible to move from the first year or something called Shell to the fifth form during the summer holidays, and then stay in the fifth form for two years; such an eccentric system left our continental neighbours bemused, understandably asking where the second, third and fourth forms had gone. This sort of consideration is why this section is called Freedom, for now we could organise the school just as we chose, within reason.

We were not obliged to follow the preparatory school's arrangements any longer, there was no charter to guide us laid down by the founding father(s), there were no staff to tell me that things had always been done this way or that way, there was no body of Old Boys or Girls to lament changes and complain about them in school magazines. Furthermore, we were an 'independent school', a description I interpreted to mean that we were generally free of government strictures too and could not be bossed around by the Ministry of Education, at least not in any detail.

What a wonderful opportunity! Let's not waste it!

WHAT SHALL WE DO ABOUT...?

When it came to deciding how the school was to be organised, all I could do was to look back on my own experience both as a schoolboy myself and in various teaching posts and select what had worked well and what was to be avoided at all costs. 'Under no circumstances will we ever do this' was just as important as 'that was a good idea and made the school much better'.

Additionally, certain arrangements were dictated by the fact that The Dicker was situated in a prominent position in the village of Upper Dicker. The nature of our students dictated yet other arrangements – clearly it would not be sensible to be a selective school with an entrance examination determining who should be kept out!

We were not very original really, for nearly every procedure was a copy of some other place's arrangements. What did make our school distinctly original was the mixture of these different ways of doing things – all the ingredients had been heard of and used before but this was a new concoction with a highly distinct flavour all its own. It developed in response to the very special needs of our student body and was not forced upon us by some educationist's Holy Grail or the educational agenda of either a founder or previous generations of students.

NEGATIVE AND POSITIVE INFLUENCES

All the schools I had attended as a boy or taught at were boys' schools; there might have been a few girls in each but essentially they were boys' schools. They had suited me well personally because I was good at the work and was a manic games player. These schools seemed to have been invented with people like me in mind and certainly the powers-that-be made no secret of the paramount importance of games and in particular the winning of matches against other schools. All the assemblies and the prize-givings made it quite clear that it was success in scholarships and in games that mattered most.

The conversations in the male-dominated common rooms were about prowess in games and yesterday's results. Schools were described as 'rugger schools' or 'soccer schools'. I can remember that when my father asked me what sort of school I would like to go to when I left my prep school, I replied 'any school as long as it doesn't play rugby'. This culture was still the predominant one in the public school world of the late 1970s. But we were an independent school serving both boys and girls, and as part of that independence we decided that there would never be compulsory games at The Dicker.

It had struck me forcibly, when looking back, how devalued those who did not play games well had been when I was at school, when in truth they were often capable of excelling in, say, art or drama. Those working with wood and clay had been treated as second-class citizens; it was assumed that those studying art or woodwork were a bit thick and therefore had to do these things.

But I felt that by the age of 13 it would surely be pretty obvious whether an individual could enjoy and play games well. In my view no one should have to risk being further humiliated if they had already spent a considerable part of each day suffering from the gibes of insensitive contemporaries and the barely disguised, generally shouted, frustrations of their coaches. There was no reason why anyone should not be proud of his or her achievements. Was it better to be seen as a maker of a fine table or a third- class footballer?

So there would be no compulsory games at The Dicker; keeping fit was important but this could be achieved in other ways. Yes, it was going to be compulsory to keep fit, but in a way that suited each individual. As head, I would give no clue as to whether I favoured games any more than any other activity, either in words in assemblies or via my fanatical presence on the touchline or boundary – even though I was, and still remain, a sports maniac, and would play every day if age and opportunity allowed it.

The time I spent teaching at Brentwood School in the 1970s was influential too, particularly in what to avoid. When I was there, apart from sport, there was relatively little on offer outside the classroom; it is probably much changed now. Then, those of us who coached games or ran the boarding houses, and we were often the same people, taught full timetables and were more than fully occupied. The majority of the staff taught really well but then retired to the staff common room where it seemed that a lot of time was spent discussing salaries. Just think what a school it could have been if all the teachers had been encouraged to reveal their many hidden skills and contribute equally to the whole life of the school.

But the power at Brentwood at that time seemed to reside too greatly with the man who composed the school's timetable and he did this year after year with a view to avoiding any extra work. The result was both a complete lack of flexibility in the curriculum and absolutely no innovation in the choice of subjects that a student could follow. What was the point in having one of the greatest mathematical brains on the staff as the timetabler if he was not obliged to demonstrate his skill?

It was important to me that at The Dicker *all* teachers would be obliged to contribute equally to the whole life of the school, which would greatly enhance team spirit. Also each year the requirements of the students and the skills of particular staff would be put to the timetabler and he or she would be expected to work until everyone's reasonable demands were satisfied.

How would this be achieved? Well, everyone would teach their own subjects but on appointment they would be required to tell me what they would like to add into the extra-curricular (now known as co-curricular) programme. They could nominate any activity they liked as long as it was both legal and educationally respectable.

Then, a part of each weekday would be designated 'club activities' time, the length of which would be sufficient to allow games to be played well. Each teacher had to contribute to this programme for four days a week. Usually they would offer the activities they had declared at their time of interview and which had been incorporated into their letters of appointment: and the rule was that if only one student opted for what they offered, then that activity would still take place. If a teacher could not attract any students to an activity that he or she had proposed – and opportunities were given for the students to be addressed with sales pitches – then an alternative could be offered, and if this still failed to draw volunteers then the teacher concerned would be 'on duty' around the school at large instead, policing the campus. The students had a completely free choice as to which activities they followed except that at least once a week they had to choose a club that would enhance their physical fitness (there were, of course, PE lessons in the timetable too).

This was a wonderful system, for the games players could play games every day of the year and be subject to excellent and demanding coaching. Those with individual enthusiasms could indulge them to the full so that, for example, would-be champion tennis players could play their chosen sport every day of the year – and three of our students did indeed become British champions. Golf could be played every day, horses could be ridden every day and those who wanted to make things in workshops or develop as artists or musicians or become farmers or horticulturalists could devote hours every week to their particular passion.

It is impossible to say just how important this freedom of choice was to the morale of the school. The staff could see the fairness of the arrangements and their standing in the eyes of the students was greatly enhanced because they could all appear as experts in more than their academic subjects. Also, in a less formal environment than the classroom, staff came to be more at ease with students; each viewed the other as 'human beings' and thus a part of real life. Whatever an individual's difficulties in class, there was always something enjoyable about the school day.

To further ensure that all teachers contributed fairly and

proportionately to the weekly routine, all general school duties of the policing variety were to be shared equally amongst the staff, whilst all were expected to contribute to the weekend programme too.

My experiences at Brentwood contributed positively as well as negatively to St Bede's development, for the arrangements for the management of the boarding houses were very sound there and we copied them.

Another plus from Brentwood was the custom that all termly reports were finished before the end of term and would therefore be sent home with the students, which of course is when they should go home rather than arriving by post too long after the events for them to be acted upon properly by parents. We adopted this habit too, for it also meant that teachers who had contributed fully and wonderfully well throughout the term would not lose any of their thoroughly well-deserved holidays writing reports in an anti-climactic atmosphere. Incidentally, the school saved a lot in postage costs!

The name 'St Bede's' implied traditional religious leanings but the presence of a school chaplain had never seemed to me to be all that helpful. In my view, the spiritual life of a community was too important to appear to be the province of one individual representing one particular strand of Christianity. This thought was highlighted by the presence in the school of boys and girls of many different faiths. For this reason it was decided that there would not be a school chaplain but that the religious beliefs of those who were fortunate enough to have them would be supported wholeheartedly, regardless of denomination or faith. Thus our boarders could attend Church of England services as well as Catholic services, services at a local free church or indeed at any church which they or their parents wished and which had a local branch.

There was also a School Meeting every Sunday for those who did not wish to follow the line of any particular creed, at which visiting speakers and fellow students led a weekly surprise session. This was always spiritually uplifting to the receptive.

We made arrangements, too, for an imam to visit the school regularly, to look after the requirements of the devout Moslems. Everyone was to go to 'chapel' once a week and we were allowed to use the village church for these gatherings. At these, all members of staff contributed by leading a weekly meeting and so it became clear to all in the school that every teacher, whether or not of a religious inclination, ascribed to the idea that the spiritual life of the community and of each individual was the foundation upon which a happy life would be built.

The teaching of religious studies in the school was also appropriate for those of all religions and for many years it was considered too important to be reduced to the level of an examination subject.

Ardingly College, also in Sussex (where I had spent five very happy years as a boarder), did not influence the approach to religious matters but it was responsible for two sets of arrangements which, looking back, had been pretty effective. The first of these was the termly record card (later a page in each student's diary) which had to be marked on a fortnightly basis by each of a student's teachers, grading the individual's effort in their studies. Allied to this was also a system of 'distinctions', whereby a boy or girl producing work which by their own standards was outstanding could be recommended to the head, who at a personal meeting would award a distinction and mark it on record card. These awards were the basis on which prizes were then judged, so that both the academically gifted and those who found life in the classroom distinctly difficult had an equal chance of winning one.

Secondly from Ardingly came their tutorial system. Each student was allotted a tutor, drawn from the members of staff attached to his or her house, with whom they would have a weekly personal meeting. Thus every single student had someone special to them, who could help keep them up to the mark, assist in times of difficulty or intercede with another teacher, as well as report on their charge's general progress and morale.

When looking back on my own school days at Ardingly, I wondered what had been the most important thing that I had gained from my time there. This was easy: a love of music of all sorts, played and sung really well, and the enjoyment of art, as well as an appreciation of just how difficult it was to achieve success in these areas when other things seemed to come so easily.

I also learnt much from an amazingly witty and inspiring teacher from Haverfordwest, an outstanding singer and more than useful games player, someone who, when he left Cambridge, could have successfully followed any career he chose. If teaching history in particular and teaching in general was good enough for Michael Watts (incidentally, his sister Helen was magnificent enough as a contralto to sing Land of Hope and Glory and Rule Brittania at the Last Night of the Proms) then it was indeed a worthwhile occupation, and something that came naturally to the best of practitioners and not as a result of lengthy training.

By far the most influential school in determining our style and approach, though, was the Dragon School, where I had spent five exceptionally enjoyable years in my first real teaching post in the 1960s. Just a few years ago, in 2003, the then government put out a policy document, an initiative, entitled Every Child Matters. How had they managed to 'discover' this when it was so obvious?! It was certainly obvious to those who ran the Dragon in the 1950s and 1960s.

The Dragon had a reputation for being a scholarly sort of school, and indeed it was, but it was most certainly not selective and the pupils were a mix of the academically very gifted and those who could be much less able in normal school terms. There never seemed to me to be any sense that one type of boy or girl was treated any differently from another or that one sort of activity or skill was valued more than another. The expectation was that every pupil would do well in whatever field was right for him or her.

In my time, the school was run by two exceptional heads, 'Jock' Lynam and R.K. Ingram ('Inky'). These were men of distinction, completely lacking in pretentiousness, whose self-confidence enabled them to eschew the comfort of conformity, unless this was to the advantage of the young people in the school. They managed to create an atmosphere in which good humour, fun and hard work went easily together. There was an easy relationship between the teachers and the taught, based on what appeared at first sight to be a lack of rules. On closer inspection, though, there were rules, but these were based on common sense, a respect for others, a busy day that left little time for less constructive activity and staff who were furiously hard at work but enjoying themselves too.

Little time was wasted on discussing the details of uniform but everyone looked reasonably tidy. If a glorious day dawned after a drab spell of weather, then Jock was likely to ring his hand-bell as he did each day to start the daily assembly and say 'too nice a day for work – holiday!' and then leave the staff to organise things at a moment's notice. This school worked because the staff shared the load equally and there was an expectation of enjoyment spiced with a strong dash of eccentricity, a pride in doing the unexpected and the confidence to be different. Jock ended the final assembly of each term by proclaiming 'three cheers for the holidays... hip hip...'. The cheers were wildly enthusiastic. I tried this myself a few times in the early days at The Dicker with very satisfactory responses from everyone – but particularly from the staff and myself!

It was an inspiring place to work. Several of us amongst the younger members of staff were given real responsibility and made to feel that we were at the heart of the team. A great friend amongst the many was George Marsh. George and I, as we engaged in the battle over whether Middle 4, my lot, or Middle 3, his lot, would emerge victorious, both aspired to start our own schools. I have been very fortunate in being given the opportunity to do so whilst George has put his stamp as a vibrant head on two leading preparatory schools at Millfield and Dulwich College. We both owe a great debt to the Dragon and to Jock and Inky.

There was a lot about meeting the great Jock for the first time that was instructive. He worked from a very small and completely undistinguished room; it was a shambles, with papers all over the place, and when I arrived for my interview he found me a chair to sit on – just. The interview started at about three p.m. and took the form of a conversation interspersed with a few questions, the first of which was to enquire whether I would like a gin. The right answer was clearly yes and thus about three hours of extremely amusing conversation began. The gins were mixed with some tonic, but the mixture was of the blue-tinged variety that denotes superior strength; they arrived in steady succession.

During the interview Jock smoked incessantly – Player's Number 3, untipped – and mainly spoke with the cigarette stuck to his bottom lip; the ash built up until it decided to fall down his waistcoat. At about six p.m. Jock had had enough of me and thought it was time for me to meet his deputy head, Keith Ingram. He showed me across the road to a place called The Lodge where I was duly greeted by Keith. 'I expect you would like a gin' he said and, wanting the job, I replied 'That would be very nice' and off we went again.

Eventually I finished the interview process at about ten p.m., feeling very happy, with a job, having heard some good stories, and with an impending hangover. I learnt two important things that day. Firstly, to be suspicious of people with very tidy desks in impersonally grand offices, for unlike Jock they clearly spent too much time tidying up and creating an impression of efficiency and thus less on doing the work that really mattered – which in schools is about people, who by their very nature are somewhat untidy. Secondly, it was clear that interviews should be spent getting people to feel at ease and in the form of a general conversation that found its own direction to some extent rather than a tense formulaic business. The interviewee could be observed more acutely when his or her guard was down and enthusiasms could be detected or, just as important, found to be lacking. It was also more likely, though not absolutely certain, that one could estimate whether the experience of having this person on the team would be a rewarding one and whether or not his or her company would be enjoyed. My own interviewing technique followed this pattern, minus the Player's cigarettes and the frequent gins, and became less and less formal as time went by.

WHAT TO DO NEXT

From April 1979 until we opened at The Dicker in September there was no certainty that everything we needed to do would – or even could – be done. We were constantly trying to recruit new students and persuading them to come, even when we could point to a building site, seemed no easier; it might even have been harder. Also staff needed to be employed and attracting top-class teachers to an uncertain venture was at best somewhat hit or miss: if an experienced teacher was on the market late in the day, possibly something suspicious was lurking.

Mary Bide and I needed at least four additional full-time teachers to join the two of us. These teachers needed to be able to teach more than one subject and to have abundant extra-curricular skills to make our activity programme work. Thus to some extent the new staff selected themselves: for example, only one potential director of music was able to teach chemistry as a side-line and so Charles Spanner got the job. We were very lucky that Paul Daly, a newly qualified PE teacher and an outstanding all-round games player, could also teach geography. Colleen Gardener was a versatile and experienced linguist who lived locally and was coming back to teaching after taking time out to have a family and whose boys had reached the age to join the preparatory school under the favourable terms open to our staff.

Meanwhile the new head of English seemed to be able to do just about everything else too and his interview in The Plough Inn, Upper Dicker, just next door to the school, went well. He was happy to move house and would bring with him his wife who could assist those who needed extra help with their English and also teach cookery/home economics. All this was, alas, too good to be true, for he was better in the pub than at work and proved to be a somewhat subversive character. It was only possible to dismiss him because Margaret Thatcher, God bless her, had extended the period in which an employee could be dismissed, without the risk of falling foul of employment law, from six months to two years.

A part-time art teacher made up the complement academically. On the domestic front Angela found a matron but, unable to cope with the

40 or so adolescents, boisterous and not all blessed with either natural charm or inbuilt obedience, she went away at half-term without any warning or even a farewell note, leaving the key to her room on the table therein having packed and removed all her belongings. Luckily this paved the way for Helena Honney's arrival; she needed a home at that time and immediately moved into 'Peggy Primrose's' room with her young daughter. She completed over 30 years of highly appreciated service as a friend to us all.

Now a timetable could be drawn up and Mary Bide created a neatly handwritten one, which read wonderfully well. There was to be French in The Boudoir; chemistry was in The Kitchen; history, English and geography were to take place in The Billiards Room, divided to form BR1 and BR2; biology and physics, along with some maths classes, were scheduled in The Stables.

Art took place in the old Pump Room, which was luckily out of earshot of most of the rest of the school, as there was rarely a peaceful sense of artistic creation there in the early days. Until David Graham joined the staff in 1984 and developed one of the leading school art departments in the country, it was distinctly chaotic. Having said that, it is only fair to add that our outstanding architect, John Innerdale, desirous for so long of being a full-time artist, did bring order to that area briefly just before David Graham arrived; alas, the constant interruptions on his mobile phone from his former clients who could not survive without him forced him to depart to Cumbria, where he became expensive to phone and of little immediate use 'on site'.

To illustrate the rumbustious nature of the art department in our very early days consider this. Our first students took their O-levels in 1981 and during one afternoon there was a furious knocking on my study door and a student burst in before I could answer. The boy was incandescent with rage and I asked him what the matter was.

'I have been fighting with the art master!' he spluttered.

'But I thought you were in the middle of your O-level exam', I said.

'I am,' came the reply.

'Then why are you fighting the teacher?' I asked.

'He had been helping everyone else and when I asked for help he

69

refused, so I hit him and a fight started.' He explained this quite matter-of-factly.

'You'd better go back and get on quietly', was all I could manage to say.

At the time we were classed as a Probationary Centre for the London Examination Board: so the less said the better!

The changes in employment law made under Mrs Thatcher mentioned above, whereby an employee could be asked to leave within two years, including any notice period, without any prolonged disciplinary procedure, was a huge blessing to schools, particularly to those in the independent sector where it was necessary to give a full term's notice under the standard form of contract. It is very difficult to tell whether teachers are effective and suited to the demands of a particular school without giving them a fair time to adapt and show their worth.

If security of employment is obtained, unless an act of gross misconduct takes place, after six months or a year (as the law now stands) then a school has to give notice either by half-term in the teacher's first term in the first case or before the beginning of a teacher's third term in the second. Thus schools have to put up with a considerable number of ineffectual teachers for ever if the head is a kindly person who does not think it fair to dismiss someone who has not had a fair trial, or is himself unwilling to face an employment tribunal and take the risk of being asked to pay compensation. Equally, a lot of teachers are dismissed summarily and in many cases unnecessarily. Unfortunately a conscientious head who wants the best for his students will always take the view that if there is any doubt about a teacher's performance after two terms, then he or she should be asked to leave. This is hard on all concerned. The law is fine for an employee or employer if a particular job is easily assessed and there is a week's notice to be given or even a month's, but for schools the system does not work reasonably.

A UNIFORM?

About a week before our first students had arrived in 1978, someone fortuitously asked someone else what the newcomers were to wear. No one had previously thought of this and there was no official 'clothes list'. As one of Peter Pyemont's children had just started at Millfield, quick thinking and judicious use of Tipp-Ex enabled the Millfield clothes list to go out under the title of St Bede's. In this way we started with no uniform for girls, who could wear any skirt with any top they chose or any dress, while the boys could wear any jacket they chose with any shirt as long as it had a collar compatible with wearing a tie; grey trousers completed the ensemble.

There was a lot to recommend these arrangements, particularly if the adults retained their sang-froid in the face of adolescent choice: but there were also some distinct drawbacks. Not only did our students have to parade in front of the deeply conservative denizens of Eastbourne and district but the vast difference in wealth and cultural and ethnic backgrounds between our varied sets of parents provided problems. 'Don't they look a mess?' sang the imperial ex-service-influenced locals. 'What on earth is wrong with Nadia's outfit? We got it in Bond Street last week', chanted another school of thought. The fact that Nadia came back each Sunday evening with another outfit even more up-to-date and in keeping with the latest fashion than the last did put an unreasonable strain on others of a similar age to keep up and, if not to keep up, at least drift towards a 'grunge' alternative in their efforts to be original and as a signal to Nadia that she was not quite 'cool' enough yet.

We felt sorry for the parents who had to fund these clothes and gaze upon them too. The boys just produced the time-honoured issues – not really grey trousers, 'they're blue!' and not really proper jackets. Shirts often remained unwed from ties and did not remain inside the trousers that were really jeans in any case, and which had been bought with an over-optimistic forecast of growth, causing them to fall down to a level that could result in a 'builder's'. In recent years there had been a male fashion of wearing trousers so low on the hips as to make this not only inevitable but actually *de rigueur*.

Staff rooms were divided on the matter of dress too – always have been and always will be. The main line of division is between the hard types who spend their whole day refusing entry to the ill-attired or getting ties 'up' and shirts 'in' or buttons done up, and those of the 'consider the birds of the air...' variety who are blessedly colour- blind and hold their gaze upon the innate beauty and effectiveness of the individual to such an extent that they don't really notice such trivial matters. Whilst personally having more sympathy with the latter school of thought, particularly when dealing with teenagers with whom there are enough opportunities to pick a fight anyway without creating too many minor issues of one's own, it was impossible to sell the school to a wide enough customer base if the students did not look reasonably orderly and business-like. Freedom of choice was a nice idea but better suited perhaps to a more 'spiritually-imbued' area such as Glastonbury; it did not work for us.

Thus it was that Angela was empowered to look into the matter of uniform; as in most things, it was imperative not to have a committee formed for this purpose. I once sat on a 'uniform committee' at Brentwood, which did away with the need to wear school caps at all times – but only took this decision after a considerable period of inconclusive debate, plus an adjournment and a further meeting as well. It also spent at least three hours trying to decide the precise measurement of the width that trousers should be at the bottom, to be laid down as law – this being particularly troublesome in the period in which the 'drainpipe' gave way to 'flares'. It was clear that there were better ways to employ teachers' time! Angela could be relied upon to come up with a solution that would be agreeable to all and aesthetically pleasing to boot, an appropriate phrase in the context.

It did prove to be a harder task for her than we had imagined for, although the boys' arrangements were just about right and just needed a bit of individual fine-tuning, those for the adolescent girls were trickier. It seemed to us that it was absolutely pointless in dressing girls of this age so that they felt even more self-conscious and uncomfortable than they were likely to do in any case. What was on offer from school uniform suppliers, from Harvey Nichols and Harrods down to the local school uniform specialists, was remarkably drab and boring and seemed to take no notice of the greatly different shapes and sizes of the teenage girl. We did not wish to appear like the old-fashioned convents and girls' schools of the area which were mostly in the process of preparing to close down, nor did we wish to submit the village of Upper Dicker to the spectacle of a fashion-race breeding a 'them and us' atmosphere as well as entertainment for passing lorry drivers.

Just in time, a parent mentioned to us that British Caledonian Airways was about to cease trading and that they had a lot of kilts that we could have at a very cheap price – would they be of any interest? They certainly were; we bought up the entire stock and thus it was that we became the first school in the area to go in for the kilt. What a success this was. Our choice served the parents well, for a reasonably priced kilt was always available in the shops and would not get out of date. The kilt served the girls well too, because they could choose whatever pattern they liked and their different shapes and sizes were catered for by being able to choose appropriate colours or to wear a long kilt, one of medium length or a short one. It worked in summer and in winter too depending on the nature of the tights worn and length selected; it upheld individuality without provoking envy, was much warmer than trousers in winter and was understated enough as long as the variety of colours and cut was retained to fit in sympathetically with the country village in which we were situated.

There were always some girls who wanted to wear trousers as a uniform. As is very evident from observing any High Street though, trousers suit some people far better than others, who would be much better served by the more versatile skirt. However, a few years later, under acute pressure from the girls to be allowed to wear trousers, we gave way and despite serious misgivings we laid down a style that would be acceptable. On the first day that a handful of girls appeared in them – there was nothing like majority support – a similar handful of boys appeared in skirts and demanded, quite reasonably in my view, that they should be treated equally and not suffer discrimination on the grounds of gender! Their stance enabled the advent of the ubiquitous and oft ill-advised wearing of trousers by our girls to be ended on the somewhat disingenuous grounds of preserving law and order!

So long live the kilt in all its manifestations. It was a pleasure to walk round the school with prospective parents and to see the versatility of the garment – a stylish, full-length cut followed round the next corner by one that was significantly shorter, each looking just right on the wearer. It was even more pleasing to be able to look at smiling faces known for what they did so well and not to have to concentrate on whether their skirts were all two-and-a-half centimetres below the knee! The girls could wear any shirt that went with their kilts and so they all looked effortlessly business-like.

What if they did not? When the sixth form developed from 1981 onwards, these senior girls were allowed to wear, if they wished, any dress in lieu of the kilt. The first hot days of summer could present the odd problem for one or two of the girls could mistake the school for the beach and would turn out in distinctly non-business-like attire! I found the best way to get these optimists and other misguided dressers to comply was to go up to them in a casual smiling way and say how charmingly they were dressed but that alas they had got it wrong. I asked them to go back to bed and lie there for a minute or two and then to pretend that they were getting up again and try a bit harder and then within five minutes to appear at my study so I could pass the improved arrangements – this technique never failed and had lasting results too!

Probably the most important consideration in deciding what form of dress the students would wear during office hours was the desire to fit in with the village. There was always the possibility that the school would grow and numerically overpower the village and thus it was all the more important to be able to fit into the scene unobtrusively as far as was possible. Our varied dress helped this for if we had had a strict uniform suitable for a school in a town it could have appeared quite out of keeping in the countryside. For example, a few hundred young people walking round the village in dark suits would have given the impression to the casual passer-by that some sort of mad film was being made or that a training camp for apprentice undertakers was in session.

There were plenty of other reasons, too, why we should try really hard to fit in with this small village. One of the triumphs of the early years was how well we succeeded, helped enormously as we were by a number of village people who were truly and influentially supportive.

THE VILLAGE

When we arrived, the village of Upper Dicker had probably surpassed in population the ten families of Saxon times but even so consisted of only just over 200 inhabitants. It had grown up alongside a track that led from Heathfield to Alfriston and Seaford following the river Cuckmere. Its older houses dated from the time that Michelham Priory was the only significant presence in the immediate vicinity and there were some cottages that were there to house agricultural workers and those who worked in the brickfields that were a feature of this deeply clayish area. Other houses reflected the presence of Horatio Bottomley, who had turned a small cottage beside the track into the 'big house' and built a large part of the village in Edwardian style to reflect the raised profile that Upper Dicker then enjoyed and to house his staff.

The village's Holy Trinity Church was served by the vicar of Hellingly, rather as an outpost of his ecclesiastical empire. The great growth of Hellingly and north Hailsham had rendered our church distinctly secondary in the incumbent's mind and Upper Dicker was in any case a poor geographical fit with Hellingly. The village had its own primary school, Park Mead, which was run by a fine head who did not have any politically unhelpful views about independent schools and no chip on his shoulder; he just did his very best for the young boys and girls who came to his much sought-after school from much further afield than Upper Dicker. There was also a pub, The Plough, run with considerable skill and geniality by Margaret and Les, who served the excellent Harvey's bitter.

The village shop (newsagent, general store and Post Office) was run cannily, to great effect, and with an abundance of good humour by Glen Carr and his chatty and financially expert wife, Phil. The shop was the centre of the village community and provided a first-class service, including all the local information that one could possibly wish for and even a bit more than that at times.

Various villagers could be seen annually in The Dicker pantomime; they formed the basis of The Dicker Players. These stalwarts included the Carrs; the head of the primary school, Roy Steadman; Sue Norris, who helped in the shop and was the mother of a very famous local speedway rider, David; Robin and Gwen Page-Wood, who ran a wonderful local nursery selling plants that were not run of the mill but always seemed to be just what we – and others from far and wide – all wanted; and also Frank Fox-Wilson, the vicar, who was a guitarist, percussionist, vocalist and all-round fine musician. The Players performed on the stage of the village hall, which was a key part of Commander Jones's 'empire'. Commander Jones RN (Ret'd) saw to it that Upper Dicker was in good shape; village spirit and *esprit de corps* were his responsibility. (Incidentally, by an amazing coincidence, Robin Page-Wood was the brother of Marcus, the school's accountant throughout our early years, a man as unlike an accountant as anyone you could ever meet.)

On first acquaintance these seemed a fine body of people to deal with and so they proved. The cooperation between school and village was a pleasing and vitally important part of our early years, as well as giving Angela and me and our family very great pleasure. A few of the villagers who had lived in Upper Dicker for generations were anxious about the changes that a school might mean and initially treated us with some suspicion; there were one or two for whom being discontented seemed to be part of their particular form of well-being, but from the very first time that I walked round the village I felt among friends and as time passed things got even better.

Indeed there was much that the village could offer us and much that we could offer the village; reciprocal offers were made and accepted on both sides.

GIVING AND TAKING

Somewhat idealistically, I was determined that our school would be different from other public schools and would not be a self-absorbed, self-satisfied, 'superior' organisation behind its own walls and detached from the community in which it lived. Why, for example, develop a school shop when we had something better than the normal school shop right on our doorstep? Encouraging the students to be part of the ordinary daily life of the village would be liberating to some extent for the boarders and would help develop good manners naturally as a result of having to deal with the real world.

We assured the Carrs that whilst we were there we would never open our own shop and that all our students would be free at certain times to walk down to the village stores. Phil and Glen knew what these times were and applied the 'rules', ensuring that their numerous customers were on time for lessons and not allowing them to purchase cigarettes or alcoholic beverages. The shop very quickly stocked a whole new range of products, mostly of the distinctly unhealthy variety such as pot noodles and a great range of crisps. Business prospered, partly because the school elected to buy certain items of groceries in bulk through the shop in those early days, as well as using the Post Office for all its mailing. This happy state of affairs continued until 1991.

Phil and Glen developed friendships with lots and lots of St Bede's boys and girls and when over the years we had visits from former students the first thing they often did was to go and see the Carrs. In 1991 Glen retired and the business of village shop and Post Office being hard to sell when just about everyone in Upper Dicker now went off to local supermarkets, we agreed to buy it and the generous living accommodation that went with it. We were able to keep a shop and Post Office running for the benefit of both school and village from that time onwards. In this way everyone benefited; the village kept a convenient shop and Post Office, the school gained valuable staff accommodation and Glen and Phil the finance they richly deserved so that they could enjoy a comfortable retirement.

The spiritual life of a school is of paramount importance. Although as has been said it was important for us not to attach ourselves to any particular form of organised religion, it was a distinct benefit to our young and small community to have a place which was not part of day-to-day work in which to meet and possibly to think, or be encouraged to think, about things other than the commonplace. The village church was just across the road from The Dicker and I made contact with the vicar of Hellingly and Upper Dicker, Frank Fox-Wilson. I asked him whether we might as a community be allowed to use the church, not only to attend on a Sunday as part of the village congregation, but also to gather as a school on at least one occasion in the middle of the week. Typically, Frank said we could use it whenever we liked and his Parochial Church Council, which I joined some time later, agreed. Without anything being written down, we agreed to clean the church, to do any maintenance that was required, to supply all the heating oil, to keep the churchyard well mown and tidy and, because we had one and they did not, to supply an organist to play at church services. Not only did Charles Spanner play the organ quite brilliantly but he also developed a choir that, in splendid surplices, sang in all the services and became good enough to embark on a tour in France in just our second year at The Dicker.

The cooperation with the church never wavered in our time at the school. We were incredibly lucky to come across such a liberal and positive thinker as Frank Fox-Wilson; not only was he multi-talented as described earlier but he preached at just the right pitch for any gathering and agreed to teach at the school. His philosophy course for our early sixth-formers was very well received and the church benefited from his efforts as all he earned was paid into church funds.

Frank and his successors were all well-known, especially to our boarders; their phone numbers were available to any student who needed to speak in total confidence to a sound guide from outside the school. At the end of our second year at The Dicker, we held a Charity Fair in aid of the church, which was opened by Harry H. Corbett, son of Steptoe, whose son was at the school. As I write, the grandchildren of Ronnie Corbett, the smaller of The Two Ronnies, are at the school. Ronnie opened a new Drama Studio a few years back so we have been honoured to have been so humorously 'Corbetted' over the years. The church profited well from the Fair and also over the years from the school's involvement with village events such as the Harvest Suppers or Lunches that Angela did much to ensure went well. These were always truly 'village' occasions, even if from time to time they were held on school premises.

Eventually in the early 1990s, the vicar of Hellingly, who at this point was Ronald Chatwin, was struggling to fulfil an almost impossible set of commitments. In a conversation with the Bishop of Lewes, I suggested that if I was able to employ an Anglican priest who was capable of teaching to A-level I would release him every afternoon and at weekends so that he could do 'vicaring' and run the church and the services at Holy Trinity, Upper Dicker. I also said that we would house the incumbent in the centre of the village for a nominal rent. Thus it was that the Rev David Swanepoel, Dean of George, came with his family from South Africa. David was not only a popular and gifted priest but with his wife Margie proved a wonderful influence in the whole community; they were crucially important in helping the relations with the village to be positive and friendly. David's successor did not fulfil the dual role quite as well and after our time no effort was made to replace him and so a vital communication helping to ensure harmonious relations with the village was sadly lost. An experiment in cooperation between the church and a local employer which could have proved an example to the rest of the country and helped the church both financially and in tending to smaller rural parishes was also allowed to disappear without any real thought.

Within two years of our arrival in the village, some of our boys and girls aged 16 and upwards were visiting those in the village who because of age or infirmity needed help with their daily household chores or with their gardens, or were lonely and needed some company. Others were helping the children at Park Mead Primary School with their reading or with things they found difficult at school and yet others were being trained to help run the Mill at Michelham Priory. These were natural activities that should be undertaken by young people in any community and they fostered fine relations between people of all ages and from all backgrounds and different ethnic groups. None of this happens any more, all having fallen foul of the dreaded health and safety concerns, Criminal Records Bureau checks, the restrictions of insurance policies and other bureaucratic necessities. Dear me!

Commander David Jones was also important in bringing village and school together. He forged the links between the school and the village hall, which lasted most productively for both parties for many years. He foresaw how villagers could take advantage of the school's facilities, facilities which were bound to increase as time went by and the school grew. For example, he founded The Dicker Tennis Club, which used the school's courts. He also saw the possibility of using the school's grounds for village events and for his much loved Dicker Day, thus setting in train a process whereby over the years the local population were able to enjoy either free of charge or for a nominal fee the use of swimming, golf and fitness facilities, and of the school's catering and hospitality potential. The good Commander was effervescently enthusiastic and Upper Dicker was his ship; he even taught maths at the school for a year but was not attuned to some of the students, who claimed that they could not do the maths he set them. The fact that they could not indeed do it never really entered his head and he put their failings down to laziness or a form of passive insolence; he would perhaps have been all right at Manchester Grammar! In truth he would probably have liked to run the school as well! As a force for good in the village he could hardly be faulted.

As you will realise by now, there was a healthy and mutually beneficial relationship between the school and the village, based partly on the fact that we believed that neither party could thrive as well without the other. I can write now that we were blessed by having so many positive helpers around us in the village; it would have been very hard indeed if there had been any powerful 'anti' feeling. But somewhat idealistically we had gone out of our way to be a real and beneficial part of the community, whether by wearing clothes that fitted in or clearing the village, on a daily basis, of all litter.

This litter clearance was a useful form of 'community service' for miscreants and indeed a certain amount of the litter could well have been attributed to our students purchasing tons of well-wrapped confectionery at the shop. However it was not all down to our students as some in the village were quick to tell me, for it was always much more scruffy in the school holidays when our scavenging parties were away.

So we had gained a shop, a chapel and an atmosphere in which we could grow happily, and we had given generously to the local community from the little we had to give. There was much to be gained by us in these early days and the school will always be grateful to the local organisations that were willing to help us in the early years. What they gave us were use of facilities and what we gave in return was a boost to their funds. In particular we were in desperate need of places to play our games, for The Dicker's small, sloping, beautifully treed park could manage only a few tennis courts which doubled up as netball or five-a-side football areas as required. Any inside recreational activity had to make use of the dining hall, which could be cleared to provide for a limited range of gymnastic and sporting activities.

GAMES PLAYING IN THE EARLY YEARS

There is always a very significant proportion of young people who enjoy playing games or sport of some kind; many of these will opt for organised team games. Our students were no exception and so before we opened at Upper Dicker we had to find places to play these games. As has already been said, the land we owned at The Dicker was not suitable for many of them. It was clear immediately, for example, that we had to play football, Association football that is, for this form of the game was the only one that suited an international school and indeed this has remained the leading winter game for boys throughout our short history. The first school fixture against another school took place in November 1979 and was an away football match for under-15 boys against Ardingly College (this being my old school, the powers-that-be were more or less obliged to be helpful!) and as coach, no pun intended, and driver, I permitted singing on the way home after a 3-1 win! So we started with a win in 1979 and in March 2009 our first team won the All England Schools Championship (that is all schools both state and independent). So it was less than 30 years since our first match, which shows how far it is possible for a school to progress in games without them becoming the main focus of life or obligatory to anyone.

But back in mid-1979 we had nowhere to play. As in so many other ways, the local community came to our aid with customary generosity. Firstly our chairman, Jack Hawkins, said we could use the sports ground that his firm Green Brothers had in Hailsham; it is now buried under an industrial estate called Diplocks or Rope Makers Park. But then it was under-used and never, like so many grounds, used at all on weekdays. This ground was suitable for soccer but not for any other games. We also from the first wanted to play hockey, rugby and cricket, and personal negotiations with local sporting worthies all proved fruitful. For an agreed and modest rent we were permitted the use on weekdays of Hellingly sports ground for both rugby and hockey and as the school grew again from 1980 onwards the use of the spacious ground at Hellingly Hospital for soccer, hockey and cricket.

Hellingly Hospital was one of those vast Victorian mental asylums which had been built with wonderful facilities so that the residents had everything they needed without the need for 'care in the community'. Visiting schools were prone to make unsubstantiated claims about us when they arrived to play at Hellingly Hospital but if you lived in Upper Dicker you were well used to such silliness and rose above it with ease.

By 1980 we had also made good agreements with Dicker Cricket Club, which had recently celebrated the playing of cricket at Dicker for 300 years (making it one of the first recorded sites where the game was played in England). A grand gala match was played against an MCC team captained by Tony Greig, then captain of Sussex and England. The agreement was that we could use the Dicker Cricket ground, rented as it was from the Parish Council, during the week in return for doing all the ground work on it, including the preparation of the wickets for the club's games at the weekend. This arrangement, so beneficial to both club and school, remains, I believe, in place to this day. We came to the same arrangements with the local football club too regarding the pitch behind the village hall, in which, incidentally, we had staged our very first drama performance and where some of our students sat O-level examinations.

I was a regular member of the Dicker Cricket Club team for 13 years (until fielding became such a gross embarrassment that I reluctantly turned to golf) and this undoubtedly helped the initial approach for the use of the ground. Since then many members of staff and students have enjoyed playing for Dicker CC, some of whom have left behind memories that have passed into club lore.

Roger Moses was a young teacher from New Zealand (now and for many years the distinguished head of Wellington College in that country) who was with us from 1980 to 1982; for a year he was housemaster of Dorms. He was also the first player for Dicker Cricket Club to stand within touching distance of the batsman at short leg and practise what was then an antipodean thing, called sledging. Roger started up our rugby too, in 1981, and his first team boasted, unusually, an all-Iranian front row. (The Shah had just been deposed and there was a large exodus of Iranians to the West, from which St Bede's benefited. Some wonderful young people came to us from Iran in our early years.)

Rugby is a good game, not helped by the convoluted nature of its ever-changing and much interpreted rules, which at school level can result in very formal approaches in both coaching and playing. One of the best memories of our very early years was the arrival back at The Dicker of our Rugby Sevens team, announcing that they had won the Sussex Cup.

Had the great rugger schools, the colleges of Eastbourne, Brighton and Hurstpierpoint – then often a mite contemptuous of those that, like us, played soccer – been taking part? I asked. Had they sent their second teams? No, they had all sent their best and done their best. What they had failed to understand was that the St Bede's team, comprising six Africans and one English boy, who was there solely to organise the scrummaging, thought that the whole point was just to run with the ball, occasionally throwing it backwards to a team-mate, and then to put it down behind the enemy line. Six very swift Africans, who ran in an informal way, backwards, forwards, or sideways with both explosive speed and no little stamina, turned the game into a form of disorganised and violent 'He' or 'Catch-me-if-you-can'.

Basically, when we got the ball, we always scored a try because our team ran about all over the place, evading the enemy by dodging here and there until a try had been achieved. Meanwhile the opposition, used to a deeply coached formulaic version of the game, was totally perplexed, left scratching their heads and wondering where their opponents were going next; what they were doing was playing intelligent rugby sevens.

Other games, too, benefited from the availability of local facilities. There was badminton on every week, first at the village hall, then in a sports hall in Hailsham and then at a community hall in Willingdon. There was swimming in Hailsham, shooting at Uckfield Rifle Club, riding at Quick's Academy in Arlington, athletics at Polegate, gymnastics at Uckfield, golf at Eastbourne Downs Golf Club and squash at a place called, mysteriously, The Blue Lagoon in Seaford.

Squash was also played at the Martlets Club, which adjoined the Golden Martlet pub in Hellingly; this place, sadly now burned down, was the venue (much appreciated by visiting staff for the quality of its refreshment) for our home matches. There the splendid coaching of

David Miles, not beaten by a boy player until well into his sixties, resulted in our becoming the winners of the Sussex Schools League within a few years of our foundation. David Miles had no teaching background but was one of my early picks as a member of staff. I had met him at an Easter Hockey Festival years before and knew he was good company and a good games player, and when he decided to give up being a bookmaker – a pick indeed – I asked him to join us. He went on to introduce IT (information technology) into the school curriculum and became housemaster of Dorms. His wife Nicky ran the school's drama department for many years – hence the Miles Studio opened in 2004.

Just think of the mutual advantages of these arrangements for our games. The local facilities were used and not just for a few hours each week. The clubs and organisations that owned them received either income or help in practical ways so that their finances were helped or considerable sums of money saved and they were grateful for this. The school clearly benefited greatly too. It did not have the capital resources to develop its own facilities or the land on which to do so. The students were able to be part of a wider community and the boarders did not feel incarcerated behind our walls. There is no doubt that the natural good manners of our students were enhanced by having to deal with a wide range of members of the general public on their own territory on a daily or at least weekly basis.

When one considers that the cost to the school for hiring all these facilities came to less than the salary of one groundsman then it is surprising that more schools that do not need to operate at weekends do not cooperate more fully with their local organisations for their mutual strength. There was of course a downside: firstly all our home fixtures had to be on weekdays and at times convenient to our landlords; secondly there was an annual insecurity about the arrangements and the possibility that changes of personnel on various committees could result in our arrangements suddenly coming to an end; and thirdly, of course, there was the need to provide transport every day of the week to get to the various venues we were using.

THE RED BUS AND OTHER TRANSPORT

How to get 20 or 30 young people to a distant ground with only one member of staff was the problem to be solved and there was no internet to track down sources of cheap buses. There must be a lot of old buses for sale, I thought, and so I phoned London Transport, who kindly directed me to the Chiswick Garage. We decided to make this a family outing on the grounds that our six-year-old son, Giles, would love to see the old buses. There in Chiswick were laid out acres of retired buses, all red and single or double-deckers. They still had their destinations on – Catford, Marble Arch, Leytonstone – which was rather sad.

But what a day we had: it was movingly nostalgic to sit in the front seats on the top deck or give the bells a double press to move off. Giles ran around from one bus to another, trying the steering wheels, dinging the bells, closing the doors, and swinging round the pole at the back. Clearly it was not going to be easy to persuade him to leave. However the promise that we would have one of them at home and that he could choose one of the single deckers which we had narrowed down to a short list of five, based on the condition of the seating fabric mainly, encouraged his full cooperation. In the end, for the sum of £2,000 we chose a flat-fronted, tough model with an AEC Merlin engine and a wonderfully smooth automated gearbox; the most evocative hisses could be heard when the brakes came on or the door opened or closed. Our new purchase was to become the mainstay of our games transportation as well as the picking up and delivering home of day students.

The bus took us to all our away fixtures, and our arrivals and departures were either much admired or laughed at depending on the nature of the audience and the skill of the member of staff at the wheel. It remained red and thus was an eccentric sight and most formidable opposition in the narrow country lanes of Sussex.

I was the main driver in the early days, partly to set an example to the more timorous members of staff (a majority) and partly because I was one of the main coaches of team games for a year or two. Another driver with sufficient skill and nerve to take on the task was David

Miles; as an ex-bookmaker he had worked out the odds and decided that the chances of coming off best in any vehicular contest were most favourable. He wore his cap, thus looking the part, and drove our Drama Touring Company complete with their staging, costumes and sets on hundreds of occasions to preparatory schools all over the south-east, often attracting so much attention on arrival that it was for the young boys and girls a longed for and exciting prologue to the skilfully amended Shakespeare that followed.

I can only say that I hope that, like me, the other drivers got a wonderful thrill from the experience – the power over other road users, the smoothness of the automatic transmission, the theatrical door opening ... and so it went on. I can still remember completely and vividly the first occasion I had to reverse 'her', adrenaline pumping, into a narrow parking place at the Green Brothers Sports Ground. I may have looked nonchalant, but the success of the manoeuvre was for me the equivalent of any goal I ever scored! In those days, though, fist-clenching and pumping were most certainly not on the agenda.

Where the Red Bus is now is a matter of conjecture or possibly spiritual insight, but eventually London Transport stopped keeping spare parts for this model and the problems of relying on her became too frequent. She was often on an extended holiday whilst we waited for a super bus enthusiast from Enfield – he had taken over the entire stock of spare parts from London Transport – to arrive, diagnose the problem and then consult his treasure chest. Eventually we sold our heroine to the enthusiast for a very small sum and she was towed away. There wasn't a dry eye in the house, as they say.

Other forms of transport were of course noticeable too, and one of the functions of school transport was to get our name noticed around the local community. We were the first school in Sussex to have a really comprehensive system of school transport and from the first until the present day this was based on the Ford Transit mini-bus.

The first two we possessed cost £2,000 each, a high price for what we got as it turned out. Luckily at that time we could not afford to have the school's insignia painted on them – for despite their vaunted 'low mileage' they were in fact falling apart. In truth they were, in the vernacular, knackered. The only good thing was that they kept us going for our first year at The Dicker, transporting all our day children to and from school. They were also part of the proof that was needed to send the dealer from whom we had bought them to gaol, for 'clocking'; instead of having done 40,000 miles when purchased as we were told, they had done either 140,000 or 240,000 miles. From then on, we decided to look for finance arrangements whereby we could have new vehicles. From 1984, Dennis Butler became our 'bursar' and he was adept at finding really good deals.

As it happened our very first new Transit mini-bus proved difficult to find for they were in short supply because of their popularity and also some production problems. We needed one within two weeks at the start of our third year, as our numbers had suddenly doubled but it seemed not a single one was available. Luckily, someone who had had children at St Bede's Preparatory School was one Sam Toy, who fortuitously happened to be the managing director of Ford in Europe – after one phone call, a bus arrived from a dealer in Aberdeen two days later!

With their dark green livery and bold white insignia announcing 'St Bede's The Dicker', these buses were truly noticeable: and 'The Dicker' made them more so. People were always asking why we had such a mad name but we rose above that because we liked it and because it distinguished us from the many other schools that invoked the name of the founder of English scholarship. Speaking entirely personally, I would rather go under the title of St Bede's The Dicker, than under the present somewhat boringly conformist St Bede's (now, in 2012, just Bede's) Senior School, a title that seems to belie our independent spirit. From 1999 it is true that after our Trust incorporated the prep school Trust we became the Senior School: a factual description, yes, but one lacking in entertainment and mystery!

What our transport system did in conjunction with the hours of our school day was to make going to The Dicker something that fitted in neatly with most parents' working days; we picked up before eight a.m. and delivered home at about six p.m. There is no doubt that this was an important factor in our growth at a time when other schools offered no transport and wanted parents to deliver children too late in the morning and collect them at inconvenient times in the afternoon or in one case at about eight o'clock in the evening!

There is now a fleet of over 20 mini-buses, all very smartly presented, and a massive presence about the county. This was not always the case, for we even owned and ran a full-sized coach or two in the earlier years. These retired and exhausted specimens had been put out to grass by Wise Coaches of Upper Dicker. They were not nearly beautiful enough to decorate with the school's name and I well remember one that had the Wise name removed and so only had the word 'Tours' on its flanks. Poor old 'Tours' leaked to such an extent that it was permanently damp and extremely humid and steamed up inside. It was said that a student getting on in Eastbourne on a Monday morning with an immaculately laundered white shirt would find that it was mildewed by the time 'Tours' reached Polegate!

For a year or so we relied on commercial garages to keep our buses in working order but by 1983 we were employing a mechanic to do the essential maintenance. In 1986 we employed a man called Kevin Read, who had just decided to give up his own garage and become an employee. Kevin could not only maintain our buses in every way so that the only involvement of outsiders was the matter of checking that all was well for MOT certification, but he also ran wonderful club activities. Students could make go-carts with him which they could exhibit and race, or they could restore vintage cars; and he has inspired literally hundreds of young people over the last 20-plus years to be inventive or at the very least to be able to understand about motor mechanics to their lasting advantage. Kevin also calmly and with superb intelligence managed the whole of our transport service, including the recruitment and management of a large team of drivers. He has proved by his professional example to be one of the best appointments I ever made and has saved the school so many thousands of pounds over the years that a calculation would be impossible.

GROWTH – 1979 TO 1983

In September 1979, you may recall, there were 65 students at the school. In September 1980 there were 160, in September 1981, 221, and in September 1982 there were 226. We had increased from 23 to 226 in just four years.

In 1981 we had to decide whether to open a sixth form and take our students through to A-level. There was not much debate about this, even though it meant that a lot of teachers' time would have to be applied to very few students and thus the costs of staffing the school would rise greatly. It was decided to offer the 11 boys and girls who were to be our first sixth-formers a free choice from all the subjects we were currently teaching, and also to open up the prospect of a sixth-form entry.

In the summer of 1983 the 11 left the school, having completed their A-levels and, as it transpired a few weeks later, passed them too. I can remember my excitement when the results of my own medieval history set of three came through and they had all passed. Two of them, Simon Risby and Aldo Notarianni, had been among the original intake of 23 and, having been through the whole five years, went off to university feeling good about things – and I felt the same way too! The necessity of fitting in the teaching of an A-level into the gaps in my busy day made the success even better than it had been at Brentwood and was a wonderful testimony to the character of the three boys who had to put up with it. Those A-level results did wonders for our confidence because we were now a complete school successfully offering a full service.

Expressed in silly terms, the school role had increased by 982 per cent in four years. Why had this happened? There was no simple answer. Possibly some parents lacked trust in the newly formed comprehensive schools of East Sussex. Others were concerned about their offspring getting in with the 'wrong' crowd and who perhaps felt that we could offer a greater degree of control and some homework! Then there were those pupils who needed a school after being asked to leave their present ones. Others could not get into the independent schools of their choice because they were unable to muster enough marks in the entrance exams. Some of the girls came from schools that had closed whilst others wanted co-education and we offered the only opportunity for that in the area. Some students came our way through the agencies or as a result of enquiries about schools that were near to where relatives lived, or near Gatwick Airport, or near the Channel ports.

As already mentioned, there was at the time a large exodus of wealthy Iranians who wanted to attend schools in the UK but who were often turned away by the more established schools, ostensibly because they could not speak English well enough. Possibly the unspoken reason was that these schools did not wish to appear to have 'foreigners' in them, as this might put off their traditional customers – who apparently believed, without any evidence, that 'foreigners' lowered standards, and would even somehow pollute their offspring with 'vices' of the sort they were 'known' to have.

There was also a large outflow of Nigerians at this time, with unlimited wealth from the recent outpouring of oil in the country (or possibly from their proximity to the governing elite). Although these young people were more often than not ambitious, certainly well capable of speaking English, and of raising the athletic standards of the school significantly as well as often exhibiting a moral sense in advance of many of the locals, their presence appeared to tell another story to a number of the indigenous population. These people seemed to think in old-fashioned terms which led them to believe that public schools were for them alone and others of their ilk, even though they were decreasingly using boarding schools.

There were some parents, of course, who had looked around at a number of schools and picked us because they liked what they saw and heard. Increasingly, too, there were those whose friend's son or daughter liked being with us, was happy and doing well, and whose own children then came as a result of such word-of-mouth recommendations, the best and only sure way of recruiting consistently well.

Importantly, we put no obstacles in the way of anyone who wanted to come to the school. No large deposit had to be paid months, or even years, in advance. We were never closed at weekends or during the school holidays and therefore would-be customers never encountered an answerphone. A surprisingly large number of schools clearly put the inviolability of staff comfort before the commercial success of their schools and seemed to have the answerphone on throughout the summer holidays, often only announcing on a recorded message that the office would be open just a week before the next term began. We picked up as many as 30 new students in the course of the summer holidays each year, whilst others 'slept'.

Neither were we going to allow the matter of the number of marks needed to get into the school to become an obstacle. Often I would be asked: how many marks will James or Joanna have to get in the Common Entrance examinations to get a place? I would always reply by asking them what they meant. Oh, they would say, we have been told that you have to get a 60 per cent average mark in Common Entrance to get into ——- (naming a well known school). What if everyone got 59 per cent, I would ask, are they going to close the school? Then we would have a good laugh and I would explain that places at St Bede's were allocated on a first come, first served basis until we were full.

Every student wishing to come did have to take one of the variety of appropriate tests, as decided by us (it could well have been Common Entrance or our own scholarship examinations), but these tests were used only to help us to understand the strengths and weaknesses of the individual and for 'setting' purposes, nothing else. However, I would say directly, and in a pointedly confidential manner, to the boy or girl sitting there in my study: 'If your head teacher says in your reference that you have not tried your very best, then you have failed and you will not be able to come.'

In my view the whole business of telling candidates that they had to get 60 or 70 per cent or whatever arbitrary number was considered appropriate was clearly both dishonest and off-putting, and it seemed to me an insult to the intelligence of the customers as well.

To deviate shamelessly, I cannot adequately express how much I enjoyed meeting those who brought their children to the school to look round and to discover whether it was the place for them. In the course of my 23 years as head there was only a very small number that I did not interview and show round the campus in person. The average length of time taken with each potential student and their parents was about an hour and a half, the actual time varying somewhat according to the questions asked or the relative enjoyment of the conversations that ensued. It was truly exciting, on opening my study door to go out to greet visitors, to catch the first sight of those waiting to see me. It was exciting, too, to determine in the first minute or two of our conversation what sort of people they were and what was likely to be the best way of speaking to them and what their priorities were, so that I could emphasise the right aspects of our highly flexible approach.

As a strict point of policy I would always address the boy or girl first and would ask them what they liked doing most and what they were best at. Inevitably they would tell me things that made it quite clear that they were better than me at all sorts of activities.

'You're much better than me at at least ten things I would say but I don't mind as I can get you (it was normally the case) at Latin and golf!'

This sort of conversation normally broke the ice and then I would quite often be told what the youngster could not do at all well.

'I'm really useless at maths', he or she would say.

'Yes, I can see that, because you only got five per cent in the Common Entrance exam and that was only the result of a lucky guess wasn't it?' was my likely reply. Normally I would get a knowing smile from young 'Edward 'or "Sophie" at this point.

'It's just as well maths is not very important', I would continue, to the surprise of all in the room. 'You are bound to get better at maths. Even if you don't have another lesson you will be better at maths in five years time than you are now.'

It was so enjoyable saying something that was obviously true when briefly reflected upon. In fact, looking back, it is very hard indeed to think of anyone who left the school at the age of 18 who had not passed GCSE maths at grade C or better, even though we would not have dreamed of demoralising the student concerned by making them enter the exam at the normal age of 16. Many aspects of maths become fairly obvious with the experience of life and those aspects that do not do so are probably of little importance to the permanently confused.

It was often the decisive factor in choosing St Bede's that a favourite hobby or interest, like making things or singing or photography or growing plants or motor mechanics or playing the trumpet, could be part of everyday life at school and be developed to the point of excellence. It truly is so much easier to try to improve real weaknesses requiring time and painful hard work if there are things happening every day in which one can excel in front of one's peers.

'My writing is terrible' would be another regular admission from potential students.

Imagine the pleasure it gave me and the young person concerned to be able to say that it was indeed terrible and was unlikely to get much better in the next 40 or 50 years, and then to add: 'Will you promise me one thing if you come to this school?'

'Yes sir.' Hope was rising.

'That you will never write another word!' A look of total amazement from the whole family. 'From now on you will do all your work on a word processor with a spell-check, including the writing of your examinations.'

'Yes, I promise!'

It has to be said that the confidence to make such shockingly un-schooly remarks came from an increasing knowledge of the nature of specific learning difficulties, on which subject more later.

The tour around the school was exciting too. Most of our visitors thought that they were going to see heavily significant buildings of the gothic revival/mental asylum variety, or at least solidly-built square blocks (schools have to have blocks, don't they?) for this or that purpose. Instead they were confronted with a large family house where the action took place in Boudoirs and Billiard Rooms and which had a large, beautiful but almost homely dining-room from which you could look out across gardens to the lake.

Boys discovered that in their first year they would sleep in Mrs B's bedroom; the girls would be in Mr B's. It was also possible to be placed in one of the four guest rooms or even conceivably in the Maids' quarters. If you wanted matron she could be found in the Bathroom on the first floor (don't get alarmed, she dispensed all medicines there from a highly secure cupboard) or in Peggy Primrose's Room.

Outside there was a collection of buildings in which the visitor could observe classes. There were Stables in which art and science lessons took place. The visitor could observe the Tack House and of course the Kennels, where Mr B had kept his Dobermans. (These buildings were at the earliest stage still owned by Peter Pickard but he had said we could use them.) There were also one or two mini-blocks of second-hand prefabricated cedar-clad buildings, either actually there or in the course of being there (they arrived in our second year at The Dicker and at this stage were initially on Pickard's land with his verbal permission). The visitor was also invited to imagine the splendours of Green Brothers' sports field and maybe they already knew where the Hellingly Recreation ground was situated.

Thank heavens these visitors always met young boys and girls who were open with their greetings and who seemed happy and smiled readily (it was of course the greatest villains who smiled the most charmingly). 'These bedrooms are not really up to the best hotel standard but the girls and boys seem to be happy in them; I expect that the Prince of Wales has a nice bedroom but he is not always that happy' – this was a line I found myself using when I sensed a mild feeling of disappointment emanating from mother and father.

In my experience, though, teenagers who board hardly notice the rooms they sleep in; their lives revolve around their work and play, around relationships, rule-breaking, deep introspection or the behavioural qualities, real or imagined, fair or unfair, purely fantasised or uncomfortably real of those that teach them. Nevertheless, as time passed, the number of parents who had themselves endured spartan conditions in rooms of multiple occupancy (I personally survived a room of 42 beds for five years) dwindled. The new generation of parents expected rather more comfort. And so rooms became smaller, offering much greater personal privacy, until the most recent examples began in their 'en-suitedness' to become almost hotel-like albeit, in the case of those occupied by boys, still olfactorily challenging, or in the case of the girls, subject to a never-ending series of wardrobe raids.

Occasionally the excitement of the parental tour was intensified. If one espied leaning out of a high window two young maidens sharing a fag, the visitors would be invited to observe the wonders of some low-lying and far off vista; if the irascible Mr —— produced an irate outburst which suddenly emanated from one of the prefabs, then it could be explained how this saintly man had an annual moment when he let off a little steam. The frequent challenges of these adrenalin-fuelled tours and the feeling of triumph when a registration followed were the highlights of daily life in these early years.

BUILDINGS – 1979 TO 1983

Whereas we had restored and partitioned and adapted the various buildings of The Dicker to the needs of the 65 of whom 40-plus were boarders, the second year at The Dicker, when there were 160 of whom 30 or more only revealed their intentions of joining us between July and September 1980 (i.e. at the very last minute) provided a different challenge. Jack Hawkins and the indispensable Mr Banks knew of a firm in South Wales called Presco Buildings, which had done some effective last-minute work at their factory in Hailsham.

Presco Buildings utilised the quantities of steel produced in South Wales to manufacture steel-clad and plastic-coated but timber-framed portable buildings, to the specifications set out by their clients. It was decided that it was likely that the boarding accommodation in The Dicker house would be enough for the girls but that another house would almost certainly be needed for the boys. Therefore a plan was devised whereby Presco (note the giveaway of pressed steel in their title) would produce a building that would sleep up to 80 students in two wings, with communal services between them, and a four-bedroomed housemaster's residence beside it. These buildings would try to hide themselves in a low-lying, tree-filled area below and to the north-west of the lake, where our land bordered that still owned by Mr Pickard. Why the planning officers of Wealden Council let this through will never be known but luckily The Dicker was not a listed building.

The building inspectors of Wealden were a rather different matter and always would be. This Presco building was going to cost about £100,000 but the foundations that our friendly building control officers wanted us to put beneath it were to cost rather more: piles three metres in depth were to be inserted to support the buildings and ensure that these wooden and steel constructions would not succumb to clay shrinkage or expansion. As each part of the structure was so light that it could be lifted by four strong men, even if the clay heave caused it to lean a bit, it was hard to imagine how there would be any measurable danger.

However we did not have the time to dispute the matter and so, not for the first or last time, our budgets were thrown into disarray;

these officers needed to cover their backs and did so by specifying building arrangements that seemed disproportionate to say the least. We had to maintain an impeccable politeness throughout for fear of aggravating these tyrants; this was incredibly difficult even if it was desirable to do so.

A Mr King of King Brothers Groundwork and Civil Engineering became my adviser in these matters. Brian King also became a good friend and even sent his son to the school. He knew the precise tactics for dealing with each officer except one, whom even Brian could only describe in deeply unflattering terms. Mr X, for example, liked a bottle of whisky from time to time while Mr Y could be persuaded by reason; on the other hand it was better to say 'yes' and then take no notice of Mr Z, for he would rarely come back to check! Luckily for the school the planning officers continued to allow our development and only rarely did our tactics fail with the building inspectors. This small mini-theme will return from time to time during this story but sometimes the stars will be firemen, or fire officers as they preferred to be called.

Despite the intervention of the building inspectors, Presco delivered exactly on time and a convoy of some 28 lorries, each bearing a section of the new boarding house, frightened the neighbours one day in early September 1980. A shower room was lowered by a vast crane to be bolted to a wash room to be bolted to matron's room to be bolted to dormitory to be bolted to house tutor's flat, to be bolted to yet more dormitories and within a couple of days there it was – functional, ugly, but luckily fairly invisible and 30 years on it is still there, now with its third felt roof.

The building's plastic-coated steel panels are unrusted and it is still partly being lived in. It has to be said that it could produce condensation on a truly equatorial scale of dampness – it was almost possible for pyjamas to develop mildew overnight in a sudden cold snap. Indeed it could be very cold or very hot inside it and although its location was low-lying, next to the lake and another rather smelly pond, it was not quite malarial. The house survived not only the hurricane of 1987 but also the general abuse of very many teenage boys, to whom plasterboard walls were not much of a challenge, particularly as they were so thin that the snoring from three rooms away was very neighbourly.

The low-lying position was a particular disadvantage, for the overflow from the lake ran away downhill underneath the structure. On one occasion a few years later, when the lake became dangerously full, it appeared that the overflow was blocked – as indeed it had been for a considerable period of time, by a large dead eel. Rather foolishly, a gardener removed the eel, whereupon thousands and thousands of gallons rushed out. The enormous volume and pressure of water was too much for the pipes: it burst forth with Vesuvian force from a manhole close to the housemaster's sitting-room, to his surprise and to the displeasure of his wife, who withdrew her services and left the marital home for a few days – she actually went off to their house in France. Another blockage occurred some months later; this time I think it was a plate from the dining-room that some enterprising youth was conceivably using for discus practice that caused the blockage.

However our first boarding house exclusively for boys was now a reality and we intended that it should be called after its first housemaster, a delightful man with a comfortably matriarchal wife who had four children, a fact that determined the size and layout of the housemaster's Presco accommodation. It was a pity that as a housemaster he was singularly ineffective so that he had to leave after a year, returning to his native South Africa where discipline was a highlight of the educational experience and administered by big strong prefects.

The next housemaster was called Roger Moses. We came to the conclusion that Moses House would be unlikely to attract the many young Arabs and Moslems who were coming to the UK for education at that time, and that such a name could prove misleading. This wonderful housemaster and his wife, Ros, are now back in New Zealand, from where they had come in 1980 for two years of travel and work experience. Roger, who has already featured in this story, asked the boys what they thought the house should be called. They replied that to them it was 'the Dorms' and so with the directness that one associates with those from 'down under', that became the house's official name, one that added no false airs and graces to the prefabs from Porthcawl!

A year or two later one wing of the building became a boarding house for girls and it was particularly satisfying to call the girls' quarters 'Dorter House', Dorter being at one and the same time a monastic term for a dormitory, a pun suggesting femininity and a perfect link with the neighbouring Dorms.

One of the mysteries of our immigration policy came to light when Roger and Ros Moses asked for their visas to be extended so that they could spend another year at The Dicker, where they were doing such a wonderful job. When I explained to the Home Office that we badly needed a first-class rugby and cricket coach and a teacher of English and that these two were indispensable house parents, the Home Office told me that we could employ a German cricket coach or a Dutch rugby man or even a Greek English teacher but a New Zealander who could do it all – don't be silly!

On the buildings front, classrooms and further science laboratories were required with equal urgency but after the financial shock of the expensive foundations for the dormitories, we could not afford much more. At this point, the buildings already mentioned earlier, in the description of the parental tour, arrived. Aware of our need, my brother, who was a governor of our old prep school in Surrey, Parkside, asked me if I wanted a building that had been put up in the mid-fifties in East Horsley but which was considered too offensive to go up in the vicinity of the former manor house of Stoke D'Abernon to which the school had now moved.

The building was lying in its sections in a factory in Addlestone and we could have it for nothing if we could arrange for a couple of lorries to go and pick it up. Pickard agreed that we could erect the structure where his battered greenhouses had lain. So the lorries collected and delivered it and Messrs Suttons the builders put it up and, lo and behold, we had a second science laboratory and three other small classrooms, which later became another lab. This estimable building was still going strong in the year of the millennium, bearing the proud label Austin Hall, who were the first makers of prefabricated cedar-clad buildings of quality in the country.

The building's life was prematurely ended when it was unceremoniously bundled away by a demolition firm to make way for the Perrin Building, which less romantically took its place, as were other worthy buildings later constructed on the same plot of land. My brother had been of great help and as a builder who ran our family business in Surrey he continued to be a valued adviser throughout our time at the school, giving us advice and confidence in the construction field.

Having fallen in love with second-hand cedar-clad buildings, the next year saw the arrival of others, for a little research revealed that there were a lot of them about and that this was a buyers' market. We weren't proud: another lorry went to East Croydon Station to collect an obscure little outbuilding, for which we had paid £250. It became yet another laboratory, a biology one this time, where Mr Gibson and Dr Allison were to ply their trade until the year 2000. A three-lorry job was next, and for £400 we rescued a large, flat-roofed building that came to sit just inside the main gate on the right (entitled the N Block, 'N' being short for New!), along with all the raw materials that eventually built the chalets and all the benching and fittings for one of the new science laboratories.

I went in person to do this deal at the Essex County Boarding School in Surrey, which was being demolished. I most vividly recall that day as a subsidiary deal was done for a large quantity of high quality teak laboratory benching. The negotiations took place with the large (very large, very strong and somewhat intimidating) head of the demolition firm that was clearing the site. Agreement was reached with him as he looked back over his shoulder whilst relieving himself over the said benching. He said that we could have it all for nothing as he anticipated burning it all on a huge bonfire the next day! I rather nervously shook his hand, to conclude the deal...

So now we were up and running to welcome the new intakes and even had a little space in hand; all that remained in that year was to appoint the necessary new staff to teach the inmates, or so it seemed at the time. Unfortunately we received a nasty surprise instead.

A SHOCK FROM MR PICKARD

It was early August 1980. With the family loaded into our car for a short break in Cornwall and an educational George Formby disc playing loudly for the children, I decided to call into the office to leave a last-minute message. There I noticed an intriguing-looking enevelope and foolishly opened it. It was an eviction notice from Mr Peter Pickard. You may recall that he was the owner of the cottage in which we lived, somewhat boxed up it has to be said but happily nonetheless.

We were commanded to vacate our house and his buildings that we were using, the Tack House and Kennels, within four weeks, removing from his land within the same short period the new buildings we were erecting with his blessing!

I mentioned this to Angela quietly when I got back to the car and she asked what we should do. Evidently I said that we were going to enjoy our holiday and Mr Pickard could wait; enjoy it we did.

Peter Pickard was over 80 years old and had spent the last 20 years winding up his father's estate in Glasgow. (His father had owned large parts of Glasgow and had been one of the great businessmen of the city; he had also been a famous eccentric, who had often had his large blocks of central Glasgow draped with banners that might reveal political slogans or even dietary suggestions for the city at large.) Now Mr Pickard was obviously turning his mind to tidying up his own affairs.

A phone call to Bill Brooke revealed within a day or two that this curt and deflating notice was Peter Pickard's way of saying that he knew we were absolutely committed and that it was time for us, now at his mercy, to buy his land, which was of course increasing in value every day as we committed ourselves further.

Through Bill Brooke we made an offer of £58,000 for the cottages, outbuildings and the seven acres that were the part of The Dicker owned by Pickard. The offer was accepted and we reached the day when contracts were to be exchanged. At this point Mr Pickard refused to sign and told us that the price was £70,000. What a consummate tactician he was; he knew far more about our plans and actions than we could have guessed and his timing was superb. There was no possible turning back at this stage and so it was agreed to buy at £70,000.

We felt pretty sore about our treatment for we had been led on and then snared and I confess that the thought 'who is a gentleman now?' crossed my mind. But when we realised in a year or so what we had got for our money (at the time the cost was half of what we had paid for The Dicker) and when one considers now the Perrin Building, all our art and CDT departments, all those classrooms that stand on what was Pickard's land, the roadway that leads round to the 2006 boarding houses and the drama and dance studios, in hindsight we had a bargain.

As an immediate consequence of the Pickard purchase, in 1981 we were able to re-roof the Tack House and convert the ground floor into a classroom and workshop for woodwork and metalwork with associated stores; upstairs there were three new rooms that were to house the art department for many years. Additionally we were able to convert the Kennels into the maintenance workshops where they remained until they were moved to the Chicken House, of which more later. At this time too the Aviary was, appropriately really, converted in a basic sort of way to music practice rooms. Kennels, Tack House, Aviary, Chicken House – is this really a school?

As a bonus of the purchase, a considerable one personally and even more so to Angie and the children, we were now in a position to join Number 2 Crossways Cottages to Number 1 to form Crossways Cottage, which remained the head's house until 2009.

Our own conversion work included the provision of a real bathroom, to replace the hurried wartime construction of the Canadian Army. This was done by Peter Howard with the help of a plumber who I seem to recall was named Darke. We remember this plumber well because he achieved a rare feat of plumbing whereby the hot water piping was connected to the WC's cistern. For a few days and in certain circumstances this was like sitting on a hot spring and probably provided a form of therapy for which some people would pay a lot.

As the conversion took several months, we moved out into rented accommodation in the spacious Cricket Field House owned by the then Dean of Exeter. He must have been a tough man, almost a medieval abbot, for we imagined him at prayer, denying the flesh – it was that cold there!

BACK TO BUILDINGS – 1979 TO 1983

The summer 'holidays' of 1981 were as misnamed and tense as those of 1980. There were far more boys and girls coming to the school than we could accommodate. Early in 1981 we glimpsed that this would be the case and so approached Wealden Council about the prospect of building a further boarding house. Plans were drawn up for a timber-framed edifice, utilising the second-hand materials that had come to us as part of the Essex County Boarding School deal and which had been carefully stored away. Eventually, in fact one year later, this durable material became a set of chalets in the same location, rather like a Butlin's holiday camp.

However so slow were the council's processes (Wealden Council was notorious in those days as being particularly difficult to deal with) that it became clear that we would not have a planning decision, let alone the accommodation, by September. The full extent of the number of students needing to be housed did not show itself clearly until about July, by which time something had to done quickly – and we did not know what that something was! Others in the village knew we were in a bit of a fix and the owners of Camberlot Hall, which was a mile down the Camberlot Road from The Dicker, came up with the suggestion that we might like to buy it. This was the same Camberlot Hall that we had looked at in early 1979 when viewing The Dicker except that it had been refurbished. It was now habitable as a result of, as it turned out, a most fortunate fire, which forced and indirectly financed the much needed refurbishment. We knew that Millfield School in its infancy had had to buy properties at some distance from their main site as the school grew and so the prospect of having a distant house from which travel would have to be arranged was not a real problem.

We had become quite friendly with the owners of Camberlot Hall, the Middletons (no relation!), through our children, for their children also travelled each day down to St Bede's Prep School and we were regularly invited to swim in their pool. We imagined then that we could agree a suitable price without much difficulty. We had not reckoned on the estate agent that the Middletons engaged to negotiate being such an aggressively astute figure. He knew exactly where we stood: we were desperate. As the weeks went by into August so Mr Leadbetter, I seem to recall that this was his name, turned down each of our offers until we were awoken from our sleep at about one o'clock in the morning to be given an alarming ultimatum: either pay £160,000 or forget it. We had to pay.

Only three weeks remained before the school year started and still we had to raise the necessary funds, sign a contract and proceed to completion. This was all achieved with a week to go and a mass of beds and reconditioned ex-government furniture was assembled thanks to the services of one Hubert Bushell, of H.H. Bushell and Co., who, from a farm in Worcestershire, sent out catalogues which praised in colourful language his furniture and offered deals on every page. I enjoyed talking to Mr Bushell for a number of years; he was splendidly upbeat on the phone and liked nothing better than a challenge. Can you get it to us tomorrow? For you, of course we can! Leave it with me! And through the night it travelled, this truly functional and unattractive furniture, and there it was the next morning. We couldn't afford normal furniture at that time and H.B. provided a magnificent service – he must have been a nightmare to work for but it was heartening to deal with someone so free of standard responses and bureaucratic handicaps.

We had a tractor and trailer on to which the furniture was loaded to a great height and it set off wobbling down the road towards Camberlot Hall. In that mile quite a lot wobbled off and had to be reclaimed from the ditch. The tractor driver was the housemaster-elect of Camberlot Hall, one Derek Newton; it was uncertain as to whether it was his loading or his driving that was the problem!

Incidentally, Derek had been my house tutor at Brentwood when we had run a boarding house there and had come to The Dicker the year before to teach languages. He was married during that year to Jo, who had been a young and efficient matron in our house at Brentwood, and thereby they had formed a fine team that would run boarding houses at St Bede's in a truly admirable fashion for over 20 years; they were the staunchest of allies as the school developed. Derek would go on to design, by way of detailed briefing of the architects, the new boarding houses of 2006 and those being built in 2010 and to be the school's deputy head. Jo continued to work in the school, running the school shop, until 2012.

Camberlot Hall was furnished as described and then curtained by Angela and her sewing machine. Rooms were prepared and ready with a day to go until the new entry arrived; we felt so relieved and pleased. Parents arrived with their sons and were shown to rooms that Angela and Derek and Jo Newton had managed to make look encouragingly comfortable, almost homely, even in the face of Mr Bushell's utilitarian furniture.

Derek and Jo were welcoming the last of the newcomers and tending to the homesick when Wealden Council suddenly sprang their ambush. Whether they resented the fact that we seemed to have escaped from their clutches or whether the matter of 'change of use' had not quite been finalised properly I don't remember, but I do remember Derek phoning me whilst the parents were still there and saying that he was just going to usher the last parents out but that there were two men from Building Control who would like to see me urgently.

Down I went to be confronted by the corpulent figure of the chief of the building inspectors, out late at night for him (it must have been nine p.m. by then). He introduced me to his colleague, who represented the Fire Service. It seemed to me as though he was panting out of excitement as much as exertion, a series of 'we've got you now' triumphant pants, as we made our way upstairs to the first and second floors. He informed us with some apparent relish that the fireman had ordered that the house be closed down at once and that no one would be allowed to sleep there. To my enquiry as to whether they were serious, they replied in the affirmative, pointing out all the ways in which the building, in particular the doors and areas under the stairs, failed to comply with Fire Regulations (1980 Revised; sections xxx).

In some desperation I luckily asked them whether if everyone slept on the ground floor it would be all right. Rather gloomily and grudgingly, and to my total surprise, they said yes. 'Well, that's settled then, gentlemen,' I said. 'Good night, and thanks for your help.'

With all the boys and staff sleeping on mattresses downstairs for a few nights, our maintenance team completed the necessary works and upstairs they all went once again. Derek Newton managed the whole process very well and the boys enjoyed an above averagely exciting start to boarding school life. The forces of Wealden Council, rather like the Sheriff of Nottingham's men, were thwarted once more and we lived to do battle with them in the future.

NOT AGAIN!

Why did we never learn? The same problem beset us yet again at the beginning of the next school year in September 1982. Once again it became clear late in the spring or early summer that the school was going to grow significantly and that still further boarding accommodation was going to be needed. As it turned out, numbers increased from the 160 of the year 1981-82 to the 221 who turned up in September 1982.

Why had we not anticipated this and taken steps to increase the accommodation accordingly? The answer to that one is simple – by Christmas 1981 there was no sign that anyone else was going to join us and, even more importantly, we had no money to invest in extra buildings. No one was going to lend to us until we could demonstrate that we would have the additional income necessary to service more borrowings.

Anyway we applied to the local planning authority for permission to put up a further boarding house near the Dorms. This new house would be hidden away like its companion, for it would not be a dashing architectural beauty – it was to be built by our own men from the aforementioned store of highly seasoned material from the defunct Essex school. So long did the deliberations of the planners take, once again, that in about July it became clear that something had to be done without their blessing. It appeared that under planning law it was possible to put up shed-like buildings without planning permission as long as they were less than a certain size. I believe that they had to be 30 square metres or less in area on the ground and single storey. It was for this reason that separate chalets rather than a boarding house were constructed; these then housed the senior students from the Dorms.

Once again, the cost of the foundations of these humble sheds set in the woods on clay was about 20 times the cost of the buildings and their services. Surprisingly, we were not asked to take them down but were invited to apply for retrospective planning permission instead. This was granted temporarily for two years, just as it had been on our other portable or prefabricated buildings. They are all still there today, having been given the accolade of permanent planning approval some years later.

Sleeping in a chalet was always popular. There were eight inmates in each, sharing four bedrooms and a shower and loo, so it was a bit like sharing a flat. As long as one was sharing a room with a friend the arrangement had a happy independent feel. The buildings were warm and surprisingly strong – one of them easily supported a huge tree that fell directly on to it in the hurricane of 1987.

It has to be said that the bedrooms in the chalets were not large and the selection of suitable pairings for each room by the housemaster or housemistress was a significant act of skill. In the first year of their existence one of these cells was shared by Haime Sasson, an Israeli who knelt in prayer each night with his skull cap on, and Wajih Murad, a Palestinian whose family had been displaced by the formation of Israel. He was the nephew of Edward Said, a fervent Palestinian and a most distinguished writer on the Palestinian problem. Their friendship was one of many examples in our proudly international school of how young people transcended the wretched issues that exercised their elders and 'betters'.

FOREIGNERS

In the early years, people whom we met at dinner parties or gatherings of local school worthies, particularly those in what one might call the independent school establishment of the area, often asked 'Don't you have a lot of *foreigners* at your school?' The question was posed in such a way that it implied that no son or daughter of theirs or any of their friends or like-minded people would ever be likely to go to The Dicker. The assumption seemed to be that 'contamination' by the supposedly backward non-English would involve a lowering of standards, as well as exposure to the undesirable habits of these incomers and the prospect of their children becoming friends with those of alien cultures. Probably, but unexpressed, was the feeling that the inclusion of those of other races and colours was unthinkable and a sure reason as to why we were unlikely to succeed.

The truth, I am glad to say, was wonderfully different. The variety of talent to which all our students were exposed was far in excess of that encountered at the traditional independent schools of the seventies and eighties. For those who felt uncomfortable in their adolescent years in the local English culture, where attitudes and hairstyles and dress demanded a conformity that rendered some outsiders, the opportunity to have talented friends who did not share these prevalent attitudes or fashions was a blessed and eye-opening relief. It was a privilege to grow up amongst people of so many different cultures and religions and appearances; it was the way the world was going and to be taken advantage of to the full. It is a great advance that so much prejudice has left us, even though one can't help thinking that for some in the independent educational establishment it was the value of these foreigners' fees in a climate that had seen boarding decline that 'converted' them! It was of inestimable value to our students to be able to observe for some of their most formative years that there were kind people of all races, villains from everywhere, funny people from different continents, extraordinary talent from all corners of the world and that honesty, dignity, modesty and the ability to have fun and laugh were equally dispersed amongst all races. Yes, we did have a lot of foreigners: thank goodness!

BUILDINGS AGAIN – THE STUD

The school year that started in September 1983 involved, believe it or not, another scramble to get new boarding and teaching accommodation ready. This time luckily all we needed was money and fortunately our bankers from Sloane Square and Pall Mall agreed to provide it. Horatio Bottomley's original estate had included his Stud Farm, situated just across the road from The Dicker, and this was still a small farm that was at that time being used as an equestrian centre.

The equestrian centre was not thriving and the original partners had split up, leaving gaps both in their manpower and finances. We had since early 1980 had an agreement to rent some rooms there where a few of our teaching staff resided and in 1982 this arrangement had been extended to include a number of senior students too. Early in 1983 Jane Lawrence (now Jane Sumption), one of the partners, in fact the only one remaining active, had had enough and was being pressed by others to sell up.

Some sensible negotiations were helped along by Michael Piper who advised Jane. Michael Piper's family had been landowners and farmers in the village over many years, although he now ran an insurance firm in 'the city'. He was to some extent the village 'squire', or as near as anyone got to that role, through his long family association and influence, his land holding, wealth and Christmas 'open house' to which the whole village was invited and indeed turned up. He was a very good companion both in the Olde Oak in Arlington and at his home and most generous with his help throughout our time at The Dicker.

The result of the negotiations was that we purchased for £140,000 in the summer of 1983 The Dicker Stud, comprising the main house, lots of stables making an attractive yard, 14 acres of fields, an enormous chicken house that had once housed 20,000 chickens, a motley array of other outbuildings and a half completed ménage. All we had to do was to get permission for change of use from Wealden Council, which we did.

In September 1983 Derek Newton was transferred from Camberlot Hall to be the founding housemaster of yet another house. We kept the name 'The Stud' for the new house and in this way it became possible for some of the boys to have as their address 'The Stud, Upper Dicker', which pleased a certain number of them!

We set to work straightaway to convert the stable yard into study bedrooms for sixth formers and Jane kept her horses in part of the yard and in other stables that were there. Jane continued to run a riding school for our students; she provided some horses but in addition students were able to bring their own horses to school so that their riding could continue during term times. We also completed the ménage; there was even a cross-country course so that equestrian events could be held and thus a facility that has helped the development of some distinguished equestrians was founded. Now in newly-built stables the business still thrives to this day, run by a successor and trainee of Jane's. She herself left in the late 1990s.

Having our own riding school and lots of horses opened up several aspects of running a school that were somewhat unexpected. Blacksmiths' bills were easily predictable but the complexities of obtaining hay were infinitely more difficult and at times produced unimaginable tension. There the grass was, growing in our fields, but would it grow enough, would it be harvestable, would the weather enable it to be cut, would the next week be a dry, sunny period enabling the cut hay to dry or would it rot on the ground? Would we be able to harvest enough to sell a surplus? In good years this was an exciting bonus. The making of our hay, all the cutting and the baling, was done by our friend, local farmer, tennis player and slow left-arm bowler Paul Rossi. He and his machines were admirable and easy to watch. However the hay could not be left to rot in the fields. It needed to be moved to our barn as speedily as possible.

This was when another aspect of headmastering at The Dicker emerged, for it was I (desperate to avoid having to pay for imported hay), my young family, Jane Lawrence, any teachers that could be pressed or inspired and any students that could be persuaded to be helpful that did the hard work, toiling against clock and weather forecasts until dark. The neatly strung bales sure looked good neatly stacked in the barn and our efforts brought on not just a feeling of acute satisfaction but a mighty thirst!

After a year, we opened one wing of the stable yard as sixth form accommodation and it was enjoyable to take visitors round at a time when students hung out on one side while horses' heads hung out on the other two sides – with the inevitable remarks about comparative IQs that such an arrangement encouraged!

As for the Chicken House, it became one of the most vital parts of the school. It housed the maintenance department and workshops, the grounds department and their tractors and all their other equipment, and of course the respective tea rooms. As is the way with archetypal workers' rest rooms, the groundsmen cosily enjoyed one of the most extensive arrays of photographic beauties to be found in Sussex. The building also housed the vehicle maintenance department and the workshops in which minibuses were serviced, go-carts built and ancient cars restored. There was still room too for the entire school furniture store and eventually for an indoor archery range (securely netted off you will be relieved to hear) in which Jim Honeysett, 'Robin Hood' to the rest of us, trained our archers to win the National Schools' Indoor Championships year after year.

This superb but ugly edifice was built by The Andover Timber Company, to its great credit, in the 1950s and was only taken down to make way for the school's multi-purpose hall in 2006. What a career it had had! I hope the chickens realised how lucky they had been.

With the purchase of The Stud we now also had some space to play our games at home and the red bus was able to spend more time in the chicken shed than on the road. A new pitch was prepared from one of the horse fields and this supplemented the pitches that we had already made on some sloping farm fields on the other side of the road from The Stud. These had been purchased in 1982 as a result of a meeting with Mrs Philpott, who owned Parkwood Farm at that time and who had been persuaded to part with some 20 acres or so.

These pitches opposite The Stud added additional 'fun' and strategic skill to the games and athletics that took place there. At the very beginning we had no planning permission to play games on these fields; of course we could all run around on them and kick balls about as the powers of the state could not stop such activities on one's own land, even if they were not truly agricultural pursuits. The problem came with the erection of goal posts. So nervous were we about this problem that high on a hill where the golf course is now we found a relatively flat area and decided, because we had a distinguished New Zealand coach on the staff who believed in it, to play rugby there. When the whistle blew to call the captains together for the toss, other participants were briefed to raise the goal posts, for we estimated that council officials would not be able to act decisively against us within 80 minutes and there was a fair chance that busybodies in the village might not notice the change to the landscape. As soon as the final whistle sounded the posts were immediately laid flat to become invisible again; visiting teams found these ceremonies stranger than the Haka!

Once we had established the right to play games on these fields we soon realised that we enjoyed a very real home advantage, for so great was the slope on the main soccer or association football field that it was difficult to fight up the hill for more than a few minutes at a time before a sense of desperation took hold. In the same way players of the home side knew that when playing downhill it was necessary to shoot along the ground from the edge of the penalty area if one wanted one's shot to enter the roof of the net; such finesse was generally not appreciated quickly enough by visitors...

In rugby, so much did the pitch fall away in one corner that shorter players could go out of view altogether from the other end of the pitch; it was possible with a good kicker on our side to keep the whole game down in this corner on the opponents' line for an entire half, the opposition having to engage low gear to get out and thus being easily caught. Most opponents persisted in their well-drilled but ineffective tactics for at least 20 minutes of each half even if they had a mildly competent coach and for longer if they did not.

My successor organised the levelling of these fields into splendidly recognisable sporting territory; it was about time that this happened but it did do away with the fun of being able to have either uphill or downhill 100-metre races and of competing in truly skilful hurdles races in which going down some hurdles were surprisingly low whereas one could encounter a very high one indeed on one of the steeper uphill sections. In a strange way these pitches and tracks reduced games-playing to what it had been originally, i.e. recreation and fun, adding a comic touch and the smiles so desirable in all games but not that evident in the present day. The competitiveness could not have been any fiercer but a degree of perspective was environmentally imposed so to speak.

The years from 1979 to 1983 had been years of manic expansion and development without the money or time to do things in a measured and orderly way. Just imagine the number of curtains that Angela made in these years and the number of aesthetic decisions she had to make. Imagine the strain on the kitchens and the desperate last-minute ordering of furniture and equipment. The last few weeks of every summer holidays were absolutely desperate in terms of the deadlines that had to be met to get things ready for greatly increased numbers of students.

As I have said, we never knew exactly how many students there would be for we were still recruiting in late August and there were always some who did not turn up. Whilst the teaching staff were away enjoying eight weeks of thoroughly deserved holidays before appearing a few days before term began to point out trivial inadequacies in the next term's arrangements, we would be hastening on furniture deliveries, quietening officialdom, seeing prospective parents and their offspring, discussing the latest issues about staffing, advising those who needed advice as a result of examination results and as a family strengthening the building and maintenance team, particularly in the matter of painting and decorating.

I vividly remember being engaged in finishing off the second coat of magnolia in one of the chalets on the day the boarders returned to school when Angela told me that some parents had arrived and wanted to see me. I got out of a back window in my painting outfit and circuitously got home via the woods and then appeared in my suit a few moments later to greet them. Did they notice the magnolia streak in my hair I wonder? I had been doing the ceilings as I was the tallest! Things didn't change for years except that from the mid-1980s onwards our children, first Giles, then Lucy and finally Sally, along with a number of their friends, all became expert in painting and decorating and labouring under the instruction of the real tradesmen.

Just to complete the picture of these frantic years I should add that in 1982 we bought another small field opposite The Stud, on which there now stand cricket nets, from Mr Emery, who had thought the land might have a future as a building plot. We installed in 1981 just inside the school's main gate, but partly hidden, a lovely Portacabin, to act as a changing room and meeting room for the boys from Camberlot Hall when they were at school.

Further excitement was caused in 1983 by the arrival on two lorries of the gymnasium from St Peter's School in Seaford; I seem to remember that we were given it as long as we dismantled it and took it away. St Peter's, a distinguished school run by Mike Fairbrother and his brother, had closed to become a building site and thus secure the futures of the Fairbrothers' families. We extended the gym by about a third under the supervision of Peter Howard, who saw to its erection. It became the gym/examination hall/assembly hall/concert hall/lecture hall/theatre for all the years until the drama and dance studios were created and the vast multi-purpose hall was opened in 2008. I believe it is now inhabited by the art and design department. What a great gift it was in our time though.

We extended our classroom capacity by commissioning new, sectional, timber-framed buildings from a firm of builders, now undertakers, in Brighton called Denyer. These buildings proved inspirational; they were known as O1 (O being short for orchard as they were situated in Horatio Bottomley's former orchard) and O2. Adjoining them was another building, initially a games/common room for boarders, which eventually became the first Drama Studio.

The buildings were inspirational because we could see that we could make others just as good, perhaps better, ourselves, and thereafter all the classrooms we added on were made in the Chicken House. This super-effective scheme, whereby we undertook our own building projects, saved us millions of pounds over the years and gave us greater control over both cash-flow and deadlines. Our architect in these years who came up with cunning plans whereby we could expand without having a nasty financial crisis was Tony Brand, whose skill enabled his talented daughter to board in Crossways, as the girls' house in The Dicker was known – and indeed as The Dicker itself was called for some time after Bottomley's departure. Payment of fees in kind was a particularly beneficial arrangement in the early years and I seem to recall scaffolding, plasterboard and commercial washing machines to name just a few of the products involved in this highly effective barter system!

WHAT ABOUT EDUCATION?

Whilst all this was going on, students and teachers in ever greater numbers were going about their business for about 34 weeks each year and for seven days each week. If it was ever less than 34 weeks that was because the staff had to work so hard and there was so much to get done in the holidays that I always ensured we had the longest holidays legally permissible.

Three students from the original 23 completed their A-levels in the summer of 1983: Simon Risby, Aldo Notarianni and Amin Mitha. They had seen the school roll grow to 227 of whom between 40 and 50 were day students. During the next five years it would increase to 341.

The feeling at the end of that school year, in the summer of 1983, was one of euphoria blended with relief. We had completed the first full cycle for students who had arrived in year 9 and left in year 13; it had not been at all easy and there had been times when our survival was in doubt. We had, though, done things as a small school that were not necessarily achieved by much larger ones: there had been a music tour to Europe for both choir and instrumentalists, a rugby tour to France, our first drama tour had included visits to a number of local preparatory schools with *A Midsummer Night's Dream*, we were involved in an engineering project to restore a water mill at Hellingly that had brought us considerable local publicity, and our first Year Book had been published.

On the games field our calendars showed us to be playing fixtures against schools that were hundreds of years old when we were only five. The first of many impressive art exhibitions had been on public view and we had enjoyed our first Summer Ball. We were looking forward to moving into The Stud, where we would have our own equestrian set-up. New tennis courts were being built and we had two players in the school (Clare Wood and Austin Brice) who would go on to win the British Junior Championships.

Overall, we felt we had really broken through. Young people were joining us from all over the world and we felt we were a breath of fresh air on the educational scene. That's how it seemed on a heady day when the summer holidays were beginning and I told everyone that we were going to become a really great school. We had even posted our best set of accounts to date and showed not for the first time a really healthy trading surplus: the governors were happy and optimistic too. In addition, O-levels, CSEs and A-levels had all been taken and most of them, amazingly it seemed, had been passed. Thousands of lessons had been taught, most of them forgotten, for, as it has always been, only those which contained a momentous personal triumph or an outstanding catastrophe or a superb act of indiscipline were destined to remain long in the mind. Yet it was the security of the unremitting everyday experience that enabled the enjoyable highlights to stand out and remain with us.

OUR STUDENTS IN 1983

When I looked on the assembled school on that summer's day in 1983 and gave them a rather over-the-top, optimistic view of past and future, I saw a truly extraordinary group of young people; they were nothing like the pupils of any other school I had had anything to do with either as a student or a teacher. Every continent was represented: mingled together were young people from Argentina and Colombia with boys and girls from Hong Kong and Malaysia. Two from the USA and two from Canada sat alongside a significant body of Iranians, Armenians and Iraqis. There were at least 30 Africans from many different African countries, from Ethiopia to Angola and from Zimbabwe to The Gambia, as well as a significant group of Nigerians. There were several Germans and Scandinavians and two Italians, one from Italy and the other from Kenya. British students came from many far-flung parts of the world, some refugees from London, others sons and daughters of military personnel posted in Hanover and Warminster. There were Indians from Ealing and Eastbourne and Uganda. There were natives of Eastbourne and Polegate and Heathfield and those from other local places like Bexhill and Hastings, all of whom provided significant variety and challenge in their own right.

Then there were those who had arrived promising to reform after exclusion from previous schools; there were extraordinarily clever academic types; there were those who, whilst clever, could speak no English and those whose inability to master any subject at all at school bemused their teachers. Some found writing almost impossible and others were so demoralised by maths that their brains fused at the very mention of multiplication and suffered total power-cuts at the mere thought of an equation. There were fine musicians and brilliant artists and gifted athletes too.

We had not really mastered the means of succeeding with the most difficult cases but we had made a start, and our provision of effective teaching of English as a foreign language was already, thanks to the brilliance of Mrs Pam Saxby, way ahead of the traditional independent schools – who nevertheless admitted and took the fees of those whose

English would not enable them to cope with a standard curriculum. Some seemed to adopt a 'let them sink or swim' attitude and thus presided over many sinkings. However we were still somewhat short of expertise in dealing with specific learning difficulties but were soon to be educated to the point where we would become really proficient in these matters.

The school maintained the pattern I have just described both academically and ethnically throughout the period I worked at the school, although the proportion of those who were not from the UK fell from about 35 per cent at its peak to about 20 per cent in the late 1990s as the number of day children increased. When we left we could boast that there were young people from 65 different countries in the school and that all continents and all European countries were represented. I have already set out the benefits of such a diverse community and will not elaborate further.

WHO SETS THE STYLE OF THE SCHOOL? THE STUDENTS!

The night before we opened at The Dicker in 1979 Angela was finding it difficult to sleep. She nudged me awake and said 'We haven't got any rules'. According to her I said 'Don't worry, the pupils will set the rules' and went straight back to sleep. There was nothing particularly profound about this reply for the general rules are obvious and are to do with being kind and honest and treating one's neighbour as oneself, being good-mannered and following the daily routine in a punctual and polite way. Particular rules tend to be created by the students, for these arise as reactions to specific behaviour in the particular circumstances of an individual school. Thus certain places become out of bounds and certain practices, such as helping oneself to disproportionate quantities of food, become the subjects of legislation or proscribed codes of conduct.

On the whole it is unwise to legislate unless it is possible to explain a rule to the satisfaction of the great majority of those expected to obey it, so that they can see that what is described is totally reasonable and in the interests of all. Making too many rules ruins the atmosphere of a school and encourages more law-breaking. It is always better to avoid stopping everyone doing something just because a few abuse the situation; rather, deal with abusers firmly.

It is without doubt a grave mistake to launch into impassioned verbal explosions against certain forms of behaviour in school assemblies. It is best to explain, for example, that swearing does upset a number of other people and one cannot be certain that such a person is not within earshot – therefore it is not acceptable to swear in public. If, on the other hand, one is in a private, adequately sound-proofed place with another who finds swearing agreeable, then one can conduct lengthy rallies of expletives to the pleasure of each other! Similarly, it was always better to explain that the writing of graffiti was wrong because it treated the work of the painters, decorators and other craftsmen that we all knew with contempt and those really nice people as things to be insulted. One thing was for certain: that a magisterial railing by the head against profanities on the lavatory walls would result in 20 more by the next morning. It was better to say absolutely nothing but to have maintenance staff redecorate without a word being spoken on each occasion, thus depriving the perpetrator of the attention he or possibly she, but generally he, craved.

And so it was that all the woodland became out of bounds unless students were accompanied by staff on a scientific quest. So much cover did it give for nefarious activities such as smoking or drinking that it was not healthy to be going on an innocent nature stroll and the staff had better things to do than permanently flush out offenders – who could easily escape justice anyway, given the protection provided by trees and undergrowth and their youthful pace. There were in any case many other lovely places for the innocent to be.

In more important ways, too, the style of the school was a direct reaction to the nature and needs of the boys and girls who joined us. Thus the daily programme and the way the week was organised reflected the fact that ours was predominantly a boarding school. It was clear to me that if the school was organised with the boarders in mind it would be a really good day school but that if it was organised for the day students it would be a very poor boarding school.

The extra-curricular side of a school is critical for boarders whose whole life is spent there and so the wonderful programme that was developed was not only a real bonus for the day students but made it clear to teachers that they had to do a lot more than perform in the classroom. As mentioned earlier, every day offered a period of at least an hour and a half for the extra-curricular (now co-curricular) programme, involving every student. For a few weeks each winter this meant that classroom lessons had to take place in the dark at the end of the afternoon.

Boarders also need to have periods of free time in each week so that they can please themselves and follow their own enthusiasms wholeheartedly. Thus there were two days each week, Tuesdays and Thursdays, when there was no teaching of classroom lessons after lunch. This system had two beneficial effects. Firstly, certain club activities that really needed a long period of time to be most effectively pursued, such as engineering projects or off-site ventures or rounds of golf or away fixtures against other schools or just really getting involved in a painting or the making of a go-cart or the rehearsing of a play, had the time needed without taking the students out of lessons. Secondly, for other boarders a part of these lesson-free afternoons provided a period in which they need not feel the pressure of the relentless school machine. Everyone who has been to boarding school in his or her teenage years can remember just how wonderful some free socialising time was.

All this might make time for a few untoward acts and might appear a bit out of control to certain teachers; it might mean that in winter for a few weeks lessons had to be taught in the darkness of late afternoons; but these small prices were worth paying to enhance the morale of the majority – even if it were at the expense of a few teachers who couldn't manage the less attentive nature of late afternoon lessons for 10 or 11 weeks in winter! Let's hope that these arrangements are never sacrificed in the interests of uniformity to the detriment of some fun and the morale of the boarders.

By the end of our first decade the Club Activities Programme had a designated member of staff to manage it and there were some 80 options running each week. As the arrangements were for each student to select an activity for five afternoons per week with the proviso that at least one had to involve serious physical exercise, the students again determined the precise nature of the programme. It was perfectly possible to be a manic games player and play organised and coached team games every afternoon of the year but equally possible to put in many hours in areas such as engineering, art, design, horticulture, animal husbandry, furniture making, drama, music, sailing, fishing and individual games, such as tennis, squash, golf or badminton. The opportunities were endless. The students had a free choice every term but an obligation to fulfil the term's course. Thus it was possible for each student to feel that the school was doing its best to allow him or her to make the best of their talents without there being any clue that this or that subject or activity was considered of greater or lesser importance in the eyes of those running the school. It was not surprising that morale was high and that generally students liked being there.

Similarly, if a school is to serve its boarders well, then Saturday morning school for all is essential. It simply is not good enough for enormous fees to be charged, mainly to pay for the services of the teaching staff, if two days out of every seven are to be reduced to a baby-sitting exercise by a skeleton staff. If Saturday morning school is to go, then what must suffer is the extra-curricular programme for the lessons have to be taught at some time in the week. Either that or the school holidays have to be shortened significantly – and who wants that! That said, and it is a personal view, times are changing and Saturday school is beginning to seem a thing of the past.

By far the most decisive and important way in which the students set the style of a school is by their skills, or lack of them. By the end of our first decade, at the very time that a National Curriculum was being imposed on state schools and which most independent schools felt that they had to follow too, we decided that a traditional curriculum was not for us and that certainly the National Curriculum was not. Those entering the school at the age of 13, or to put it more simply in year 9, were to follow a very broad course so that we could find out all about them. Those that needed extra help with English could receive this in the time set aside for the majority to study two foreign languages. The staff were in place not only to provide the extra tuition in English as a foreign language but also to look after the needs of those who were clearly, from our own testings and those of educational psychologists, dyslexic or with other specific educational needs. All who entered year 9 followed courses in information technology, art, design and technology, cooking, music and religious studies in addition to the standard subjects. From year 10 the GCE O-level (GCSEs as they are now known) and, for a short time, CSE courses started and lasted for two years. There were to be only three compulsory subjects and these were IT, maths and English. Three modern languages were on offer in the main curriculum but it was possible for any modern language to be studied and we guaranteed to provide teaching in any language that was desired; the proximity of Sussex University was particularly helpful here. The three sciences were to be taught separately and there was an additional option in agricultural science. There were several options within art and design, whilst PE and food and nutrition were options too. Latin and Greek were available outside the normal timetable for those who wished to study the classics and enjoyed them and who were strong enough academically to do so.

It was felt at this stage that religious and spiritual education was far too important for it to be reduced to an examination subject and so we had a compulsory course called REPS (religious, ethical and philosophical studies) and in a two-year course this also included education on sexual matters and drug-related issues that we felt it was important to treat in a thorough way.

At the end of year 9 each student was interviewed thoroughly by his or her tutor and a programme involving the three compulsory subjects and between three and seven other subjects was recommended. If it were necessary to plan for extra mathematics or extra English classes then these could be arranged for those who took a total of five, six or seven O-levels or GCSEs.

TEACHING

In 1980 there were six full-time members of the teaching staff and three assistants/ part-timers. In 1990 there were 44 full-time teachers and a few assistants/part-timers. In 2001 when I retired there were 82 full-time teachers and a small supporting staff. I believe that by 2009 there were over 120 full-time teachers on the staff.

Throughout my years, the ratio of staff to students remained consistent at around 1:7.5. Finding the right people to join the team, who would subscribe to our philosophy and look forward with enthusiasm to managing much more than students in classrooms, was always an enjoyable and exciting part of my job. The enjoyment came from talking to someone I had never met before about their life and career to date and finding that the conversation often led down interesting side-streets, to mutual acquaintances and to rare coincidences. It was also enjoyable to describe the school and its particular style to strangers and to see if they would get caught up in our enthusiasm. The excitement came in opening the door to a stranger whose CV I knew by heart but whose appearance was going to be a surprise. The anticipation intensified when we had decided to offer a job to someone whom we really wanted to join us and I phoned them to ask if they would like to accept the post: would they say yes? The main excitement, of course, came later when they arrived and showed us what they could really offer.

It was important to me to follow one's instincts rather than apply any strict rules when appointing staff. There was far less red tape in the seventies and eighties than there is now. There was no school inspection system then to check whether written references had been gathered and systematically filed away, or to put a black mark on a report if there were any petty failings in this respect. In my experience it was much better to phone up referees than to write letters to them for they found it much easier to provide details and even to tell the truth on the phone than they might have done on paper; they could be asked what they meant or to give an example to back up a general statement.

It took me quite a long time to realise that it was what was *not* written that was often the key. One particular case comes annoyingly back to haunt me. On receiving a reference written by the head of a really prestigious and famous school, I failed to understand and, for some time after, to believe, that this was a letter aimed primarily at ridding him of a moderate teacher, one of his 'mistakes'! To further illustrate this point, the best teachers may well be those without any formal teaching qualification but it would be a truly brave head who took on someone who was not formally qualified nowadays.

Several of the very best and most inspiring teachers that we had certainly were not formally qualified and two of them had no degree at all. They would of course have been very good even if they had had PGCEs or similar but they may not have been quite as good – for their experience in the commercial world or their pure love of what they taught helped to make them really impressive, and possibly that little less likely to operate by the book or a set of inculcated doctrines. In short their natural self-confidence, built up by successfully following their instincts and imagination, might have been unfruitfully challenged and diminished to some extent by the apparent certainties of courses delivered by 'experts'. Of our small senior management team in the late 1990s three of the six, including myself, had no formal teaching qualification. I do not make this point as a matter of pride but to emphasise that it was necessary to be flexible in one's thinking and opportunistic too if the best teachers were to be had.

Sometimes letters would come from those who were replying to no advert but who just wondered whether their CV might be of interest; these were people always to be interviewed. It was always possible to create a post for someone really good who just turned up and who was bound to add to the quality of what we offered. Sometimes there would just be a phone call and it was nearly always of interest to see the caller. On two occasions I employed a teacher via the telephone without seeing them at all; both turned out well. One, Lou Belhriti, she was called Skofic then, so well that she is now in charge of all boarding at the school and has for many years been a quite outstanding teacher and housemistress. The editor of a local newspaper, Sally Wellings, who had no degree, turned out at interview to be just the person to take on marketing and PR for us and then became a wonderfully successful A-level teacher and a very good housemistress before returning to the marketing. Originally she had come in response to an advertisement for a school secretary and was converted in the course of the interview! A good salesperson who can act and who has a real love of their subject and other true enthusiasms that will help to enrich their own lives as well as those of their students is likely to go far, though they might not necessarily be the product of a university department of education and its all-too-often rather formulaic training.

One of our most respected and successful teachers and housemasters springs to mind at this point. Mark Rimmington was on the sales team of the Reed Paper Group but was called to teaching partly by the desire to coach and play cricket and to a lesser extent football. An outstanding teacher, he rose to be a Deputy Head at the school although it has to be said that his forte was his ability to help and inspire our students both in the classroom and, aided by his wife Dawn, when housemaster at Camberlot Hall.

We were not a famous school, in fact hardly anyone had heard of us, and therefore we were not necessarily going to attract the very top, newly qualified staff, so it was important that we were opportunistic and imaginative in our appointments. It was also a help that we, from the very start, always paid our staff significantly more than the standard rate in recognition of the fully committed job they had agreed to do and also we would always endeavour to accommodate them free of charge.

It was difficult in the 1980s for teachers to be able to afford to buy homes in the south-east even if they were paid over the odds. This affected our ability to appoint the best people as we sometimes had to go for our second or third choice just because they already lived locally. It was for this reason that we started in the mid-eighties to enter into shared equity schemes with certain members of staff whom we really wanted and who had families to house. These schemes involved the school and the teacher paying agreed shares of a mortgage, with the school having the option to purchase the teacher's share of the house if they were to leave our employment.

The usual way for staff to join us was by answering an advert that was placed in the *Times Educational Supplement*. Applicants were required to apply in writing, enclosing a CV and providing the names of two referees. A number of appointments that were to be of real importance to the future development of the school were made in the 1980s. Of these, three came as a result of answering an advert in the *TES* and three came without such formality, either because we knew of them or in one case because he turned up and asked for a chat.

In 1982 it was becoming clear that we were doing all right but were somewhat under-organised. Some members of staff put it more strongly for it seemed to them that the head was running the school, in the day-to-day sense, from the back of an envelope that he occasionally mislaid. To be honest there was some truth in this, for the deeper levels of bureaucracy have, I admit, never appealed. It was decided therefore to engage a deputy head who could provide a greater degree of day-to-day leadership of the teaching staff and begin to develop formal procedures that would be of help to everyone: things like staff handbooks, and overt systems of recording student performance.

The performance of the staff, too, could be more closely monitored; the duties and extra-curricular programme could be more formally set out, as could the details of the daily procedures which could be more formally displayed.

Having replied to an advert in the *TES*, James McArthur joined the staff as the first deputy head in January 1982. He came from being a housemaster at Denstone College, a traditionally run Woodard school, and what a difference he made. St Bede's felt as though it had made a great step forward. James not only ran the day-to-day aspects of the school with admirable sensitivity and truly remarkable efficiency but also, having the natural qualities of a top geographer, with great neatness.

Now we really felt like a proper school. For six years James added quality, energy and good humour to our operations and indeed I believe that he came round to our rather less old-fashioned way of looking at the education of our students. He was also a very accomplished teacher of geography and enjoyed coaching rugby. His loyalty and ability rightly meant that he left after his six years to be a head himself and retired only a few years ago after a long and successful spell as head of the Reading Bluecoat School.

There were two other deputy heads in my time and both deservedly went on to take up headships. In one case the style of St Bede's was exported almost in its entirety to East Anglia and caused the revival and subsequent flourishing of a long established school which was not really thriving when he arrived. This was the work of my second deputy, like the first and third a geographer, Jim Malcolm; there is more about Jim later. In short he was a quite outstanding leader of an increasingly large staff, who was not only much loved by the students as a teacher and mentor but also was a fine promoter of the school. Firm, utterly calm, and bureaucratic enough, he ran very good parties at Hogmanay and also forced us to observe Burns Night! Both staff and students found him to be fair and compassionate; as a partnership we thrived and so did the school. He was described by one of his referees as appearing a little like an Old Testament prophet and indeed he did have a beard of significant length. When, after a few years, he shaved it off, there were days, even weeks in some cases, before he was recognised. As a stranger he heard all sorts of comments about the old deputy head!

The third deputy, Andrew Fleck, was tireless, multi-talented and more of a 'systems' man, a valuable asset in the late 1990s. He went on to be the head of a large school in Yorkshire and is now head of Sedbergh College. It was so important that we found deputy heads from outside the school at that stage in our development, for they added true value and took us forward so that we did not get stuck in our ways. They were ambitious and therefore it mattered that we were successful, for that rightly took them through to their own headships.

Derek Newton came to St Bede's in 1980. I knew him from our Brentwood days and asked him if he would like to join us. He became the leader of our boarding side and the most reliable aide in the planning of the school. He was also by far the best at running the discipline side of things for he seemed to be able to see into the minds of the villains and so was able to anticipate their next moves. He was the most cunning of detectives and enjoyed solving cases. The final denouement of a crime or series of crimes often came during a combined interview by Derek and myself during which I occasionally gave him a rest from his intuitively subtle pursuit of the truth, thereby allowing him to come back refreshed and stronger for the final showdown!

I recall with some pleasure one occasion when he tracked down a Chinese student, who had gone missing for several days after half-term, to a lodging house in Hastings where the young man had been staying with a number of Chinese girls. Jackson Wong was surprised to be woken at 11 p.m. only to find himself staring into the faces of Derek and his own housemaster, Roger Moses. It transpired that he had been delayed not by the ministrations of the Chinese maidens but by the fact that he had got through to the last eight of the Hastings Open Snooker Tournament and was therefore in with a chance of some prize money. We did arrange for him to return from school the next evening to play his match but unfortunately he lost!

Derek's tactical mastery meant that many villains were able to stay on at the school and reform their behaviour, for he was adept at devising ways in which they could save themselves; this was not only much appreciated by the boys and their parents but also was a big advantage to the school's 'bottom line'!

Andrew Barclay was another teacher whom we already knew; he had taught previously at St Bede's Prep School. He was persuaded to become our director of music, arriving from Shiplake College in January 1986. The next 15 years were just exceptionally enjoyable, as we listened to musical performances of the greatest quality. It was perfectly possible to close one's eyes and forget that what one was hearing was a school performance. The singers, including teenage boys, believe it or not, sang in small groups, as well as larger choirs performing some of the greatest choral works as a choral society: how typically English. The orchestra could perform large works from the classical repertoire and there was also a string orchestra numbering about 20 that gave us some wonderful baroque music; there were string quartets too that were a pleasure to listen to and a number of highly talented soloists. But that was not all, for by 2000 we had a superb jazz band, numerous groups playing highly complicated electric-based music, a swing band, a didgeridoo group, crooners singing in 1950s style, and in addition the ability to stage musicals wonderfully well. Before Andrew's arrival the choir had taken a whole term to learn how to sing a well-known hymn, and although those who had survived the tedium of relentless rehearsals did sing it well, they performed somewhat mechanically. Indeed, music then had become an operation of much planning, frequent letters of request for more and more equipment, but more and more excuses as to why nothing was actually happening. This was hugely disappointing after the bright start that music had made under Charles Spanner.

What Andrew Barclay realised was that putting events in the calendar and making them happen gave a real point to all the practice and lots of excitement to the performers. What also helped him not a little was that he had real charisma and if that is needed anywhere it is most certainly required in abundance by directors of music. There really is little point in learning music if it is not to play or sing for the enjoyment of others. Through performing our musicians thrived and we were able to send them out with confidence to act as representatives of the quality that was in the school.

Andrew also realised that although he himself was a fine conductor and motivator, he was not primarily a classroom 'academic' musician. He was however able to attract some serious young talent from the Royal Academy and had the good sense to marry one of these talents: Penny Jones, as she then was, became responsible not only for good GCSE and A-level results but also for the precision and outstanding teamwork of string ensembles. Incidentally, Penny, now Penny Barclay, later combined all this with being a very good housemistress to the Crossways girls.

From time to time when Andrew felt that he should further his career by becoming a housemaster or a deputy head or a head, it was my job to tell him the truth – and that was that there were thousands of potential heads, deputy heads and the like around in schools in the UK but there were very few gifted directors of music in the whole world.

David Graham answered an advert in the *TES*, arriving as head of department for art and design at the beginning of 1984. He was the first full-time artist on the staff and served the school inspirationally for 28 years until his retirement in 2012. By the time I left in 2001 there were six full-time artists on the staff and, thanks to David, art was the most numerically followed subject in the school after the three compulsory ones. Under a highly respected and thoroughly disciplined leader the art department became one of the finest in the country. Some of our students were even allowed to go on to enter top art schools without having to do their foundation courses, because their achievements in GNVQ advanced courses were so outstanding. The department trained students in ceramics, in photography, in graphic design, in painting and drawing, in textile art and in any combination of these things.

The art studios were always open in the evenings and at weekends and there was an atmosphere of serious concentration at these times even when no member of staff was present. Many artists gained the highest recognition in the school even though they were finding much of their academic work really difficult; their contemporaries just marvelled at the range and breathtaking quality of their creative output when it appeared in the annual exhibitions.

It has always struck me that art is a wonderful subject, for like music and unlike a number of other aspects of school life that often seem to gain more adulation and recognition, it is a training in something that will truly last a lifetime as a participant and not just as a spectator (rugby and cricket for example) as one reaches more advanced years. It is also clear that when looking at the portfolio of an A grade A-level artist, one is looking at hours of the most meticulous and professional application. It might be possible to pass a maths or French exam and get it half wrong but in art getting it half wrong doesn't count at all. One might ask – which is the better preparation for the real life after school?

As already mentioned, I appointed another member of staff, Lou Belhriti, on the telephone, whilst she was in Morocco. She is in fact a down-to-earth and talented Lancastrian but at the time was teaching English in North Africa. Within a year of her arrival she took over the running of Dorter House, our second house for girl boarders. She continued to do so with consummate skill for more than 20 years and has been the school's director of boarding in recent years. She has taught English, has been the head of the department of English as a foreign language, and has been a real leader in the school as a fount of practical common sense. I mention Lou because of what she has given to the school and also as an example that making appointments must at times, as I have said before, be allowed to be a calculated risk and not subject to any particular system or rules.

In 1985 I gave a job as a teacher to a local farmer (he had come in for a chat). He walked into my study and proposed that he should join our staff to teach farming or parts of it to those of our students who might be interested. Let's see how it goes, I thought. This appointment did open the way to the keeping of chickens and a few sheep and pigs and to the learning of hedge-laying skills and other activities that benefited a number of our students enormously and hopefully ensured that occasionally labour-intensive jobs on the farmer's farm were more easily completed.

The students also had to understand farming as a commercial enterprise. They might help the ewes to give birth to their lambs and then help to rear them, but after that they knew that lambs would have to go to market to be sold for meat. This was not a problem for the majority of our other students, who in any case did not appear to know or really care about what was going on.

However this was not the case with a batch of eggs that lay incubating in the classroom known as S1 where the farmer taught (it had been Bottomley's Pump Room). These eggs became chicks and at some time after that a number were sold as 'point of lay' and the remainder, now at large in a run in the grounds, grew fatter. The day came when the agricultural or, should I say pastoral, students were told to prepare these chickens for the table so that they could fully appreciate the full cycle of poultry husbandry. They duly set to work wringing necks and plucking, not merrily but certainly noisily, in S1.

This was not well thought out in a school where there were lots of girls, some boys and teachers who were squeamish, and in certain cases vegetarians to boot. There was an invasion of my study by a highly passionate and outraged group of petitioners who demanded that I should rush to S1 immediately and put a stop to the barbarity. Tears were being shed. I managed to persuade the farmer and his tutees to stop the carnage and promise not to do that again in such an indiscreet place. The relentless process whereby the human race is fed did go on back at the farm but the farmer's courses were less healthily subscribed for a time!

The appointment of the farmer was a stroke of good fortune in a different way too, a way that changed the school profoundly by affecting the thinking of all of our teaching staff. Graham Jaggers was not only a farmer but he was also acutely dyslexic. He was a successful entrepreneur with two farms and plans for developing a major adventure and leisure attraction not far from the school; it is still there, thriving and growing, in 2012. He had two sons who were also dyslexic and wanted them to have an education that gave them a realistic chance in life as opposed to his own which, even though it did not seem to have mattered, had not. What is more, Graham not only knew about dyslexia at first hand but had also studied the issue in some depth and was thus able to help his fellow sufferers.

As a boy at Dulwich College Preparatory School in south-east London in the days when schools were not expected to have heard of or in any case to give credence to, dyslexia, Graham had reached the age of 11 without being able to read. His teachers all thought he could, for Graham's very high IQ enabled him to develop effective tactics to disguise his shameful secret. The fact that he got extremely low marks for learning preps, and very low marks for most things as it happened, and seemed permanently unenthusiastic in class was put down to the 'fact' that he was extraordinarily 'thick', a dimwit in other words. That Graham tended to get about two out of ten in the tests on learning homework should instead have been seen as a testimony to his extreme quick-wittedness, for this knowledge was gleaned by picking up clues from what he had heard. Fortunately for Master Jaggers he was struck down by scarlet fever and in the three weeks he was forced to be away from school he taught himself to read by applying himself for hour after painstaking hour to the study of *Alice in Wonderland*. Even in his forties when he joined our staff his spelling would fall apart if he were to be put under any pressure of time and his handwriting was terrible – about average-GP-minus!

However within a few months of knowing Graham we as a staff understood about dyslexia and even the arch backwoodsmen amongst us, who thought it was just an excuse for being bone-idle, began to change their outlook.

Students who might once have been dismissed as lazy or immensely stupid were now being thought about differently. We were introduced to the idea of using educational psychologists. These experts, in turn, were able to demonstrate by testing that certain of our students who found reading or writing very hard, or who could not do maths at all, or who could not really read, had weaknesses in the functions of their brains in such testable areas as coding or digit span. An inability in coding (one of the 20 areas of brain function tested in an IQ test) rendered the teaching of linguistic skills by traditional methods virtually impossible, equally frustrating and demoralising for both the teachers and the taught. If a student's digit span failed the test disastrously, it meant that such was the weakness of the student's short-term memory that he or she could not reasonably be expected to follow a chain of instructions. It was mathematics as traditionally taught that became the problem in these circumstances. Thus adding up columns of long numbers was virtually impossible, whilst the processes of adding fractions or even worse, solving simultaneous equations, would cause the brain to cut out completely. 'You stupid boy!' 'Why don't you listen?' 'You're not trying.' One can hear the frustrated teacher yelling. But the student was far from stupid: could listen but not recall the instructions, and, having tried desperately hard, gave up in a frustration which equalled, or probably surpassed, the teacher's. Within a short time of Graham Jaggers' arrival we were, even more than before, an 'up-to-date' school.

Those who had special needs were detected early by our testing. The nature of their weaknesses was circulated to all the teachers who taught them and instructions were given to each teacher as to the most effective way of teaching that individual. So, for example, it was often important to issue instructions on a printed sheet rather than writing them on the board, as certain students found reading and copying a slow process. In short, students had a statement of their needs circulated to their teachers and, what is more, any failure on a teacher's part to follow the recommendations in the statement was seen as a serious professional offence.

What helped even more was that our curriculum allowed for each student to follow courses that played to their strengths. They certainly had strengths, for throughout my time at St Bede's the highest IQs were always possessed by those who were dyslexic; it was just a matter of setting them out on the right course and, like Richard Branson, many a top actor or indeed Graham Jaggers himself, they would rise to the top. What could be noticed time and time again was a relationship between dyslexia and the form of tunnel vision that enables a person to drive almost manically at their goal. A surprising number of our best artists, actors, makers of clever pieces of engineering, inventors and indeed farmers had in mind the all-important vision of the end product and the practical drive and determination to get there. It was hardly surprising that with their morale lifted by their courses and the wonderful assistance of our professionally trained teachers of those with special educational needs that all our students found the courage to tackle their weaknesses and before they left to pass GCSEs in maths and English. Unlike Graham Jaggers, and thanks in no small measure to him, they were able to win recognition for their talents and to enjoy their school days.

It was rewarding by the 1990s to be recognised as a first-class school for those with learning difficulties or, putting it better, those with special needs. We were far ahead of the game in education nationally in this, for the state system would not face up to the fact that to run schools properly as comprehensive schools, they had to put a lot more money into teachers and specialists to allow much more time for the teaching of certain students in very small sets. Most of the independent schools appeared not to want to be thought of as schools where there were difficult students who might 'lower the tone' even though they actually raised it if treated properly. It has always seemed to me that only Millfield among the leading independent schools has managed to combine, as we did, the teaching of the academically most naturally gifted and the student with acute special needs without doing other than good to both categories. Strangely it was often the academically most naturally gifted who found the achievements of the outstanding dyslexics most inspiring; after all, those in both categories have special needs.

It was possible at St Bede's for public examinations (GCSEs or even A-levels) to be taken as early as 14 or as late as it was necessary to achieve a pass and yet feel comfortable socially whilst staying on at school. It did not take years of educational research to bring this about: just a small amount of common sense.

Enough said on an opportunistic approach to staff recruitment. As a final word, on a rather eccentric note, there was one surname that we never seemed to have much luck with and the appointments of those with this name always seemed to end disastrously. After the third failure I confess to deciding that any application from anyone called by that name had to be basketed. What appalling prejudice and unfairness – I am sure it was probably me that caused the problems and I trust that my successors have exorcised this particular ghost!

Anyone interviewed for a teaching post went off from our discursive and hopefully settling chat to meet the deputy head and the head of the department in which they would mainly work. At some point later in the day (there was no time limit involved) the candidate would come back to me and I would ask them how they had got on and as a matter of course whether they were interested in the job. This was a key question, because if there was the slightest hesitancy or any talk about 'thinking it over' there would be no offer. A discussion with the other staff involved in the process would then ensue and possibly an offer would be made and accepted. What we wanted in every area were enthusiasts, almost maniacs, whose subjects were just the most important things in the world to them and who would sell them to the students with not only zeal but a lot of humour too.

Of course some truly poor appointments were made along the way, particularly when there were few applicants and an urgent need to fill a vital gap. Some new teachers did not last long. The record for short tenure was held by a man from Sheffield who had been appointed to run the design and technology courses. We always had a meeting of all staff on the Friday before school term started on the following Monday. This gentleman listened to the description of the duties that were expected of all staff, concluded that they were too onerous, and arrived in my study two minutes after the end of the meeting to resign. There was never any point in arguing in such cases, nor indeed was there any point in prolonging the career at the school of anyone who was clearly performing badly; if necessary it was worth paying up to finish the contract or even to risk an industrial tribunal.

Very often the best way to discover whether any teacher was going to be a success was to ask one or two of the students quietly and they were never wrong in my experience. Another sure sign each year were the numbers who chose a particular subject, for the word got around quickly amongst the students if the chances of success under a particular teacher were not rosy. These things never changed for the teacher concerned was inevitably one who blamed the students and kept on doing so year after year; such people were in the wrong job!

DEVELOPING OUR OWN CURRICULUM

The St Bede's curriculum came from studying our students and taking full advantage of any developments that helped them; it was never static. Given that the only reason for going to school is to leave, it follows that it is better to leave feeling something of a success than to leave feeling rejected. With this uncomplicated thought in mind it is clear that a good school will so organise its curriculum that each student has a really good chance of feeling a success. Entrance exams will tell you much and if a young person scores lots of marks in all subjects and has a good reference from the head of their junior school then it is likely that such a one will be able to deal with any curriculum. It is equally clear that for those who did not score many marks in any of the subjects tested, or in particular subjects, then an analysis needs to be made and a policy developed to rectify the situation.

Putting those who are deemed by exams to have failed on the right track to success is essentially a simple matter. First, it is necessary to make a proper analysis of the individual student; there are many professionally devised tests to help with this. All the newcomers to our school would sit certain ones so that we could determine their potential (the results would also provide a useful benchmark against which, to use the jargon, a school's delivery of 'value added' could be assessed). Incidentally, it was just as valuable to have confirmation that a young person was indeed extremely gifted in this or that area and there were subjects in which it was extremely likely that he or she would achieve excellence. Such a clear message could not be ignored by our teachers.

In extreme cases, where the student clearly had deep problems to overcome, an educational psychologist's report could be obtained; often one already existed but some junior school had failed to act on it effectively, either because it would cause problems within the system or because the school's attitude was still so old-fashioned that all failures were put down to idleness! Once we knew where we were, either a skilful confidence-building approach had to be taken by teachers to rectify the problems by winning over the student, so that he or she could see a reason to succeed and would therefore develop the will-power to work hard to do so; or things had to be arranged so that certain subjects were avoided altogether. This latter course of action seems at first sight a bit defeatist but it is not pig-headed and it is certainly intelligent. What on earth is the point of banging one's head against a brick wall when there is nothing significant to be gained from doing so?

The view that we developed during the 1980s was based on thinking clearly about what could not be avoided when the boy or girl left school. Our conclusion was that maths to a certain level, English, and the ability to handle information technology were the only subjects taught at school that could not be avoided in the real world. All the other subjects were truly wonderful and highly desirable but not if one was bound to fail in the end, however admirable one's character. What on earth was the point of spending hour after hour in GCSE physics classes if one found the basics of maths virtually impossible at the age of 14? Similarly, an inability to read or write one's own language with any fluency because of the make-up of one's brain was hardly a passport to the study of more languages or those subjects that particularly relied on the writing of English to succeed.

These arguments could be applied to many students and it was impossible to imagine lives being lived in the future based upon what a person was useless at. Was it better in the future to be able to say, with cheerful honesty, I was totally inept at French or chemistry or that I was really good at drama and pottery and still enjoy them? The answer is so obvious that it is surprising that the national curriculum was treated like a holy grail for so many years.

The time saved by not following certain subjects was quite naturally used to give extra help either individually or in very small groups (threes or fours) in those subjects that could not be avoided without a problem emerging later in life. I am still amazed by those who say that everyone should learn a foreign language or learn a science. Have they not noticed that it is possible to lead a perfectly successful life without speaking French or knowing any chemistry? In any case it is certainly true that a few months in another country or a course based on learning to speak another language via CDs will result in anyone learning far more in a short time than they would do at school with the handicap of dyslexia! In the case of chemistry, someone will tell you if you need to know something relevant at any time.

One of the major problems facing teachers and learners in schools is that, totally understandably, the content of courses is dominated by the adults who set them up. Additionally, and understandably to an extent, these adults are the leading professionals in that particular subject and therefore might possibly lack the imagination to feel what it is like to find the subject really difficult. Furthermore they are rightly enthusiasts for their subject and like it to hold its head up in respect of its rigour and intellectual challenge. Who are they trying to impress? Is it other high-flying academics in their own world or really able adults or politicians who can talk of falling standards or rising ones? These are almost certainly the targets; the 13- and 14-year-olds have been forgotten. The geographers want young people to become 'geographers' and the historians want them to become 'historians'. The result of this misplaced enthusiasm is that two really lovely subjects, that so many of us loved, are now made unapproachable for very many young people.

History used to be taught as an exciting story. It evoked wonder, stimulated the imagination and opened the way to enjoyable discussion; it encouraged finding out, made excursions exciting and provided, in the hands of a good teacher, plenty of humour. Now the 13-year-old is told about sources, primary and secondary, and does exercises in empathy, being confined to those periods of history where there are plenty of sources and it is easy, therefore less exciting, to empathise – notably the Second World War, or in extremely enlightened schools the First World War!

As for geography, so determined were the geographers to escape from the jokes they had to bear at university concerning the academic strengths of those studying the subject that they forgot just how many enjoyed their subject and how many leaders of industry emerged from the schools of geography and team games (take St Edmund Hall at Oxford for example). Instead they ruined the subject for many by re-inventing it as a 'science' and filling it with graphs and economics and so much maths that the audience was sure to decline, at least among 14-year-olds and the A-level students who wanted at least one enjoyable subject and had previously chosen geography.

You have probably detected that I have gone off on a major deviation, so I might as well finish it. In the late 1960s, maths got a makeover after it fell into the hands of proper mathematicians and New Maths came about. The result was a subject that ceased to be one at which most Dads, and Mums, could generally expect to help their offspring to one in which they had little, if any, chance of doing so. There were always topics in maths that failed the test of usefulness for a very large proportion of the population but there were not enough of them to cause rebellion. Now were added topics like vectors, which arrived early in a student's time at school. The word was bad enough but as a topic it singularly failed the usefulness test, becoming a companion for simultaneous and quadratic equations. Have you had to use one of those recently, I wonder?

Maths is an essential subject, but why not teach all children a common course up to, say, the age of 14. Then, having discovered who the gifted mathematicians are and those who are not, let there be two distinctly different courses at GCSE level. The first would be compulsory for all and would be called Maths for Citizens: it would deal with adding and subtracting, with working out interest and percentages and fractions, and how much wallpaper you will need and how to make a right angle and the like. Its usefulness could be sold to all students with ease and force of logic as part of one's armoury for life. The second course would be Maths for Mathematicians: it would either be taught simultaneously or at a later date to those who were good enough to do it, or who needed it or wanted to do it, to see if it was for them. This sort of flexibility would cheer up a lot of young people and stop the question 'what is the use of —' when the answer is far too complicated to be convincing at that age, and, in many cases, during the rest of their lives. (Bravo – Carol Vorderman discovered all this in 2011; even I was preaching it at the Dragon School in the 1960s, it was so obvious!)

To return to the narrative though: during the 1980s there were students at St Bede's at The Dicker – and there still are, one hopes – who set out to do five GCSEs, some who do six, a lot that do nine or ten and a few that do 12 or 13. There was no snobbery about this as there was demonstrable success all round. We also introduced a lot more subjects so that there were several courses of art and design, different forms of science such as agricultural science, environmental science and human biology, which, like the other sciences, could be taken either singly or as part of a package. As has already been said, any language could be studied and there were over 30 subjects in all to choose from. Examinations could be taken at a time that was suitable in each individual case. It must be said that the vast majority of the students followed courses and did exams in just the same way as happened in the rest of the country.

Closely related to these considerations is the matter of age. Isn't it amazing how it is almost an immutable norm that students take GCSEs at the age of 16 and A-levels or whatever equivalent at the age of 18? Most of the schools in the UK adhere inflexibly to the notion that in year 10 GCSE courses are started and in year 12 A-levels or their equivalent begin. What is wrong with doing GCSEs aged 14 or 15 or 16 or 17? Or A-levels at 16, 17, 18 or 19? The answer is that there is nothing wrong, except that it takes more organisation.

After all, as I have asked already, what is the purpose of going to school? The purpose is to leave! Is it best to leave when ready to move to the next step in life with a record of success? Yes! What age is this? Don't know! Obviously it would be impractical to have schools with too long an age band but surely a little flexibility would not hurt. Whatever the case, students at St Bede's had that flexibility and there were, and, I believe, still are, students taking all versions of the public examinations at all ages between 13 and 19.

TEN YEARS OLD

We reached the end of our tenth year, in July 1988, full of confidence; mainly because we had survived! We had had to refinance ourselves four times in those ten years but now, at last, we felt somewhat more secure. Our main loan, secured against our property with Alliance & Leicester, was repayable over 25 years rather than five, or on demand, as had been the case with the banks. We had even survived the hurricane of 16 -17 October 1987.

That had been quite an event, for we had woken at four in the morning to the sound of persistent crackling and when we emerged we found that all the roads were totally blocked by the most enormous trees that had been uprooted by the storm. Bottomley had planted lots of pine trees to adorn both the village and his estate, and these had grown to very impressive heights but they had very shallow root systems. With the ground being wet from a lot of rain and the trees, not just the pines, being either evergreen or in leaf, provided plenty of wind resistance and were uprooted or severely broken in their hundreds. Our twelve-year-old daughter, Lucy, having gone out later to catch the bus to school, came running back into the house shouting that the roots of the trees were higher than houses, and indeed they were!

There was no electricity, nor was there to be any for the next two weeks. As we were predominantly a boarding school we decided to carry on as normal. Luckily Angela was so quick off the mark that she reached Hailsham in time to clear the town's supply of candles. Luckily too we cooked by our own supplies of propane gas and our heating was supplied by either oil or propane. Whilst most schools closed, we carried on, eating evening meals by candlelight and illuminating dormitories and studies in the same way; staff went round blowing the candles out at bedtime. Health and safety officials had yet to make their appearance in our lives!

For a week, life went on in this way and we had all adapted in an exemplary fashion to the circumstances when finally the lack of electricity beat us, for the sewage from two of our boarding houses relied on electric pumps to empty a large subterranean chamber into which it flowed and to push it uphill to the main drains. An unceasing battery-powered alarm bell started to ring, telling everyone within half a mile that the chamber was full. At this stage I decided that we would break for half-term a few days early and give all the students a few days extra holiday (they were not unhappy about this).

We also decided that the staff should come into school as normal until the official start of half-term so that we would use these days to clear the grounds of the hundreds of trees that we had lost. There was not universal glee about this decision but it was obvious that the ground staff could not cope alone. By this time there was a really strong team ethic in the school and the ground staff and all who worked in the school in whatever capacity were seen to be part of the team just as much as the teachers, and this was their time of need. It was interesting to see who considered themselves to be above such menial work (two of our best known socialists were the main objectors!) but they were in such a minority that they were shamed into action. At the end of two great days of chain-sawing, dragging, lopping, bonfiring and lumberjacking we were proud of ourselves, somewhat fitter and definitely very well set up for Bonfire Night on 5 November. It was a great team effort and just the sort of thing that made us a little different from the general run of schools. There was an even greater sense of being together when we met for our Christmas parties, which at St Bede's always involved everyone who worked there in whatever capacity; this particular year the celebrations reached new heights of unrestrained jollity, which was extremely difficult to achieve!

Now I was telling you how we finished our tenth year full of confidence and indeed, as we gathered on 8 July 1988 in the large marquee that accommodated students and parents on the final day of each year, we had every right to be feeling good about ourselves. We watched our touring theatre company perform a skilfully compressed *Macbeth* and then we were treated to excerpts from *South Pacific* that were wonderful in quality, humour and design, providing just the right light touch to send us away happily for the summer holidays. We could reflect that we had had an exciting time and achieved more than most people would have believed possible when there were just 23 students in a converted garage or 65 about to inhabit a near-derelict mansion. We had increased in numbers every year and were now over 300. We had also produced surpluses on our trading accounts every year since our third year of existence.

At that year's end we could report that one of our students, Geoff Wiginton, was the first Oxbridge success we had had. He later proved the selectors right by leaving Corpus Christi, Cambridge, with a First. Counting the number of students that get to Oxbridge is not a reliable yardstick for the quality of any school but it was reassuring for us to know that anyone with the necessary aspirations and talent could get there as a result of choosing St Bede's.

We also had an orchestra that had played in public, and successfully too, for the first time; there had been an acclaimed production of *The Crucible* amongst other lively shows. The enthusiasm of Andrew Barclay, our director of music, and Nicky Miles, our head of drama, was uplifting to us all. For the first time our artists had been noted publicly as being quite outstanding, which they truly were and still are. In our brief history we had had two National Under 18 tennis champions, in Clare Wood and Austin Brice, whilst another former student, Julie Salmon (now a most successful coach at the school) had reached the third round at Wimbledon. Clare Wood went on to reach a world ranking in the forties as a singles player and considerably higher as a doubles player, and represented Great Britain in the Wightman Cup.

Spencer Pession from Brighton won the Under 15 World Championship as a skier and his sister, Heidi, went on to do so as well as I recall. It was a pleasure to say goodbye and good luck to Spencer and Heidi at the end of the Christmas term and tell them how much we looked forward to seeing them at the start of the summer term the following April. They did their school work by post and their teachers rose to the challenge; both Spencer and Heidi produced outstanding results, so don't let anyone tell you that missing lessons is all that important! Our boys had also reached the National Tennis Finals at Under 15 level and indeed all our boys' and our girls' teams were thoroughly competitive.

There were other things, too, that enhanced our confidence. We already understood more than virtually any other school, apart from the specialist ones, what was involved in successfully teaching those with learning difficulties. We were a proper international school with the best systems in the area for dealing with the particular needs of those with English as a second language. We were undoubtedly a long way ahead of all our rivals in the provision of and use of information technology. Thanks to the work of Iain Barr we could justify a healthy level of investment in this area and developed compulsory courses for all our students.

It was a great help to have a settled board of governors and the board of 1988 was with only two significant changes the board of 1998. They were real friends to Angela and me, they were truly supportive and we laughed a lot at meetings – not an experience I have enjoyed at the many governors' meetings I have been to myself in that capacity, where it can all be a bit heavy and 'important'. There is a list of all those who have served as governors in an appendix to this book and it would be inappropriate for me at this point to single out any of them for special mention; in truth they were a wonderful team.

In 1988 we produced a new prospectus, which was colourful and had a cover designed by one of our talented young artists, Fay Beaumont. Her design became a sort of brand image. With careful amendments and the addition of Dicker News, the prospectus as a whole became a much admired one by those considering St Bede's, for it said things directly and clearly and had obviously not been produced by one of those professional marketing firms that everyone else seemed to go in for and whose products all seemed the same. It is good to see that Fay's version of the St Bede's bird still remains in 2012 the school's emblem.

Perhaps the greatest indicator of our confidence in the future was that Camberlot Hall was taken off the market for the first time since the year after we had bought it! Banks and planning authorities had urged us to get out of Camberlot from 1981 onwards and the house had nearly sold in both 1987 and 1988, to Andrew Lloyd Webber's orchestrator. However, this excellent man's inability to sell his own property in London (the first signs of the market downturn that was to produce the rash of negative equity in the 1989-1992 period were just showing) and the shock of learning just how much a firm of builders wanted to build us a new boarding house, next to The Stud, meant that luckily we had kept Camberlot.

Sadly, as we go to press, the house has been sold: I hope for a very large sum. In our time it had provided a somewhat more homely experience of boarding school for a group of boys for whom this was appropriate, and a refuge for those who liked to be somewhat distanced from the main sources of authority! It was also important as one of the many factors that made St Bede's unlike other boarding schools and a bit less predictable. However, there are now new, state-of-the-art boarding houses at the school, all wonderfully equipped and one nostalgically called Camberlot; in truth, though, the 'Arthurian' period in the school's history seems to be over as the romantic qualities of this secluded and slightly mysterious pile are quite irretrievable.

It was in 1988 too that St Bede's at The Dicker, or to be pedantic its headmaster, was elected a member of SHMIS – the Society of Head Masters (and Head Mistresses too, it should not be forgotten) of Independent Schools. The Society (now known incidentally as the Society of Heads) and the GBA (Governing Bodies Association) sent inspection teams down to see if we were fit for membership and it added to our confidence when they said that we were – the school, its head and its governors too were all, so to speak, kosher.

Usually my instincts tell me to shy away from such organisations and 'clubbery' but if we wanted the valuable services of ISIS, the Independent Schools Information Service, we had to be a member of one of the organisations that made up the ISJC – Independent Schools Joint Council.

It is possible to be totally acronym-ed out in education and still be none the wiser! The poor teachers in state schools have to put up with such a welter of acronyms, jargon and general gobbledygook that they must seriously doubt the competence of their elders and betters sometimes: and they do!

However as there have always been political opponents of independent schools, the schools have an understandable desire to try to ensure that their names are not linked with latter-day Dotheboys Halls; hence a further reason for being part of an association. Membership was a form of approbation, a sort of kite mark.

As it happened SHMIS would prove to be a thoroughly helpful organisation, one that made very little attempt to interfere in the affairs of its members' schools. It held a conference each year at which there was always some good company and some interesting and valuable ideas to be heard and discussed. There was also an enjoyable golf competition (which I was pleased to win on one occasion) and some good food and some top-class refreshment too – that is if you took care to manoeuvre into a seat at the table manned by the insurance men from Holmwoods (now HSBC Gibbs) who were both very good friends of long standing and thoroughly amusing late night companions, as befits men with deep expense accounts who are the modern day rulers of the world. (If you don't do as they say – which means employing at least one person to do nothing else but risk assessments – they won't pay out!)

Some of our members were also members of HMC (Head Masters Conference) and by and large they felt that they enjoyed the SHMIS meetings more as they were less stuffy and devoid of any snobbery. However it may not have been a disadvantage that one of my best companions at the SHMIS conferences came as part of the inspection team that passed St Bede's fit to be a member of HMC in 2008, thus rendering our school super-kosher.

In 1997 it has to be said that HMC had declined our application for membership: more on this later. I confess to having found this something of a relief, when I considered matters in the cold light of day; there was a scent of regulation and 'this is how it's done' about the HMC and we were not ready for any restraints at that time, however well-intentioned.

If on reflection it could be said that our first ten years had gone surprisingly well, we had also suffered rejection as well as acceptance. In 1984, full of self-belief, we had applied for The Queen's Award for Export Achievement. Putting this application together took many hours that should have been spent on more urgent matters but the governors thought it a good idea and one that, if successful, would have gained us much valuable publicity; indeed it would have. It was not a frivolous application, for by 1984 we had brought into the UK millions of pounds worth of fees from all over the world, having sold our product in every continent. We had made a small but not negligible contribution to the country's balance of payments figures.

It was a disappointment when the letter came saying that our arguments had not convinced the judges but it was interesting to note that we were told that the Queen was unable to make the award as it would seem that by favouring an independent school with royal approval she would be entering a field of contentious politics and appear to take sides. The admirable nature of the British Constitution was revealed quite excellently; there was, rightly too, to be no return to the days of the House of Stuart!

DIFFICULT TIMES

Once one allows the thought to enter one's mind that things are going really well, then it is normally a sign that there is trouble afoot. As all good housemasters know, it is when things have been quiet for a spell and it seems that all is in perfect order that a major drama occurs or a can of worms is revealed. Indeed three years were to pass before the school was to exceed the number of students we had had on 8 July 1988 and in two of the next three years we recorded the only deficits on our trading account since 1979 and up to the present day. There was a severe recession economically and the number of people sending their children to boarding school in the UK declined rapidly. The local economy was weak, interest rates were very high at this time – bank rate hovered around 15 per cent – house prices were falling and independent education was after all not compulsory. Our day student numbers were very weak and local prep schools were not sending us the numbers we had grown to expect.

Thankfully we were truly international and thus we suffered less than most. As the pound sterling was weak there were countries around the world where the St Bede's fees were getting lower and lower, as they did throughout most of the nineties; the Germans, for example, thanks to the strength of the Deutsche Mark against the pound got a fee reduction each year whilst the British got an uncomfortable rise. More German students came as a result and fine students they were too. They enjoyed the freedom that the English method gave them. Also, once we had systems in place whereby they were able to qualify for university either here or back in their homeland, they came in ever greater numbers and stayed for longer.

Ironically, at a time when our politicians were preaching that we must follow the superior German system, more Germans were coming to take advantage of what they perceived to be the superior English system. At least it could be argued that they became totally fluent in speaking and using English, which, thanks to the USA and possibly the World Wide Web, is the only viable international language. What an advantage we had as a nation and what an advantage we had at The

Dicker with the superior flexibility of our curriculum and our outstanding programme for those who needed to learn English as well as qualify for universities.

However difficult things were, it should not be thought that these matters weighed much upon the school – its students and teachers that is – even if they did on others, such as the head, some of the governors and poor Dennis Butler, who had to wrestle with the finances and withstand the unremitting daily torment provided by banks, threatening creditors and those unwilling to yield up the fees they owed.

Indeed, so little was the general morale threatened that in July 1989 we celebrated ten years at The Dicker with a wonderful ball held, of course, in a marquee beside the lake. The setting was superb and Angela was responsible for not only an artistically beautiful scene but also for bringing the very best out of our talented catering staff, who liked nothing better than a chance to show off. She also created an atmosphere that was stylish but lacking in self-importance, as she always did. With nearly all the original students present and lots of other former students there too, we, our staff from all areas of the school's workforce, as well as lots of friends and parents too, were, as usual at St Bede's parties, unrestrainedly celebratory. Horatio would have been proud of us!

DO IT YOURSELF

One important factor in seeing us successfully through hard times was that we had learned to do things for ourselves as we could not afford to pay others to do them. Fortunately the extreme hardship of the early years had bred in us a tendency to thriftiness and to find less expensive ways of reaching our goals. I have already recounted how we were able to manufacture classrooms in the Chicken House and assemble buildings from other people's cast-offs. By 1988 it had become clear that our library was inadequate for a school of our size, as was our staff common room and its facilities, while the provision for recreation and quiet study for a sixth form that had grown from 11 in 1981 to approaching 200 in 1988 was not good enough.

We needed a sizeable new building and not just another second-hand prefab. We decided that we should seek estimates from building firms and at least one of these had long connections with Peter Pyemont and the prep school so we were optimistic. This esteemed firm did indeed provide the lowest estimate and I reported to the governors that we needed at least £800,000 for a building designated 'quick build', a timber-framed construction. I also reported that we could not afford this but that we had a little experience in timber-framed buildings, we had a carpenter on the staff and could get another, and so we could produce a 'slow build'. All we needed to do was to get an architect to draw up some plans of what we wanted and to help us through the planning and building regulations stages. I was sure that good tradesmen would follow the drawings as they always did, pointing out errors to the architects and suggesting sensible and cheap ways to solve the problems that emerged.

My brother, running the family building business in Walton-on-Thames, thought my analysis was right. Fortunately we had a firm of architects in mind that would treat us well, for John Innerdale had been on the staff as head of art before David Graham and his firm, Innerdale Hudson, contained Richard Hudson, with whom we were to work over many years and who was responsible for the imaginative nature and aesthetically excellent quality of several of our buildings.

In November 1988 we were granted planning consent for a building that would contain a new and unbelievably luxurious staff common room (compared with the existing one), complete with subsidiary offices and services, a large library of a height that would permit at a later date a mezzanine floor, a common room for sixth formers complete with services and a bar, and furthermore a number of small rooms which would act as study rooms or small teaching rooms and which soon became the headquarters of special needs teaching. These rooms became known as the T rooms (they were close to the S for Stables rooms) and several of those who taught in them inevitably became known as the T Ladies.

This building was to be situated beside the main lawn but was to detract as little as possible from the beauty of the landscape. It achieved this wonderfully well and when it was finished we had a building of unimposing proportions that did not appear at all 'schoolish'. What is more, it was built entirely of wood so that even the roof was covered in cedar shingles. The wooden construction fitted in really well with the garden landscape but, primarily, it was made of wood so that our two carpenters could build it as we had planned, with a little help from a plumber and an electrician.

During 1989 our friend Mr King and his company provided us with foundations and drainage, discovering at the time that we were proposing to build over the top of a set of large, brick-built chambers that had stored the water supply for Horatio Bottomley and his household. There being no mains water in Bottomley's time, all the rainwater from the roof of his house collected in these chambers, situated deep under the lawn, and was then pumped back to the storage tanks in the house from the pumping room, now classroom S1, any excess water draining off into the lake. This admirable system did not make the laying of foundations a simple task!

The building first came into partial use in November 1991 and was then officially opened by Admiral Sir Lindsay Bryson, then Lord Lieutenant of East Sussex, at the end of term in July 1992. The entire structure had been built by Eric Rogers and Mick Richards. At times they had had to stop, to complete other maintenance jobs around the school, so it all took quite a long time.

The whole process, though, had been a highly instructive one. Because it did take a long time, the costs were spread and this suited our cash flow. It also showed that if something was really wanted then there was always a way to get it; and, furthermore, the staff realised that they could survive perfectly well during the period of waiting. At all times we were in charge of our own destiny and so if it was inconvenient to carry on, we could stop. By purchasing all our own materials we saved about 20 per cent on the amount we would have had to pay to a contractor. We could also hire in tradesmen directly, as and when they were needed, at about half the cost they would have been charged to us by a contractor.

At the end, when all the bills were added up, the building had cost us just over £350,000, against an original estimate, and they never tell the whole truth, of £800,000. There was a real sense of pride around the place and a process had been started that was to be repeated regularly from that point onwards.

The innovative and enjoyable science building (no science 'block' here) was another all-wooden construction. Later, we complied with the increasingly complex health and safety legislation and were our own 'main contractors' for the creation of The Dorms boarding house from the six Stud Cottages, the stylish Perrin Building, various buildings to house the grounds and maintenance departments, the all-purpose Hall, and latterly important new buildings at the prep school.

There were times when the technical difficulties involved in producing a building meant that we had to call in a main contractor – the swimming pool building with its complex engineering was a case in point – but I cannot tell you how exciting it was, in the days when the school was still extremely young and not at all affluent, to produce top quality buildings at about 45 per cent of the commercial contractor cost. How fortunate I felt to be able to take a daily part in the direction of these projects and to live, very temporarily, in another world, amongst very capable people who all seemed to have a refreshing brand of humour.

We were so lucky to have at our disposal an inventive, imaginative architect who was truly sympathetic to the history, atmosphere, landscape and structure of Bottomley's estate. How fortunate we were, too, to have the expertise of the likes of Shaun Pantry, a carpenter with a well-organised mind whom I had first spotted when he came to do a couple of minor jobs in the school as a self-employed tradesman. He and Derek Wingrove, proper builders both, ran our projects in a truly professional manner that impressed architects, engineers, building inspectors, sub-contractors and even firemen. They filled me with confidence too for they clearly set high standards and knew what they were talking about. How even more fortunate we were not to have a bursar flapping around, feeling the need to be important!

The thought of a traditional bursar's role makes me think of another area in which doing it oneself reaped rich rewards. In our very early days, one of our only governor-appointed bursars felt it was necessary to make his mark and impress the governors by extolling the virtues of contract caterers. The fact that such a move would rid the bursar of considerable hard work, responsibility and a certain amount of anxiety was not mentioned in the presentation and I listened, head in hands, to such phrases as 'budgetary certainty', 'responsibility for all employment matters', 'full responsibility for all aspects of environmental health, quality control' and 'bulk purchasing savings'. I knew, as did the trust secretary, the omniscient Penhallow, that our governors were going to be taken in: and they were! It all seemed too good to be true: and it was!

I can't remember now whether they were called Grand Metropolitan or Compass Services. I can remember Penhallow telling me that contract catering would cost us an arm and a leg. The first manager we had was absolutely first-rate but after a period he left to start up a new site for the company and it soon became apparent why this was the case, for he was possibly their only excellent manager. His successor needed a manager himself. So much for 'management expertise' offered in the presentation: Angela was still our manager and, luckily for the school, an unpaid one. When the monthly bills came in and I questioned the bursar about 'budgetary certainty' – for they were inevitably higher than we had anticipated – he fidgeted about and said someone had asked for an extra match tea and we had given a sandwich and a cup of tea to a visiting speaker. (Neither of these had been in the contract – oh no!) To cut a long story short, the bursar fortunately left and we soon terminated the contract with the catering company.

From then on we employed our own team. Of course there were moments of anxiety over the years. For example, the first, admirable catering manager did very well until his side-line of running a dating agency outgrew his ability to do his day job and he sadly left. His immediate successor unfortunately saw all his staff, whether female or male, as immediate sexual opportunities: I remember explaining to him as I sacked him that even if the allegations were not true, the fact that most of his team thought from personal experience that they were true meant that the style of his leadership was not good for team spirit. Then for the next 20-plus years, the catering manager was Michael Wallis. The team consisted of Michael, who liked to beat his budget forecast, his brother Trevor, who was a gifted chef, David Solomon, who was a master of the pudding and of course Angela, who, until we left, inspired great quality, particularly for special events. She also ran the committee of students who presented suggestions regarding all aspects of their food every term. Together these people were a truly magnificent and a highly respected part of the whole school team.

To round things off, the only good thing the catering company did for us was to employ Michael Wallis. When we produced the figures for the year after they left, we found that we had employed more people, produced much larger portions for our students, given them all a far greater choice at all meals, produced the most outstanding food for special events and saved ourselves over £30,000 to boot. Don't let any bursar tell you otherwise. That Penhallow knew a thing or two and we each had a small smile on our faces when we revealed this outcome to the governors.

It was a sad day indeed when 'Pen' retired as our secretary and clerk to the governors not that long afterwards. He had done an enormous amount to assist with the setting up of the school and as a source of good-humoured wisdom and support both Peter Pyemont and I had found him truly invaluable.

Even in matters of health and safety and environmental health, it was far too easy to put management teams into an unjustified state of fear and trepidation. Any self-respecting catering manager knows the form and in any case the council officers come round and they tell you what to do and give a time limit to comply. Frankly I could go on and on about health and safety legislation for a long, long time. The school now, I am led to believe, employs a person who does nothing else but go around assessing risks. We all assessed risks quite naturally as part of life, having been taught by our parents and our experience to do so. We pointed them out to those who could do something about them if we could not do so ourselves. We applied common sense and did not need someone to spell out to us that sharp edges were dangerous. I wish sometimes I had become involved in one of those profitable ventures making silly notices of the 'THIS IS A RIVER; IT CONTAINS WATER; DANGER OF DROWNING' variety. Unfortunately insurance companies make us put them up and also force us to produce lengthy documents, the products of even lengthier committee meetings, to prove that we go about being both conscious and generally sensible!

Whatever else may or may not be true there is a great and thoroughly merited pride that is engendered in any organisation by the knowledge that the team is made up of people from all walks of life who can manage their own responsibilities and do so really well. All these marvellous people, so expert, were part of our daily life and our friends, not just people who flew in because we could not cope. We knew them all and shared their ups and downs.

I have talked in some detail about the DIY aspects of our building and catering but I could just as easily have talked about the preparation of our accounts, done without external aid save auditors, or managing the maintenance and repair of all our vehicles and machinery ourselves. When I saw one of those small white vans labelled Partco or Unipart or the like arrive on site, normally driven at urgent speed by a young woman, I thought with pride that we were as good as any garage. Thanks to Kevin Reed, who was mentioned earlier, and Simon Richards, St Bede's was and still is.

HOLIDAYS – WHAT HOLIDAYS?

It was really irritating when friends not involved in education said how much they envied our long holidays and assumed we were off lying on beaches or travelling the world for weeks on end. The days of 13 weeks a year in our house in Cornwall ended when the school started and for the first few years we were lucky to be able to escape for three weeks in a year, although that improved to about five in the second decade. Not only were the pursuit of customers and the managing of building projects reasons to remain at The Dicker, but the school was also so short of money that from the earliest days, the premises were let out not only in the summer holidays but also at Christmas and sometimes at Easter too. Luckily The Dicker was a lovely place to be for our children and their friends. Those that rented the premises were a very mixed group of organisations and mixed blessings too on several occasions.

Ideally we would have liked to run beautiful summer courses at which talented young musicians gathered for weeks at a time in the idyllic setting of The Dicker and played and sang and finished with a wonderful open air concert before a happy audience on a balmy summer's evening. Both Charles Spanner and Andrew Barclay drew up plans for such events and publicity material and mail-shots and advertising took place; Charles even enrolled Lady Barbarolli as patron. But there were never enough takers and both programmes failed to get off the ground. It was disappointing and the reality of using our premises for profit during holiday periods was more mundane.

We started by making an agreement with an Italian based in Eastbourne who wanted to bring large numbers of young compatriots to Sussex to learn English by the seaside. He could see easy money and we naively believed in his plans. Nothing materialised and our dreams of reaching August without a financial crisis melted away. However the following summer the school *was* filled with Italian youths from another source and they were with us for about a month. It was on balance slightly better the year before, when no one came. For these visitors might have learnt a little English but they also certainly experienced the joys of a holiday away from home and parents – sun, perhaps, sea at times yes, sand not much, sangria not at all, but sex in abundance, which they recorded, along with other recollections and points of view, in an outpouring of graffiti. Although this showed that a certain amount of English had indeed been assimilated, it was mainly scrawled in easily translatable Italian. Clearing up and repairs bit deeply into any profit but the village shop did sell a lot of ice cream!

Faith in human nature was restored the following Christmas when the followers of Gurdjieff, those who had used The Dicker as their English headquarters until 1976, came back to relive old times. These students and followers of The Work weaved and spun and painted and created and cooked and discussed for a week. They were admirable and positive and highly intelligent and a pleasure to have around, and they paid modestly but promptly. They spent three happy Christmases with us. We also had good luck and happy relations with an evangelical church group from Cuckfield who stayed for part of the summer holidays for many years.

On two or three occasions the religious theme was maintained by the presence of summer holiday camps for Orthodox Jewish organisations from North London. At these events young people, mainly teenagers, escaped their urban surroundings to, in theory, enjoy the country life, give their parents a rest and imbibe the teachings of their rabbis and cultural leaders. They managed their own catering, purifying in a proper manner our cooking pots and utensils and delivering strictly kosher fare.

One group ran a string round the whole of the grounds at The Dicker, thereby creating symbolically 'holy' territory, or that is what I assumed to be the case. They also placed in the trees at various strategic points loudspeakers, which were wired up to broadcast at an impressive volume ethnic music and chantings throughout the day and into the evening.

Whilst this may have been satisfying to the initiated, it was not to the taste of the inhabitants of Upper Dicker, for the sounds provided an unwelcome background to family lunch parties, gardening, doing the washing up, walking the dog, shopping and village cricket matches. You can imagine who had to field the complaints! 'It's in hand', 'they have given assurances...' – I practised a string of diplomatic utterances without having any confidence that anything would change.

I just hoped that their cheque would not bounce and that none of their black-suited, hirsute and skull-capped members would be addressed in an uncomplimentary way by a villager or that nothing worse might befall them. It has to be said that for a few weeks the village took on a theatrical look for the black-suited outnumbered the orthodox, if I can use that word, citizenry. Needless to say, Glen Carr at the village shop with his customary meticulous judgement, was quick to stock the appropriate items of appropriate or rebellious foodstuffs, and was well pleased once again!

On one occasion I came out of our house to get into the car but caught sight of a head protruding from behind a pillar of the school's entrance and thus beyond the string, but only just. The desperate figure waved a plaintive hand in my direction. I went to see what the problem was, only to be asked if I could possibly carry 100 or so books to the drama studio. The service was about to start and the congregation were expectant but the Leader had forgotten to put the books where they were needed the day before and now it was the Sabbath. He was forbidden, in accordance with the strict rules laid down in Old Testament times, to do any physical work on this day. I enjoyed helping but got the impression that the waiting youth would have enjoyed their day better if I had not! Fundamentalism of any sort and its 'laws' has an impractical quality and sometimes fails the test of 'treating one's neighbour...'; it becomes clear why the New Testament was necessary!

Despite some of the blips in public relations with the village, the governors were still keen for us to continue our quest for additional income. For a few years therefore we entered into a contract with PGL Adventure Holidays, leaders in the field of summer camps for the children of hard-working and affluent parents. They were organised as well as their university-age keepers could manage, enjoyed themselves, put on hearty shows, never reached the levels of attendance that they promised, paid when pursued, did a lot of damage and had to be pursued yet again. It has to be said though that we were grateful for any extra revenue at this time.

In the beginning ... there was Peter Pyemont (PP) (*above left*) whose idea the school was, the 'advertiser' in PO Box 315 and whose garage was to be converted to house the new school. Among the original Board of Governors were Jack Hawkins, chairman 1979-1980 (*above centre*) and David Baker (*above right*), seen here dressed up as High Sheriff of East Sussex, who was Chairman of the St Bede's Trust from 1980 to 1999, giving endlessly encouraging and timely service. There were buildings: inside the converted garage (*below*) and the first boys' boarding house in Darley Road, Eastbourne (*left*).

There were teachers too: Mary Bide (*above left*), now Rector of Wimbledon, Peggy Metcalfe (*above centre*) and, as we saw The Dicker for the first time (*below*), Stephen Barnes, second from the left, and the rest of the school! Exploring The Dicker: outside (*bottom*), and inside (*right*).

There (*above*) is The Dicker house and here we are (*below*), the Perrin family surveying the scene on our first visit to The Dicker.

Early buildings at The Dicker: the church, Holy Trinity, Upper Dicker (*above*); the Stables, housing amongst other things the first science laboratory (*below*); Crossways Cottages (*right*) our family home for 22 years, although Peter Pickard only allowed us half of it for the first two years; and (*far right*) the Upper Dicker Village Shop.

Horatio Bottomley's Conservatory (*below*), the Aviary – later music rooms (*left*) and (*above*) our first new buildings (all second- or third-hand and all free of charge!).

Some early staff: Peter Spiers (*left*), first groundsman, wellington boots in the bag, with Peter Howard, first maintenance maestro: Derek Newton (*above left*), untiring, constructive ally throughout the early development of the school, a boarding house master, assisted mightily by his wife Jo, for 20 years; and there I am (*above*) established in my study, half of Horatio's drawing room (economy bookcasing courtesy of Peter Howard).

Buildings of the early 1980s: the first Dorms house 1980 (*facing page bottom*) cheap steel-covered, bolt-together pre-fabrication from Presco Buildings, Porthcawl; Camberlot Hall boarding house 1981 (*above*); The Dicker Stud boarding house 1983 (*left*); and (*below*) The Dicker Stud stable-yard 1984, converted to study bedrooms.

Some key arrivals of the 1980s: Dennis Butler (*above left*) looking a little coy amidst his financial team (Tricia Russell, who succeeded Dennis, on the right, Sam Bennett on the left); our financial saviour and long-standing governor Mervyn Griffiths (*left*) looking piratical and, to enhance his financial credentials, pictured with the then Governor of the Bank of England; Lou Belhriti (*above, she's on the left!*) very long- serving housemistress to the girls of Dorter and later Head of Boarding; John Berryman, our spiritual guide, pictured in a characteristically colourful tie as part of the day house (*below, ringed*).

On the facing page Andrew Barclay (*top left*), director of music (that's what you saw as a chorister!); David Graham (*bottom, ringed*), leader of a superb Art Department, as housemaster of the Dorms House; Graham Jaggers (*middle right*), dyslexic entrepreneur, who inspired our understanding of those with dyslexia and other learning difficulties; Dr Colin Tourle (*middle centre*), our wonderful school doctor, pictured here with his team – Angela – doing their daily business; a proud catering team (*top right*), managed by Michael Wallis, at the top of the steps on the left, and inspired in culinary terms by his brother Trevor, seated second from right; and (*middle left*) Kevin Reid (Transport Manager, pictured with some of his go-kart builders and vintage car restorers).

Do-it-yourself buildings of the 1980s and 1990s: simple ones (*left and below*) the chalets for sixth-form girl boarders and (*bottom*) classrooms made in the Chicken House being assembled and spreading down a concrete road through Bottomley's orchard, hence the 'O' rooms.

Not helpful! The hurricane of October 1987 (*top and above*). More ambitious and increasingly stylish: the entire construction team in front of the Library and Staff Common Room building (*right*) and (*below*) its opening with Admiral Sir Lyndsey Bryson, Lord Lieutenant of East Sussex, and Eric Rogers, Head of Building and Maintenance, having cut the tape.

The swimming pool (*above*) opened outdoors before being covered and attached to squash courts and fitness rooms. Converting the Stud Cottages into the new Dorms boarding house (*below*) and (*right*) the team that did the job, including seven students of the school. Can you spot two Perrins and future senior housemaster Ed Dickie?

Even more stylish, new Science Laboratories (*above*) and (*left*) our construction team leaders: Shaun Pantrey flanked by, right, Derek Wingrove and, left, Rupert Cain. Finally, thanks to the same team, the Perrin Building in the course of construction (*below*), displacing the lovely free buildings of old.

Those that made things work: three Deputy Heads, all of whom went on to headships of senior schools; (*above left*) James McCarthur (1982-1988); (*above centre*) Jim Malcolm (1988-1997); and (*above right*) Andrew Fleck (1997-2002). Arrivals of the 1990s: Sally Wellings, first Head of Marketing and PR (*below left*); Kim Reed (*below centre*), my PA extraordinaire and international tennis player; Jill Ho (*below right*), the founder of St Bede's International Summer School; Leigh Bennett, head groundsman (*bottom right*), pictured making a putting green from part of a cow field; Wendy Vincent-Smith (*bottom left*), the Principal of the Legat School of Ballet, part of St Bede's from 1999.

Celebrating and partying: Dame Felicity Lott (*top left*) helps Andrew Barclay to cut our 21st birthday cake after a concert to celebrate the event; Christmas duties at the annual party for the whole work force (*top right*); Tenth Anniversary Ball (*above left*); Angela's preparations for '20 Years at The Dicker' Ball (*above right*); end of summer term annual marquee on the lawn (*below*).

Christmas party with Roger Hyde-Peckham (*top left*), Upper Dicker character and leaf mover par excellence; end of year BBQ for the whole work force (*top right*) and (*above*) a house staff dinner. Angela and Roger Perrin (*below*), and (*left*) enjoying their retirement party with Griff Rhys Jones.

Then one day in 1992 a lady asked for a meeting and sitting in my study suggested that we start a Summer School at The Dicker as a partnership. She said that she had learned how these schools worked in a previous job and that they could produce significant profits. The proposal was that we should form a partnership and that the St Bede's International Summer School be founded. St Bede's and Mrs Jill Ho would be equal partners and would share the launch costs. Mrs Ho would run the show and be paid a salary but all costs would be shared equally and the profits divided equally too. The school would get rental income per capita per week and would charge for its catering and cleaning services.

It was agreed that each party would put in £17,000 towards the start-up costs of the enterprise, including the publicity, brochures and development of the network of agents needed to bring in the students. Mrs Ho certainly knew what she was doing and before we had paid our £17,000 entrance fee in full she announced that there were already enough deposits paid to make it unnecessary to put any more money in.

In this way a wonderful venture was started. Jill Ho was an outstanding organiser. She ran things with true professionalism and without any fuss and I was left to look after the school. We never had any disagreements; the project prospered and we developed other centres at St Aubyns in Rottingdean, at Lancing College and even for a brief period at Wycliffe College in Gloucestershire. Jill's husband Harry started a sister International Summer School at the preparatory school in Eastbourne, in which we enjoyed a 25 per cent share of the profits.

Our Summer School was accredited by the British Council and was one of few upmarket operations in this often doubtful area of commercial enterprise. It was a great success because Jill knew what good standards were and laid on really top courses run by able directors. She was an expert in managing the costs and maximising the profits without losing sight of quality. Within a few years we had developed a fine international reputation in all the continents, except of course Australasia, and were making profits that amounted to over £100,000 in a six-week period of the summer holidays – and that was just our 50 per cent share. We had rental income as well as the profit and the days of wondering if the salaries were going to be paid in August were well and truly over.

When we left The Dicker in 2001 the school bought out Jill Ho's share and the Summer School still flourishes, with the school enjoying 100 per cent of the profits. If ever anyone deserved the profits of a venture it was Jill; she was a model of calm efficiency and honesty; everyone who dealt with her knew where they stood; she enjoyed every aspect of business and enjoyed greatly being able to announce record profits.

We all went out and enjoyed a marvellous celebratory dinner once we had clearly reached game, set and match! Here was yet another example of how well things went when we did them ourselves. As a by-product of all this, Angela and I remain firm friends with Jill and Harry and I still enjoy playing a weekly game of snooker with Harry and other friends at his house in Eastbourne. He is as optimistic of profit at the table as he is in business but he is undoubtedly better at business than potting!

1992

Apart from the Summer School, 1992 was a truly notable year. The number of students reached 350, the first rise in numbers since 1988. At this point steady progress began, whereby the numbers rose every year. In 2001 the school roll passed 600 and in 2009, I am told, it reached 900. In 1995 when we reached 450 the governors called a special meeting for the sole purpose of reviewing the numbers in the school.

After much discussion it was agreed, put to the vote and recorded that the school would best be served if it did not exceed 450 in number. Two months later, at the first governors' meeting after this solemn decision had been made, I apologised to them and said that there were now 465 students in the school. The board, being practical people, decided not to express a view on the subject again: and I asked for guidance as to how I could refuse entry to the charming boys and girls who applied, some of whom needed our help really urgently.

In 2001 when I left the boarders made up about 60 per cent of the school. In 2009 the number of boarders remained more or less the same as in 2001 but they comprised only 40 per cent of the total. These ratios should not make any difference to the school's way of doing things and the steady rise in day pupils was clear proof that what was being done clearly worked and impressed the local community.

Let us hope, however, that in the future the proximity of so many of the parents will not have a misleading influence on those in charge. It should always be of paramount importance that those who board at the school are thought of first. As stated earlier, a really good boarding school will always be an outstanding day school whereas a good day school is quite likely to be a poor boarding school. What really counts for boarders is a well-balanced week and well-balanced days. Thus the extra-curricular programme is, for the boarders, essential, as they have no access to local clubs, and the club activities that form such an important part of each day at The Dicker help to make it a very good boarding school. If the extra-curricular programme is to be allowed to flourish, involving all members of the teaching staff, and if the week is to be well balanced for boarders then the academic teaching programme has to be spread across more than five days each week and teaching has to take place on Saturday mornings.

Strong pressure can be put on schools by day students and their parents who do not want Saturday school. Some have given in to this pressure and are then left wondering why their boarding numbers have withered away. Some schools do argue that they still have Saturday games programmes, but most students are not in school teams and if they are, I wonder if they really want to be! Lots of members of staff would like to leave Saturdays to a few of their colleagues and also go home on weekdays at three or four p.m. like other day school staff they observe. And, if they do this, what happens to the boarders whose parents are far away and who cannot be a nuisance at the 'school gate'? What the boarders then get is a form of babysitting, so that the quality of their experience at school is seriously diluted. Discerning parents will look for a real boarding school and easily detect a day school that 'has' boarders. Even more importantly, perhaps, the morale amongst the school's staff will decline, slowly at first but inexorably, as there is perceived to be a failure to distribute the tasks that form the daily running of the school fairly amongst all the teachers.

Certain things always follow from the abandonment of Saturday school. More boarders are at a loose end and they inevitably fill their time in other ways – and not always in the library. In fact our own daughters for a while attended a boarding school in which for the staff's convenience (and most of these were married ladies who had families to look after at the weekends), the library was only open at certain hours at the weekend, whilst the facilities for art and information technology were firmly closed on Fridays to open again at nine a.m. on Mondays. Both Lucy and Sally left and went to a real boarding school.

Small wonder that the lure of local towns and the temptations that are such an attractive part of adolescent life become a troublesome *raison d'être* for many boarders far from home! A few hours each week spent experiencing the 'real world' is a welcome respite for boarders who have been really busy, but any more than that tends to lead to all sorts of unproductive preoccupations. In any case, if Saturday school is abandoned (incidentally often paving the way for weekend jobs for the day students that have never had other than a weakening effect on exam results) then the holidays should be shortened by four or five weeks each year; this does not seem to happen in those schools that have abandoned Saturdays and weak reasons are given for it not happening. However what I have just said is just a personal opinion and could be hopelessly out of date but boarders do pay enormous fees and most of what they pay is for the services of the whole staff during the whole of each term: perhaps the fees should be lowered in compensation!

In 1992 St Bede's at The Dicker suddenly made a surplus of over £300,000 (the previous high had been about £90,000). For the first time the surplus that the school had generated was to make a real difference to the capital plans that could be carried out. Previously, if there was anything substantial that needed to be purchased or built, then all the money had to be borrowed or the overdraft stretched to dangerously high levels. As it happens not only did the number of students attending rise every year, at least until 2008, but the annual surpluses also rose, certainly until we left in 2001, and by that time they had reached on one occasion seven figures.

Somewhat earlier, in 1989 to be precise, we had received planning permission to put up a new building to house a swimming pool, ancillary changing-rooms and three squash courts; it was also to include a gymnasium containing modern fitness equipment, so that those who were inclined to work out, or who needed to, were catered for. We could not afford this, nor could we claim that it was essential and therefore it was pointless asking any organisation to lend us the money.

Somewhat 'tiresomely' – I say this partially in jest – one of the governors said that he knew someone who ran appeals and who had been very successful in doing so. Shortly afterwards an appeal was duly launched: fund-raising dinners were held and other events organised. Personally we felt a little guilty because we didn't happen to know lots of people with large sums of money who were looking for somewhere to put it. Also it seemed to me that there were much better things to do with one's time than to assemble groups of people in London and other centres of population in order to try to persuade them to part with their money for a swimming pool – and that wasn't just because I had always hated swimming.

The appeal leader had indeed done well at other places but he had not previously worked in the middle of a serious recession, or for a school with very few former students – those that we did have were no more than 26 years old at the oldest! In 1992, David Summers, one of the most recently appointed governors (whose son, incidentally, was a first-class tennis player and also won the sixth-form prize for history in 1989), decided to run the London Marathon on behalf of our appeal for funds for the swimming pool. He managed to raise the quite amazing sum of £4,000 and with this generous help and the appeal fund having reached about £100,000 out of the £250,000 we had hoped for, we decided to call it a day. We closed the appeal and, armed with our new-found financial confidence, decided to get the pool started.

Work began in 1993 and on 1 June 1994 we held an inter-house swimming competition in what was by then an open air pool. The superstructure was completed in 1995 and a fine building it was too, enabling serious swimmers to train in a competition-sized pool and for local swimming clubs to do so too. Local residents formed a club and we also allowed the local primary school, Park Mead, to use the pool completely free of charge; this was, of course, entirely at one with our determination that the school should be of benefit to the village and local community.

Indeed we greatly enjoyed doing so many things to help the primary school at that time. Not only did we offer the use of various buildings in which to hold their events but also we sent in senior students to assist the teachers in the afternoons. I hope these excellent relations persist and are part of normal life, not just seen as a means to maintain charitable status. Incidentally, the year 1992 also saw us running the village shop, having purchased it from Glen and Phil Carr late in 1991. There is more about this and what it meant to the school a little later in this account.

In addition, 1992 was notable for the completion and opening of the library, the staff common room and the sixth form common room, as well as the teaching rooms and offices that also comprised this unusual and picturesque building. As I mentioned earlier, Admiral Sir Lindsay Bryson, the Lord Lieutenant of East Sussex, performed the opening ceremony but Eric Rogers, our carpenter, cut the ceremonial tape.

What made the year even more notable was the help we received, without any warning, from John Clare, then the chief education correspondent of *The Daily Telegraph*. He asked if he could come down to see the school, having got wind of us from one or other of his London contacts. He was enjoyable company and clearly approved of the school's philosophy. Our reward was even more unexpected for he produced a double page review in his paper that was really favourable both to the school and, even more surprisingly, to its management. We were included in *The Daily Telegraph Good Schools Guide*, an entry which was free to the school to prove that such favours could not be bought. This was a great boost to our morale and coincided with my decision that we ought to make much more effort on the marketing and public relations front.

I was a bit ashamed of my efforts in this respect for most other heads seemed to be holding highly publicised events to promote their schools; they entertained furiously and jetted off to distant parts of the globe on recruitment campaigns; they were constantly in the Education Special Reports of local newspapers making what seemed occasionally to be highly exaggerated claims and held frequent Open Days. All I was doing was staying in Upper Dicker. I did sense that this was not a totally misguided policy, for our numbers still seemed to go up – this was probably something to do with ensuring that we did a good job where it really mattered. But it would be nice if we did some of the more adventurous things, too, to ensure that the school remained in the public eye and that ever more people heard of the service that we could offer their sons and daughters.

In the event I found that I did not have the time to do all, or even one or two, of these functions justice. If I was honest I would probably have admitted that I did not like the prospect of travelling around as a salesman either. And so it was that in 1992, as I have already mentioned earlier in this account, when interviewing for a new school secretary, I found myself talking to a candidate who seemed to me to be a powerful character, likely to be a thorough nuisance as a school secretary but, as the recently resigned editor of the *Sussex Express*, one of our local weekly newspapers, a person who might help me out with this marketing and public relations business. Such an appointment might well help the cause and salve my conscience.

As the interview progressed, it changed direction, with the role of school secretary fading away altogether. Sally Wellings, for it was she whom I was interviewing, and I, together with Jill Ho, then spent several productive years as a really effective marketing team. I only had to leave Upper Dicker to go to events and exhibitions that were set up for me by those who knew how to do these things. We had lots of prep school heads to lunch, and we appeared constantly in the press showing what our students did and thus what we offered. Unlike the local competition, we did not just crow about victories on the games field, although we did make sure that national successes by our games players were well publicised. We showed off what students were making, we showed off our vibrant drama and music. We showed off those rearing sheep and laying hedges. We toured with plays and also ran events in which a play was chosen and then put on to a large audience for charity within 24 hours of the play being announced – 'Twenty Four Hours to Showtime' they were called – and the marketing team made certain everyone knew about them. We went to lots of exhibitions around the south of England and spoke at prep school events. Sally and Jill went off to far away places and recruited for both school and Summer School. Believe it or not, having a full time director of marketing and PR was virtually unheard of in 1992 (everyone has got one now) and by pure luck we were once again ahead of the game. Mrs Wellings, a true journalist and unearther of information *par excellence*, certainly made a very important contribution to our growing prosperity and reputation.

These were exciting times. But not everything was that exciting, for 1992 also saw the introduction of school league tables and the beginning of a period still not ended in which central government meddled and fumbled with the country's education, producing initiatives as knee-jerk reactions to perceived problems or to prove that they believed in schools and education whereas in fact they knew little about them apart from ideas to which their prejudices led them.

GOVERNMENT LEADS A MERRY DANCE

The idea of a comprehensive school seems a pretty sensible one to me. In such a school young people of all different types, from different backgrounds, of different ethnic groups, of different creeds, come together. They have abilities and skills and difficulties in all sorts of different areas of life and learning. Having come together and, being equally valued for each one's particular talents by those that run the organisation, they, through meeting together over a longish period of time, learn to appreciate each other. They should learn that everyone they meet at this school may well be better than them at any one of the different activities but that that is something to be happy about, for the others know that about them too. It is a type of school that a few enlightened politicians have aspired to make the norm but alas they have failed.

They have failed because the majority of their colleagues do not have their imagination or courage and because education in the civil service and in the town halls is managed very often by those who because they have been successful as young people in their particular schools think that everyone should be like them. It follows in these narrow minds that the schools that they associate with their good fortune and success must be the right pattern for everybody. There is at large a form of educational chanting that puts out populist but entirely untruthful messages to appeal to the prejudices of a largely Middle England audience that has been partly, but importantly, responsible for undermining the comprehensive schools from the beginning.

Let me give you one example of a recent chant. This misleading rant concerns A-levels: we are led to believe that some A-levels are superior to others. Supposedly there are easy A-levels and hard ones and the only reason that the grades that students achieve are getting better is that more and more of these inferior A-levels are being done. Would it be better if young people were to specialise in courses that interested them little and for which they had little or no aptitude? Has it not struck these chanters on automatic pilot that to get a top, almost perfect, result is difficult to achieve in whatever course is followed? To do so requires time and trouble and interest and skill and ambition and almost certainly good teaching. The same personal qualities or characteristics are needed to get a top result in physics as they are in art or chemistry or media studies; however different people have different sets of skills and it is fatuous to imply that someone who gets an A grade in physics or French or history would find it easy to get a similar result in art, agricultural science or food technology. Unfortunately much educational thinking seems to be befuddled by making comparisons that are intellectually unsound. As my grandmother used to say, with some intensity, 'comparisons are odious'. Yes, people and courses are all different but surely, to be intellectually honest, incomparable.

Comprehensive schools in the UK got off to a poor start. All too often an enthusiastic central government told the local authorities that the policy was to have comprehensive schools. In many local authorities there was an equally enthusiastic response; it was felt unsafe to decide at the age of 10 or 11 who should be selected for a form of education that led to universities and jobs in the professions. Quite right so far; but so far it was easy, it was just rhetoric and talk and reasoning. The real difficulty, as in all ventures, is not having the idea but making it work. In many cases making it work meant combining grammar schools with their long history of gown-wearing academic excellence and conservatism (after all grammar was Latin and Greek grammar) with the local secondary modern from whence came our plumbers and tradesmen and labourers and scaffolders.

All too often, to soften the blow and appease the snobberies, and, it has to be admitted, the genuine concerns of the ambitious grammar-school-aspiring parents, the head of an existing grammar school emerged as the head of the new comprehensive. All were told that standards would not slip, i.e. it would be business as usual for the 'intellectuals' from the grammar school. The staff of the two merging schools joined forces and in many cases the message that those who taught PE or art or woodwork or cookery were second-class citizens came over, more or less subtly. In the early days it was the students from the secondary modern and their parents who should have felt anxious.

These early years of comprehensive schools often set the worthy project back and there has remained a critical, and often opinion-forming, body of people who have never seen the amazing potential in this most obvious of systems. This body of 'pundits' talk of 'bog-standard comprehensives' and 'sink' schools and it is precisely the same sources that decry 'easy' A-levels. Such views have contributed to a loss of confidence in the system that has resulted in a welter of governmental acts to try to improve matters but which in reality have been efforts to turn the clock back to the good old/bad old days before comprehensives came in. Key Stages and their tests, league tables, and national curricula are all meddlesome efforts, which have distracted a generation of head teachers from concentrating with uncluttered minds on allowing comprehensive schools to thrive.

When in 2002 the government pushed an initiative called Every Child Matters, what had the world come to? Surely it was blindingly obvious to the teachers and their leaders that this was the case. But perhaps it was not, and the reason it was not was that for decades only lip service had been paid to the comprehensive ideal in too many places.

Let us for a moment consider the much publicised gross mismanagement by the local authority responsible for the organisation of secondary education in Halifax in the 1980s and 1990s. This took centre stage for a few days in the national media, partly I sense because particularly fine examples of classroom indiscipline were on film and all of us enjoy having our early and often fond memories released. The local department of education had allowed a form of backdoor selection to take place and the result was that one of their schools had a very large number of those who found academic matters very difficult and were therefore prone to be tiresomely behaved. Bureaucratically and politically unable to escape from this mess for fear of upsetting their systems and the voters whose children went to the other schools in the town, the local authority compounded matters by insisting that all schools followed the same curriculum.

The school concerned certainly appeared to have discipline troubles, indeed it seemed unmanageable and successive heads had failed to master the unruly elements. A large posse of suited gentlemen from Ofsted was sent in and they decided that tough measures should be imposed. At this point the school disappeared from the nation's television screens. There had however been some memorable moments when the students had been filmed in splendidly disruptive action. In particular a French lesson was shown in which the books were being hurled around the room in a sort of 'pig in the middle' game. The teacher was palpably powerless and almost certainly deeply unhappy, wondering why she had to be submitted to such distress on a regular basis.

The whole scene summed up what was wrong with much of the 'comprehensive system' and that was that those in charge had no idea how to manage it. The scene portrayed was totally unfair to the teacher and her pupils. Almost certainly this particular school contained a high proportion of the children of Halifax who had learning difficulties, some of whom were almost certainly dyslexics and still being treated as 'thick'. It also served a considerable body of those who were not that well-disposed towards school in any case unless it offered something of practical consequence to them. Why on earth were such students being asked to study French? It was not a prerequisite to a satisfactory life in Halifax, or anywhere else that was not France, come to that. Why were they being asked to study French when they could see no practical point in the subject and in any case found it really hard to have any mastery even over English because of their specific problems? Would any body of adults sit in a room unquestioningly when what was being offered to them was clearly of no relevance or benefit? Of course they would not; they would politely, or otherwise, walk out, and certainly not come back for the next session. I thought the behaviour of the captive boys and girls was really quite mild in the circumstances and could be attributed almost entirely to the mismanagement they had to endure.

And now we have 'academies', a word possibly suggestive of better education to many and beloved of the Scots, but in reality unlikely to produce successful comprehensive schools. These will emerge only as soon as the talents and difficulties of each student are far more carefully considered and, freed from all preconceptions as to whether one field of activity is superior to another, the staff goes full out to exploit those talents and, having done so, help the individuals with their difficulties. Nothing should be allowed to deflect the minds of all those concerned in teaching from this central concern. But will there be one good teacher to every seven or eight students? Will there be setting and much smaller teaching groups, particularly for the inescapable subjects such as maths and English? Will the national curriculum be dismantled? I doubt it!

How did St Bede's stand in all this? Well, we certainly were a truly comprehensive school in the purely educational sense. In the 1990s we were sending students to Oxford and Cambridge and all the leading universities. We were also made up of a student body which at one count had within it boys and girls of 65 nationalities. At least 15 per cent of the school students had recognised specific learning difficulties, needing to a greater or lesser extent the attention of special needs teachers, or as we called them our learning support department. We had students who had been sent to us by various local authorities because they were far too difficult for their schools and had been excluded repeatedly. Within our ranks were those who adhered to all the major religions.

It was during the 1990s that the school really began to refine its approach to the programmes that we would offer our students. We finally decided to abandon any attempt to follow the national curriculum and thus arrived at the point where the only subjects that had to be studied by all from year 10 were English, maths and information technology. There were, as has been said before, no other subjects that we thought would be unavoidable in at least some post-school careers. There was an obligation to give all students, for their future good, courses that were not examinable in aspects of religion, personal relations, including sex education, and living in the community.

As regards the various Key Stages that the government introduced at this time, we decided that as soon as there was a pilot scheme we would get involved; there was no question of rejecting them out of hand. Let's try it and then decide was our attitude. What particularly concerned us was Key Stage 3, under which at the age of 14 all students were expected to undergo a series of tests to see where they stood in relation to national objectives. We went through the pilot scheme and after it was completed I asked the staff to let me know whether they considered it to be helpful. The unanimous response was that it had been a complete waste of their time. Endless hours had been spent following a cumbersome procedure laid down from on high with little imagination and it told us what we, as capable and conscientious teachers, already knew. It lessened the time that we could use to apply that knowledge to something useful, such as moving students towards a point at which they could take GCSEs which was Key Stage 4. So that was the end of our involvement with Key Stage 3. It was all so typical of government policy at that time whereby it seemed to be believed that constant weighing of the pig would miraculously increase its weight!

These years were a period in which alternative forms of qualifications to GCSEs and A-levels began to emerge and of course they were viewed with mighty suspicion by the 'not like that in my day' brigade. These advances, for indeed they were advances, included BTECs, NVQs and GNVQs. A number of certificated courses were available which were practically based in IT. We embraced such courses wholeheartedly and were the first independent school to become involved in them. The courses were given a value equating to a number of GCSEs or A-levels, and enabled students to take a line of study more directly related to activity in the world outside school. Naturally they were viewed with deep suspicion by traditionalists, for they involved a lot of independent research by the students and the assembly of much course work for each of the modules that made up the course. The work was assessed as students went along and if it did not come up to scratch in a particular section they were allowed to do it again to make it better.

What the courses undoubtedly had was a direct relationship to what students would encounter when they left school and started work. They had to be self-motivated, they had to work on projects on their own, they could improve on their efforts if they were not wholly satisfactory and were subject to close scrutiny as they went along. Now all that seems to ring a bell for those of us who have been employed, or indeed self-employed.

The courses were particularly well suited to those who were interested and talented in art and design, in business and related courses, in agriculture, horticulture and related areas. All of them involved elements that improved literacy and numeracy in practical and thus clearly acceptable ways to those who wanted to succeed.

It was telling that our successes in the Young Enterprise competitions in the 1990s were led by those who were involved in the GNVQ courses in business and finance, ably supported by the students of media studies and those from the design courses. The winner of the south-east area competition one year was a team of our GNVQ business students who were almost exclusively dyslexic; our other team of highly academically able A-level economists came nowhere – they were good in theory though! But the point I make is that both teams were comprised of excellent young people, all of whom were different and whose talents were incomparable. By the end of the 1990s some of our art students, through their GNVQ qualification and performance, were being accepted into the degree courses of leading schools of art and design without the need to do a foundation year, as I have already mentioned.

These were confident young people who were recognised around the school for their evident abilities. The fact that many of them were also being helped to combat serious difficulties at the same time did not really register with their contemporaries, who were only aware of what they did so excellently. Would they be able to go on to higher education without GCSEs in English or maths or both? Amazingly if one has the incentive and a high level of self-esteem based on what one *can* do, it is much easier, with the right help, to put in the supreme effort necessary to overcome one's failings. At the age of 18 or even older all these students seemed to be able to gain C grade passes in English or maths; and great was the celebration, both by the boys and girls concerned and by their teachers, long-suffering and truly heroic they were! What these superb efforts meant was that the school was organising things to the advantage of the students' long-term benefit and their morale. The one place that such eminently laudable behaviour would gain no credit was in the school league tables.

From 1992, all state schools had to submit their GCSE results to a government agency and the independent sector felt obliged to follow suit. The agency then entered these results into a giant database from whence there emerged league tables; thus all schools, irrespective of their different characters, could be put in order of achievement. It was a thoroughly simple and doubtless lucrative contract for the agency to have won. It was a pity that the results of this effort shed little light on the performance of schools and certainly did no credit to those schools that tried to look after their students intelligently. I have to say that naively I thought for a few years that the tables were based on our actual exam results and I believed also, not naively, that the general public believed so too. Although we seemed to get good results, indeed excellent results, when we were a totally non-selective school, we always came surprisingly low in the tables of GCSE results.

Where were we going wrong? The answer lay in the small print. The tables gave the results of all those in the school who were aged 15 on a certain date in the year before they had taken their examinations. The government compiled these figures from the annual return all schools had to give of those on their roll each year, including their ages at this magic date. Because of our concern for our students, we arranged that GCSEs were taken at a time that was appropriate to each individual; thus, if a boy or girl was particularly able in a particular subject, they could take the exam when they were young, sometimes aged 15 or 14 or even 13. Indeed there were those who took all their GCSEs a year early if it was right for them to do so. If, on the other hand, a student needed extra time, a further year, before taking these examinations, to ensure that they had a realistic chance of passing them, we would arrange for them to have that extra year.

This latter consideration was particularly relevant for two categories of our students. Firstly it was right for those students who came from other parts of the world and who had to master English first before realistic exam entries could be made for them. Secondly, there were those who had specific learning difficulties, often highly intelligent boys and girls, whose prospects of passing a significant batch of GCSEs would be enhanced by taking an extra year to enable them to overcome those difficulties. Now this seems to me, and possibly to you, to be an intelligent, nay, common-sense approach. After all, the object is to pass the exams rather than to preside, with excuses blaming the young ready to hand, over inevitable failures. It enrages me to think of the thousands of young people each year who, schooled in an inflexible system, either become 'switched off' by the dreary tediousness of work that is not sufficiently challenging or, perhaps worse still, come to realise that they have no real chance of success so give up altogether.

As far as the computer print-outs of the league tables were concerned, many of the St Bede's students who were aged appropriately did not get any passes at all, not even a single grade G. But how could they score, when they had not yet taken any of the exams? The computer credited them with a big fat zero and with so many of these our average pass-rate went down and with it our position in the league tables. I once grouped for the press a body of 20 students, surrounding our MP, Norman Baker. They photographed well, looking bright, smiling and intelligent. All their 'results' were counted in our league table score but not one of them had actually sat a single examination that year.

I explained this point, in writing, to three different Ministers of Education. I told them that the public believed their tables and that therefore they were doing us a great disservice by printing false information. The only suggestion I had in reply was that we should enter all our students at the right age! What can one say? Apparently, what the government really wanted to establish was the state of the nation's education system when everyone reached 16-plus. Every year this was revealed and people across the country were disappointed. But what is this fixation with age? Can you tell the difference between an 18-year-old and a 17-year-old? If the answer is 'yes' then you should go and sit in the nearest off-licence and do something useful! Is it better to have a world full of successful and confident 18-year-olds or one full of defeated and demoralised 16-year-olds?

The A-level tables were a different matter. It was possible not to submit results at all and there are some schools that do now refuse to submit them and their reasons are to be respected. What the A-level tables became was a form of beauty parade, whereby the independent schools that were the most selective could 'surprise' us by coming top and say 'look at us, are we not glorious and grand, we have beaten St Cakes by 0.023%'. To the credit of Eton College, amongst others, they

177

have now declined to take part in this annual farce. On the other hand it could be argued that it is encouraging to know that a school can ensure that their students do pass exams. If a school considers a student able enough to embark on an A-level course then that student really ought to pass the relevant exam at the end of it.

The other notable fact about the A-level tables is that they were relatively easy to fix to a school's advantage. There were even some schools that in an utterly reprehensible fashion suggested that certain students left after GCSEs or even after the first year of an A level course because the schools feared that these individuals would have an adverse effect on their league table position. What a disgrace! Here we have young people, whose families have paid thousands of pounds in fees, being let down just when they needed the help of the school the most.

Of course it was also possible to gain a few extra places in the tables by bringing in a few top performers on scholarships for the sixth form. I do remember we once 'imported' a girl from Romania (not for that reason), who came in on a scholarship awarded to those from the newly freed eastern European countries and deservedly so. The fact that she passed 6, or was it 7, A-levels, all at grade A, probably advanced us up the tables by about 50 places. When we decided to enter all our German students for German A-level, which they could pass at grade A without really doing any significant work or using up lots of a teacher's time, we were rewarded with a leap of over 100 places in the tables. What a farce! And to think that the public take these tables seriously, when, for example, shortly after the tables were introduced, Portsmouth Grammar School for Girls came top, I seem to recall, with only a small number of A-level students being entered, albeit very able and conscientious girls. The only proper test should be the individual consideration of each young person's results, asking the question whether each one did as well as he or she was capable. If they did, then every single one of them was equal first!

The 1990s, then, was a period in the history of St Bede's at The Dicker when, as has been said, we really started to organise our academic programmes ever more specifically to the needs of the individual. During this period a number of programmes were being developed at some universities to try to perfect tests that could act as benchmarks of a student's ability and potential at a certain age, thus enabling schools to be able to tell whether their students were doing better or worse than was to be expected. Clearly such tests were not 100 per cent reliable but they fitted in with our approach, which was to find out as much about each student as was possible so that our efforts and guidance could be most effective. We chose the programme called ALLIS which came from the University of Durham and which proved very helpful in determining whether or not we were, in the current jargon, 'adding value'.

It was also at this time that we investigated whether or not we should offer the International Baccalaureate as an alternative to A-levels. To do so it was necessary to have a really large sixth form, at least 300 it seemed to me, so that the need to employ a large number of extra staff to serve a very few students was avoided. It was also a course much vaunted by the 'clever' people, who spoke the loudest because they had the most able children and thus they had the most to boast about – in a subtle way, of course.

These opinion-formers had to be treated with great wariness because they influenced people to think that their children were being disadvantaged if they did not do the same as those of the outspoken ones. In fact we discovered that the IB was a fine course for those whose abilities were excellent across the whole spectrum of academic subjects. For example, maths had to be studied at a high level and it was necessary to be an efficient linguist too. Just as we were on the point of signing on as a centre for the IB, the introduction of AS-levels and the option of broadening the A-level courses came about. It was now possible to follow, say, six subjects for at least the first year of a two-year course, which seemed to enable students to get the best of the IB approach whilst still retaining the narrow focus of the A-level courses that was distinctly helpful to many of our students.

We therefore dropped the idea of offering the IB at that point but the option could still be taken up if it was certain that students would not be wooed onto a course that for them was not the right answer. For the brightest all-rounders it is a marvellous course, developed by truly intelligent people. As in so many educational matters, though, the idealistic course-makers and the think-tanks constantly devise new and better curricula, getting carried away with their enthusiasm, and then schools and parents cannot resist jumping on the bandwagon. Before any true thinking takes place the chanting starts and the poor young people are being bent and moulded to fit the necessary pattern. What of course should happen is that a school should look at all the options and then decide how to advise each individual, in the light of a deep and considered knowledge of the strengths of that particular individual. All the courses make perfectly respectable and practical stepping-off points to the next stage in a career.

BACK TO EARTH

Early in the twentieth century Horatio Bottomley, at the height of his fame and wealth, had built an imposing terrace of six generously sized cottages to house his stable lads and other staff that served his stud farm and other racing activities. In 1989 Number Six Stud Cottages was offered to us and we agreed to buy it for the then top-of-the-market price of £90,000. This was the start of a slightly more strategically planned, as opposed to opportunistic, approach to acquiring the necessary property in which a strongly growing school could operate. It is probably misleading to claim that there was much detailed planning to our acquisitions but there was certainly more than had existed in our first decade when purchases were made to answer desperately urgent problems.

The new emphasis was on buying properties that were close to the heart of the school and disposing of properties that were scattered in other parts of the village. At the same time, any large property that came on the market was sure to interest us. These opportunities came up infrequently and needed to be taken if the long-term future of the school was to be served wisely: and who knew what that future might bring. The success of the owner of Number Six Stud Cottages in getting a really good price for his property at a time when a notable decline in the housing market had just started, prompted the owner of Number Four to offer his property too, and this was acquired later in 1989 although at a lesser figure.

Number Six was right next door to our Stud boarding house and, as numbers were rising, it appeared to have good potential as overflow accommodation. This soon proved to be the case, for my policy of always admitting five or six more boarders than we actually had room for, on the grounds that roughly that number always failed to show on the day, was a risky one and luckily we had Number Six when the exception proved the rule.

The no-shows were nearly always those from distant lands who had either failed to tell us that they had registered at three other schools and had chosen the cheapest or a more prestigious one, or had failed to persuade little Carlos to get on the plane at the last minute, or, quite commonly, could not come because young Wilhelm's mother, demonstrating her unwillingness to be parted from her darling, had made a scene of decisive emotional intensity, also at the last minute. All these reasons were quite understandable, particularly as in most continental countries the notion of boarding school was regarded as a desperate last resort for those in discordant families or those who had very exceptional special needs.

My over-booking gamble having failed on one occasion, Number Six became a Stud annexe with a tutor's flat on the ground floor and six sixth-form students in the three bedrooms above. All went well until a local spy informed the planning department, so that we then had to face the consequences of owning a house of 'multiple occupancy'. Much hasty work on doors and staircases ensued until the fire officers were happy and the crisis passed.

Number Four soon became similarly useful and the germ of an idea was formed, whereby the whole of the Stud Cottages terrace would become a boarding house enabling the Dorms House to move from its Portacabins. When in 1993 Number One came on the market, complete with planning permission for two semi-detached houses in its garden, we could not resist and for a bargain £120,000 it was ours. An agent was then employed to negotiate with the owners of the other three cottages and, to cut a long story short, by early 1996 these had been safely acquired too. The prospect of converting the entire terrace and its wonderful roof space into the new Dorms was now a real possibility and in September 1997 the new house was opened. The conversion works had all been done by our own in-house building operation. We had produced a thoroughly luxurious house (certainly by 1997 standards) for about 70 boys at a total cost of little over £1 million.

Amongst those labouring on the site, developing an expertise with the Kango hammer and the dumper truck and generally providing youthful strength, were two future housemasters of the school. One of these was Ed Dickie, who had at one time in his extreme youth lived in Upper Dicker at a time when his father was Operatic Director of Glyndebourne. The other was our own son Giles, who had become friends with Ed at university in Edinburgh and had enrolled him on the building site. Ed was also our lodger, a most welcome one with his detailed knowledge of current events and all things sporting! He was persuaded to do a teacher training course at Sussex on the understanding that I would give him a job when he finished and he has proved to be a great success. Now a housemaster, Ed also introduced the politics course to the sixth form and played a vital part in helping the history department to shed a rather poor reputation to emerge as one of the strongest and most successful.

Our son surprised us by saying one evening after a tiring day on the site that he thought that teaching was quite a good life but that he was only prepared to work at St Bede's. I told him that I could not give him a job myself but that if he were to hang around and go to see my deputy head, Jim Malcolm, in the week before the school year began, there would be a chance that Jim would be desperate for someone to do something to make his timetable work. That duly happened and I told Perrin G. that we would pay him half a salary for a year and if he was any use he would have a proper salary thereafter. Having studied religious matters at school and throughout university, he was familiar with the parable of the labourers in the vineyard and accepted the offer.

Within four years Giles had become a housemaster, introduced the GCSE and A-level courses in religious studies to the school, and taught a number of students to play the didgeridoo, amongst a number of other valuable contributions to the musical side of our affairs. He also pioneered the development of recreational football. After six years at St Bede's, two under my successor, Steve Cole, he spent five highly enjoyable years at a large state comprehensive. What is he doing now? Why, believe it or not, he is now married, to someone who was at school with Ed Dickie, and with four young children he became involved for a few years in starting a new school from scratch in India! It is as they say a small world. Uncannily, believe it or not, he has since then been invited to become the first head of a new foundation in Sussex!

Ed and Giles were not the only valuable 'signings' from the New Dorms building site. Whilst I was observing the finishing touches being put to the car park, a chance conversation with the expert ground worker resulted in his joining our staff in early 1998. Rupert Cain has contributed mightily and with immense good humour to every building project the school has taken on since that day. We bought him a JCB and a dumper truck and the foundations, drainage and subsequent finishing touches of paving and tarmac of our new buildings, including those of the preparatory school (more on this later) have been looked after with a precision and expertise, in all weathers, that leave one speechless with admiration. Rupert has saved the school hundreds of thousands of pounds. What a bonus that it is possible to talk to him about all aspects of British history from the Middle Ages onwards, about poetry, which he writes, and about all matters concerning the natural world.

In 1996, the year that work started on the Stud cottages, the house next door to the building site, called Fairfield, also became available. After its purchase it became the housemaster's house for the New Dorms. Before that, in 1993, Mr Penfold, a local friend whose family owned Berwick Service station (used in those days by the school for refuelling our vehicles), died, and the school had first option to buy his house, known as The Cedars. This property had a sizeable garden and occupied a site right opposite the school's main entrance. Subsequently it was rented to the estates bursar/caretaker, Herbie Wodehouse, and on his departure became offices. These purchases were of property that was close to the heart of the school; thus in the mid-1990s we were able to dispose of Numbers One and Two Cooper's Cottages and a bungalow called Fairlands, all of which were situated in more distant parts of the village and which had been bought in the 1980s when we were desperate for accommodation for teaching staff who could not afford to buy in our part of Sussex.

In 1993 another piece of property adjoining the school's land fortuitously came our way. This was the field on which is now situated the all-weather pitch and the main cricket ground. We acquired it from a former parent who had bought it when money was no object to him so that his son, then a student at the school, had somewhere at hand where he could practise his golf! This gentleman's business foundered in 1993 during the development of a hotel and golf course complex; his timing was just wrong and, like so many property developers, he was over-extended, believing that the good times would go on for ever. Needing ready cash quickly, he phoned me up and asked if we would buy the field quickly. Luckily or wisely for both parties we agreed;

£20,000 was a lot to pay for agricultural land but what a bargain it turned out to be.

Apart from a desire to consolidate the school's holdings around the crossroads in Upper Dicker, we were naturally interested in any major property that came on the market in the village. The school grew very quickly during the period from 1992 and there was no telling where we could expand to, particularly as the planning authorities did not seem to favour allowing us to develop the gardens and parkland of The Dicker itself. In any case there was no appetite on our part to develop the gardens as they were tranquil and beautiful and hence a wonderful selling-point for a boarding school.

In 1991 Glen and Phil Carr decided to retire from running the village shop and post office. We had agreed well in advance of this that we would buy the property known as Providence House in which they and their family lived and of which the shop formed an integral part. There were two motives in wishing to buy it. Firstly, the shop was essentially the school's shop: the major part of both sides of the business's income came from its links with the school. Secondly, we felt strongly that the village should not be deprived of either its shop or its Post Office, which provided a valuable amenity, especially to the pensioners in the village and for those unable or unwilling to make a three-mile journey to the nearest alternative. There was no public transport at all in the village at this time. There was also a dearth of potential purchasers prepared to scrape a living, at best, from such a shop, as the supermarkets were beginning to exert their stranglehold.

There were no buyers apart from us who would have paid a price that would have helped the Carrs to a well-deserved and comfortable retirement. We particularly valued the friendship and support they had always offered to the school, its students, who loved them, and to ourselves and the school's staff. From the moment we arrived in 1979 they had made us feel welcome and we shared much laughter at the shop, in the village hall where the Carrs were much involved with the Dicker Players and as families with children who got on well.

Additionally, and not insignificantly, Providence House would provide significant space for members of staff, whether as family or bachelor accommodation. Thus the school found itself involved, through a company called Dicker Enterprises which was generous enough to donate any profits to the School Charitable Trust, in running a newsagents, post office and general stores.

The first couple we employed as managers were good but the second were too lazy to get up to organise and deliver the newspapers, thus losing a lot of guaranteed revenue. It was clear that running such a shop was not a profitable thing to do if there were employees, so the shop was then rented out to people who were free to develop it but were assured of the school's business. And so it was that Upper Dicker kept its shop and post office for much longer than other villages in the area. It was sad to learn that in 2008 the post office closed along with many others in rural villages.

Other major properties that came on the market during the latter years of our time at St Bede's included Malvern House, which had been the vicarage until Upper Dicker ceased to have its own vicar in the early 1970s when the parish was amalgamated with the more populous Hellingly. The property became available in 1998 at a time when the school was growing very rapidly indeed and when it was certainly quicker and less costly to buy a property rather than go through the tortuous planning process and then fail to get what we wanted. Malvern House was not only spacious but was also readily developable as there were derelict buildings on the site as well as the house itself. The property had been accorded light industrial use, which the planners really did not like; they far preferred to grant use as a college or educational establishment or offices or further housing – anything, in fact, apart from an industrial use. We considered it as a replacement for Camberlot Hall as a boarding house, as a centre for a linked international study centre or as a spacious headquarters for our special needs provision. We also considered it as a head's house, with a small flat or two for single resident staff. In the end, though, overtaken by other more pressing needs, it became a staff residence for a family and several bachelor members of staff. It did good service in this capacity for some ten years until it was sold in 2009 for £600,000 having been purchased for £400,000. Let us hope that this sale will not be regretted in 50 years time.

Another major acquisition bordering our property was that of some 50-plus acres of fields that ran down from our small golf course to the River Cuckmere by the bridge at Michelham Priory. We imagined that these fields would prove valuable in the long term; perhaps as an extension to our playing fields, perhaps as additional or alternative grazing land for the riding school's or students' horses, certainly as an area to expand our five-hole golf course into nine or even 18 holes.

The small practice golf course had been made in the 1990s by the simple means of mowing and treating a large and suitably undulating farm field. It remains a tribute to Leigh Bennett, our head groundsman, who before he joined us had trained as a green keeper at Willingdon Golf Club. No great earth-moving was involved, just the creation of a number of practice holes of variable length and the development of some really good greens by persistent work. A number of very talented golfers joined the school from the UK and from continental Europe just because of this facility and the ability to be attached to the academy at the East Sussex National Golf Club. These students could of course play golf every day of the school year as part of the daily club activities programme.

The last purchase of any significance made before my departure was that of the large site of Wise Motors, situated next to the Cedars. Wise Motors was a long-standing village institution and had been set up by Ben Wise decades before the school existed. It was originally the village garage and filling station. By the time we arrived in 1979 the filling station was nearly a thing of the past but the pumps still existed and they filled the coaches that Ben Wise's son Dick operated. The workshops were still in action looking after the vehicles of a favoured few but not generally commercial, except for the maintenance and repair of the coaches. There was also, spreading down behind the garage and the cottage in which Ben lived, a scrap yard, which was busy in the sort of slow and rusty way that characterises such places.

The scrap yard was run by an old retainer of Ben's who was hard to involve in conversation and possessed quite a hostile demeanour. I noticed that it was not just me that he brushed aside, for he only talked at length to about three men. It was clear that he was only at ease with those whose families had lived in Upper Dicker for at least three generations and who were interested in scrap. Mind you, to keep a scrap yard secure it was probably necessary to give off reasonably hostile vibes and to appear as someone not to be 'messed with' – for those who frequented such places were not just DIY motor enthusiasts seeking a wing mirror for a 1974 Escort but included those having a good look round with a view to returning after dark! If they had decided to do so, they would have found things more menacing still: for if Ben's tellingly noisy dog did not deter them, then Ben himself, who was an old man by this time and not that mobile, would fire his shotgun from an upper window of his cottage in the direction of the intruders. Any thoughts of free tyres, wheels, wipers or starter motors promptly vanished.

Ben had a number of horses in training and he followed their progress with great enthusiasm until his death. He really seemed a natural link with the world of Horatio Bottomley and spent most of his days, until he moved away to Jevington to be nearer his horses, in his cottage following the racing on television. I spent a considerable number of hours talking to Ben and trying in vain to persuade him to sell us the scrap yard when he wanted to close down his business in the village. His memories of Bottomley's day and of Horatio's racing trainer, Jimmy Hare, were fascinating and our discussions were discursive, covering nearly every aspect of his youth and village life but rarely about the scrap yard. These meetings were facilitated by a glass or two of whisky, regardless of the time of day at which we met. What became clear was that Ben was going to sell the yard to Berkeley Homes, who were going to pay him a lot more than a young and somewhat impoverished school, but that he also liked a bit of company for a good chat.

Ben's son, Dick, ran the coach company and his son, James, now runs it from an office in Hailsham. The company always did good business with the school. Additionally both Dick and his son were fine cricketers and I played in the same Dicker CC team as them for a number of years, becoming a good friend of Dick's. Thus when he wanted to retire and needed a pension fund we did the same service for him as we had done for the Carrs, buying the whole of the Wise Motors site, including Ben's cottage and on which Dick had already got planning permission for ten houses, for £600,000. The year was 2001 and the departure of Wise Motors marked the passing of an era in Upper Dicker, an era when the village had a vicarage with a vicar in it, two shops, a garage and a village policeman.

Whether these acquisitions prove to be wise ones (better perhaps in this context to say prudent!) remains to be seen but I would argue that if something major comes up the school should always be interested. There is no guarantee that it will come on the market again and the school must be treated as an organisation that will still be going far beyond the imaginative scope of the present governors or head. Will future generations be grateful to current management for passing up an opportunity? It's not worth the risk of letting down those who come in the future for if a rainy day should come these are, after all, saleable assets.

In property terms, the school that had first occupied The Dicker and its 12 acres with its 65 students in 1979 was left in 2001 with many properties all individually marketable and about 150 acres of land. Other developments were under way at that time too and plans laid down for other ambitious schemes. Most of these have been excellently carried out.

As soon as I think of Malvern House sitting there next to the village cricket ground, I think of the Reverend Johnson, the last vicar of Dicker (don't the two go together beautifully) and how the world has changed in the last half century. I also think of Providence House and its evocative name. Why was Providence House not the vicarage? It seems more suited to the task. Malvern House is slightly set back and aloof from the mainstream of village life whereas Providence House is right there at the hub of things. It was clear that at the centre of the villagers' world was the shop and post office, that domain of gossip and material concerns, whilst on the periphery were the affairs of All Saints, Upper Dicker. But for a period between 1994 and 2001, or possibly 2002, Providence House came into its own.

PROVIDING PRIESTLY SERVICES

In the years immediately preceding 1994 it had become apparent to the villagers who noticed such things that Upper Dicker saw very little of its vicar, who rushed in to take a service and rushed off again. This was not the vicar's fault, for he had to run the much larger parish of Hellingly, where he was extremely busy, and the two or three miles to Upper Dicker, which was on the other side of the busy A22 road, deterred him. From talking to the Reverend in question, Ronald Chatwin, I came to understand the strain on his life and conscience that Upper Dicker posed. As the school organised confirmation classes (for both Anglicans and Roman Catholics), I came into contact with the Bishop of Lewes from time to time and, as has been mentioned before, suggested to him that it might help the Church and the people of Upper Dicker if the school was to find a suitable priest and employ him. Apart from teaching in the school he could run All Saints church in the village. Not only would the Vicar of Hellingly be relieved of considerable responsibilities that he could barely fulfil but also the proposed priest would not cost the church anything, so the idea appealed to the Bishop.

I therefore found myself penning an advertisement for insertion in the *Church Times* for a priest who could teach to A-level in any subject he would like to offer and who would take charge of the church in a small rural parish. Within a week or so I was interviewing a series of young, trendy, evangelical would-be priests-in-charge, none of whom would have been able to keep order in any class. Most would also have caused a revolution in our dress code as they seemed to favour either the pony-tail or the earring – and seemed at first stunned and then distinctly hostile when I politely asked whether they would be able to consider some modification to their appearance if appointed.

However, all was not lost, for an application came through from South Africa from a man who had been a distinguished journalist on the *Rand Daily Mail*, a paper well known for its anti-apartheid line. As a priest he had risen to be Dean of George and additionally had at one time been a teacher at and chaplain of a major South African school. He put forward the Bishop of Portsmouth as his main referee. I offered him the post, which he accepted, and David Swanepoel (he has been alluded to briefly earlier in the story), his wife Margie and their two children came to live in Providence House.

Six mornings a week David taught English and did so very well. Each afternoon, as his club activity, he did 'vicaring' and on Sundays he ran the services in All Saints church. The church was revitalised, the sick and dispirited amongst the villagers were visited and helped, and now there was someone of immense experience and humanity in the very centre of the village to whom anyone could refer. What a great move his appointment was, and not just for the Church. David's presence, allied to that of his amazingly charismatic wife, pulled the village together very effectively and linked it most definitely with the school. Margie entered into village life with lots of charm, enthusiasm and no little skill and their children were popular too. It was a sad day in 1999 when David and his family went back to South Africa to find a climate more suited to David's health.

The experiment continued, but after we left it was unfortunately allowed to lapse when David's successor lost his calling but remained on the teaching staff. No effort seemed to be made to find a replacement priest. What a pity for both school and village that this initiative came to an end. Such a venture, whereby a local employer of significant size took on a priest who could be allowed to work part-time for the Church, was a template that could have been reproduced all over the country to the benefit of small parishes which had had to be combined to their mutual disadvantage. A real disadvantage it was too, more importantly, to those in the parishes, who lost a leader and a force for harmony in their midst. There are those who would love to combine a job with a leading role in the local church and be paid for it. The Church as a whole, financially unable to support the salaries of additional priests, would have been more than happy with such arrangements too.

BACK ON HOME TERRITORY

During the 1990s and in our last ten years at St Bede's we were not only involved in purchasing land and property within the village but were also developing our own original property, The Dicker, with a series of buildings that ranged from the beautiful and architecturally ambitious to the truly unpretentious – small structures to be hidden away out of the sight of all authority but which solved the immediate needs that came up suddenly and almost unpredictably as the school grew so rapidly.

All the distinguished buildings were erected by our own construction team, as I have explained, having been planned by gifted architect Richard Hudson and his partnership. The starting point was the building housing the library, staff common room, offices, teaching rooms and sixth-form common room that has been mentioned already and which was opened in 1992; it was a building that looked perfectly at home in a garden setting as it was not at all school-like. It was our ambition, and one in which Angela took a powerful leading role, that the character of the gardens and small park should not be sacrificed to the school's mundane needs. We followed this policy successfully during our time and the relaxed beauty of garden and lake were responsible for much recruiting; it was good to imagine one's children boarding in such an environment.

The next building, started and completed in 1999, was also stylish and was certainly not a block even though it did house the science laboratories. Just like the library, it was made by our carpenters and was of wooden construction. It was built on the site of our first tennis and netball courts, on what was called the astroturf, a floodlit play area, and necessitated the construction of a further bank of three tennis courts across the road near to the Stud House. These new courts (now submerged beneath the new boarding houses built in 2011) were urgently needed as we were emerging as one of the leading tennis-playing schools in the country. Gradually, all the school's sporting activities were being moved away from the original Dicker site and across the road on to the land that had come with the Dicker Stud and other purchases already chronicled.

Our new building was to be the least science-blocky creation in any school in the land. It also included a lecture theatre, to introduce a wider world of culture and aesthetics to the world of Bunsen burners, dissection and pulleys. It was a cost-effective building too, created for only 45 per cent of the total quoted by an outside contractor. One or two interesting battles had to be fought with the authorities to keep those costs down. We were now in an age when any two-storey building had to have a lift in it for the disabled. The disabled were very well cared for at St Bede's – it was possible to lead one's whole life at school on the ground floor – and we objected to vast areas of space and huge expense having to be put into facilities that were unnecessary. Fortunately, after months of time-wasting debate, we were able to win that battle, saving us a much-needed £25,000, the cheapest quote we could get for installing a lift. I wonder how many people, lacking energy for the fight, just follow the demands of the planners and their rules and regulations and waste vast sums of money in consequence.

Another wooden building created a dance studio in the late 1990s and this, coinciding with our provision of a home for the Legat Ballet School (more on this later), was another modest building designed to fit into a wooded environment. It is a widely held view that buildings made of brick and block are superior in some way to wooden buildings. This is a sad fallacy, for both sorts of building methods have their advantages and disadvantages. Both types will last as long as each other provided that they are properly maintained. Consider, for example, the wooden buildings of New England and, indeed, the many wonderful medieval timber-framed buildings in this country. Whereas wood can rot more easily than concrete, concrete and brick can more easily crack and are less resilient when there is movement in subsoil. What is undoubtedly true is that wood has a gentler feel and somehow looks more in keeping with a garden scene.

By the late 1990s it was clear that the admirable (largely because they had arrived free or at negligible cost) buildings that greeted visitors as they entered the main gate had to be replaced. The growth of the school and the expansion in popularity of subjects such as food technology and the diversification of art-related skills meant that we needed a lot more space. Richard Hudson therefore designed what is now known as the Perrin Building; it could have been a block but Richard ensured that its style fitted in well with the Tack House and Stable rooms. What emerged after two years of high quality work by Rupert Cain, Derek Wingrove, Shaun Pantry, and the rest of our own team was a building that not only housed various academic departments but also two day boys' houses and all their changing-rooms. It was a complex building to construct, particularly in the areas of drainage and foundations, and Rupert was a particular hero in that aspect. The buildings it replaced had served for some 20 years and they were most certainly much handled, second- or even third-hand, when they were put up at The Dicker. One of them, the 1950s Austin Hall building, went away to start a new life, I believe on a farm, but the others regrettably became reclamation timber or even firewood. It was unbelievably sad to see them go.

Temporary homes for the departments of business and economics had to be found whilst the new building was being built and therefore some additional Portacabin types found their way on to the site, being squeezed into any available space. Two of these were metal and were quickly christened the Tin Cans – any 'banging of heads against a brick wall' sounded like a distant call to dinner.

A private habit I had was to analyse the A-level results according to which room a particular teacher taught in and it was particularly pleasing to note in one year that the best results were gained by one of the Tin Cans. It goes without saying that the teacher concerned was extremely good at his job and made certain that within his Can any appropriate technology that would help was available: it made absolutely no difference to him where he worked. The more I saw of teachers the more obvious it became that those who blamed their accommodation had failed to notice the real handicap – themselves!

I was talking to a head recently who told me that he really had to get rid of certain wooden prefabricated classrooms because the teachers would do so much better if they had really spacious state-of-the-art rooms in which to operate. What a load of nonsense. When we all look back on our schooldays we are very hard-pressed to remember the state of the rooms in which we worked. But memories of the people taking the classes are as clear as crystal, either for the great fun and enthusiasm they engendered or conversely for their particularly lamentable performance.

The only comparable modern foundation to St Bede's at The Dicker is Millfield School. Founded in 1935, it has prospered to be one of the largest and most effective independent schools in the world. It has always been happy to educate young people from all over the world and looks after the gifted and those with serious difficulties with equal enthusiasm. It does not worry whether it beats this or that school in the league tables – why should it? It has a clear conscience. When I went to visit Millfield in the 1980s there were still many round-roofed Nissan huts in use; they testified to the strength of its early growth and the urgent need for more accommodation. By then the school had been going for 50-plus years and yet there they still were, these huts, replete with scholars and gifted teachers that made these humble rather ugly buildings of supreme unimportance. We parents are not silly. We know what we want for our children: appropriate opportunities, inspiring teachers and a vital community, even if the buildings do little else but keep the rain off and the cold out. If one has to keep up with the Joneses it is important to choose the right Joneses.

At St Bede's in the 1990s sundry other growths, apart from the Tin Cans, of a more or less pleasing appearance came into being. A hideous dormer window was put on top of the charming Aviary so that the musicians had more room. Various unofficial hut-like structures were hidden behind the gym into which the art department percolated. A new art department of several rooms was also fitted in behind the Tack House and further obscured the 'unofficials'. This building, the last to be constructed in the Chicken House, was mainly notable for the tasteless nature of its roof; it is clad in a red felt which attempts to look like tiling but fails, even when observed from a long distance away in failing light!

Finally, an extension was added on to the back of the Stable Rooms to provide a mixture of male and female loos and a suite for the study of food technology. The most memorable thing about these buildings was the discovery that Thermolite blocks, although extremely light and a pleasure to handle for builders, don't work well in school toilets and changing areas. There is something about boys sitting in loos; they spend too long there, probably to avoid going back to class, and at the same time need some employment, favoured forms of which are inscription or carving. Thermolite blocks are highly prized by carvers. Starting with a random gash and moving to a proprietorial chiselled inscription, the boy, forgetting the purpose of his visit, soon notices that the Thermolite block can be burrowed into with ease. Whether it was this particular boy, sitting there securely bolted in whilst his peers completed a test, who realised the full potential or a disciple we know not, but persistent burrowing resulted in a smallish, almost unnoticeable hole through to the girls' changing-room. Eureka! Next move, this time from us, was the swift application of some granite-like render. A golden rule – never mention the felony or start a hunt for the culprit, or the result will be the honeycombing of the wall in question within hours and/or a mass outbreak of carving and offensive graffiti.

YEARS OF AFFLUENCE

The late 1990s and the first two years of the 21st century were indeed years when, to my immense surprise and delight, the school found itself untroubled financially. We were able to add the new and stylish buildings as well as to purchase significant additional property without borrowing. Indeed our original borrowings were now moving towards being paid off. It was particularly gratifying to be able to receive more in income from our bank through funds placed on the money markets than they received from us in interest payments on loans.

There are two attitudes of mind that are commonplace at times when there is no shortage of funds. The first of these, and one that we tried to follow, was to ask ourselves why we were so fortunate and then to resolve to maintain the discipline that had brought about this happy state of affairs. The second approach is to lose focus on the control of relatively minor items of expenditure, on the grounds that they are now easily affordable, as indeed they are, and to allow everyone who wants anything to have it without the usual tough and detailed scrutiny. The second approach can often be accompanied by delusions of grandeur and, whenever it appeared that we were doing well, then these would surface. Two such instances spring to mind.

The first was quite early in our history, when one or two of the governors decided that Herstmonceux Castle would be a better site for a truly distinguished school. I recall listening to the arguments in favour and patiently going on a visit. 'Think what we could make of that ballroom!' 'Look, we would have access to all these telescopes: the school could be a centre for the study of astrophysics!' What a waste of time! We would almost certainly have been bankrupt before we started and would also have had the millstone of a Grade One listed building around our necks for ever. But at least we could have appeared grand for a few moments ...

On another occasion, much later on, it was proposed that we should try to find a way to convert a large institution that was for sale into a new, additional preparatory school. After years of just about surviving and for the first time having the capability of developing some much needed facilities at The Dicker, here were some of the governors, not many of them thankfully, wanting us to go off on a wild goose-chase, committing our funds to an unnecessary cause in an area of East Sussex where we had already won the trust of the existing preparatory schools.

OLD HABITS DIE HARD

When this period of relative affluence occurred, we were firmly rooted in a way of thinking that disliked waste and resented paying over the odds for anything. Michael Wallis, then our catering manager, took pride in buying extremely competitively and beating his budget. Herbie Wodehouse, the self-styled 'estates bursar', had a weekly discussion with me about his needs and if, for example, brandishing a catalogue, he suggested buying six new waste-bins for the campus at enormous cost, he would be invited to try harder for three new bins that were undoubtedly the best value on the market and see if the suppliers would give us a fourth one free. Often he would return the next week bubbling over with his success and the school would be a few hundred pounds better off. It should be within the powers of anyone in a buying post in any organisation to save their whole salary by their diligence. It should also be the role of the chief executive to lead the way in this respect, demanding that money needed for important developments in the future that directly relate to the lives of the students and their learning should not be wasted.

Angela, for one, could not be faulted in any way in this respect. Despite our easy financial situation she continued to charm and cajole the representatives of those companies supplying medicinal, cleaning and housekeeping supplies to 'sharpen their pencils'; they did not mind this, for they enjoyed the banter and, as they told her, they would not get the same hard time at the next school down the road, so they could make up there what they might have lost at St Bede's!

I continued to sign every cheque that left the school. I returned a few invoices for further and better particulars to be provided and even refused to pay one or two when we had not received a satisfactory service. I recalled last autumn how reluctant I had always been to allow the school's central heating systems to be switched on, for they cost us hundreds and hundreds of pounds each week in oil and propane gas. The clamour each year for heating in the houses and classrooms would start on the first slightly chilly day, the request being presented to me annually by Pam Saxby. This was a sign that something might have to be done in the next two weeks, when even those less affected by the cold or those possessed of thicker sweaters and thermal underwear joined the chorus. I remember one particularly favourable year in which I managed to avoid switching on the heating until the October half-term break, when it was not needed anyway. I am slightly ashamed to say I was mildly triumphant! In such ways though was Pam Saxby's pay ensured! Unwelcome bugs were killed off and there was no danger of nodding off in the classrooms; at least that was my story.

Basically I oversaw the spending of every department. I was never persuaded that giving any department or individual a budget and letting them have the freedom to spend it over a year was a sensible idea. It was certainly a time-saving one and an easy option; but in my view it was far better to ask the spending departmental heads to justify the need for what they wanted, to say why they wanted it and to explain the real difference to the quality of what was on offer to the students that the purchase would make. Next I would seek proof that the market had been thoroughly researched and ask how the expenditure would be phased throughout the year so as to work within the constraints of the school's cash flow. Sometimes it was obvious that a large sum needed to be spent in a particular area and conversely sometimes obvious that too little thought had gone into a department's planning and that money and resources were going to be wasted or ineffectively applied.

I cannot resist recalling at this point, in the context of careful financial management, a very pleasing victory over a provider of photocopying machines. We, like all schools, paid thousands and thousands of pounds each year for photocopying machines and the service that went with them. This entertaining contest started when I decided to check on whether we were getting a good deal and I discovered that we most certainly were not. We were next told that we could get out of our contract by paying £150,000 or thereabouts. We cancelled the contract, returned the machines and duly received the demand accompanied by dire threats of much legal activity. Another rival organisation, run by a disgruntled former employee of our opponents, keen for business and offering highly competitive rates, suggested that we contact a certain solicitor who was in the process of organising a class action against the company concerned. This lawyer, a sole practitioner, I met in a scruffy office just north of Oxford Street. The papers might have been scattered around and piles of files were covered in dust but this man's brain was in neat order and the result, after many months, was that I was able to report to the governors that instead of us paying the very large sum to escape we were to receive a gift to our charitable trust which, when tax was recovered, was worth about £40,000. It was an entertaining and instructive venture into a rather grubby and somewhat threatening world of unscrupulous, fast-talking but absolutely charming salesmen and sharp practice. But it was a pleasing outcome.

This concentration on the relative minutiae of expenditure bred an aware community and one proud of its skill in finding the best solutions. It was always a huge pleasure to read the school's trading accounts and to see that we were consistently producing the funds to make significant improvements for the benefit of our customers.

Throughout the affluent years we redoubled our efforts and concentration so as to consolidate our hard-won advantages. We were, so to speak, two sets to love up in a five-set tennis match and our opponent was there for the taking; it was time to keep the successful tactics going and to make an even fiercer effort to finish things off. Thus any increase in student numbers resulted in an increase in the number of teachers and a willingness to pay really well for the best. It did not result in an increase in bureaucratic staff or administrators.

I personally continued to show virtually all the potential customers around the school, being unwilling to deprive students of their teachers or students of their lessons to do something that was palpably my responsibility. Why should others who had not been employed for that purpose take the responsibility for keeping the school filled and therefore the salaries of themselves and their colleagues paid? They might succeed, but if they did not then they deserved no blame, whereas I had taken on the potential for blame and would deserve it if I failed.

When one side of the administration needed a helping hand in a crisis, at St Bede's others would always step in to assist. Too often in organisations, those feeling the pressure will not come forward and ask for help – understandable perhaps, but a sign of weakness nevertheless. Once help has been sought, though, people will inevitably find that others like to help them, and those others in turn will feel better about asking for help themselves. When the temptation arose to hire another person to alleviate a difficult period, we resisted that temptation. Those under pressure were always helped, either to think of better ways of doing what they were doing, or given the temporary assistance they required. This can only happen when the feeling of teamwork and pride of being part of a good team exists. By the late 1990s we were undoubtedly, looking back, a good team.

A GOOD TEAM

As soon as a team starts to think it is good, then defeat is just around the corner. Most really good teams know what their main purpose is and concentrate on it; then, if the players know their jobs and the captain keeps them positive and intent, a team will probably win a lot more contests than it loses. In the context of a school, the judges of a good team are the students and the parents: school inspectors do not really count, for theirs is an artificial process aimed at salving the conscience of government or local authority. In any case, things can always be set up for their pleasure in advance of their arrival.

Good teams in schools do not try to imitate rival schools; they are fearless, never thinking of whether they are better or worse than the competition but serving their students by applying themselves to the different needs of each boy or girl in the school *today*. Good teams avoid making comparisons, focusing instead on the positive qualities of all the students for whom they are responsible.

All our teachers were available to meet the parents every term on a morning specifically set aside for such consultation. That these were all highly pleasurable events, at which over many years I had to meet very few complainants, was a testimony to the quality of our team. So too was the universally high quality of termly or half-termly reports produced by our teachers. Positive, constructive reports were insisted upon and the very few that failed this test were returned to the writer who was asked to do better. These reports were never based on comparative tables of results or other scores but spoke of students doing their best, and included encouraging suggestions as to how to raise their attainment levels even further. Given that each student followed an individual course based on his or her strengths and was able to choose the nature of their extra-curricular programme, our young people were inclined to pass a favourable judgement on their teachers too.

Teams in schools are made up of many different people and to pick individuals out is always a risky practice. As the school grew in numbers and confidence, so did the teaching staff take pride in the fact that we had no intention of selecting pupils on the basis of their

203

academic attainments. We were pleased to be exceptionally comprehensive in our intake and to seek out and welcome all nationalities; by the 1990s this mission was firmly embedded in the school's ethos. The fact that this was so was due not just to the leadership but to a very talented and committed 'middle management' if I may call them that, when in fact they were very 'high management' in the eyes of the students.

No school, especially a boarding school, will succeed without top quality house staff; all our houses, both day and boarding, were very well run in the middle and late 1990s. (There is an appendix to this volume that sets out the names of our house staff.) These leaders had to deal at very close quarters with all our students and all their parents; they were part of a boy's or a girl's life every day, and for seven days a week in the case of boarders. To do this job for any length of time required a quick and subtle mind working full out, lots of wit, much patience, the ability to bear disappointments which could come thick and fast, unblinking self-confidence, the ability to appear totally unruffled and of course massive energy, for the day could last from seven in the morning to midnight and even later on occasions.

The house staff also had teams of tutors to run and, in the case of the boarding houses, matrons and cleaners to keep happy as well. The phone always had to be answered and the man or woman in charge was expected to know whether Jim's arm was better or whether Tina still had a temperature and what time the train left Polegate. Just look at the list of house staff in the late 1990s and you will not see a weak one there.

A sign of real strength in house staff, and indeed in all of a school's middle management, is the willingness to bring matters to the attention of the head if they are in any doubt. I was fortunate, as were the boys and girls in the school, that this group of staff, deputy head, house staff and departmental heads all had the confidence to bring any problem forward. There are those who think it is a sign of weakness to consult the head but in reality such people are unhelpful, both to the head and to the students, particularly if a degree of parent management is required. The last thing a head needs is a parent making him or her aware of a serious problem for the first time; it could precipitate hasty action not to the student's advantage.

One of the greatest sources of discipline, for teenagers in particular, is the prospect that their parents will find out. There are occasions when it is better that they don't but the prospect that they will next time hangs over a miscreant. It was noticeable that the less effective house staff tended to involve the parents far too quickly in a problem, out of fear that they might find out about it anyway and then raise a complaint. This is a risk that should be taken, for most parents will take the view that they have sent their children to boarding school so that trivial issues can be addressed by others and thus could well lose confidence if it appears that the buck is being passed back to them.

A minority of mothers or fathers, if invited to become involved too often, would almost try to run a house, or even a school, by proxy. There were others who, feeling some guilt because they had sent their children away, would become fussily involved and then become in many cases an embarrassment to their offspring. The golden rule had to be that following an incident, the head was consulted and a plan of action agreed and, if it was a serious matter, the parent informed and told what was being done. In the case of illness, parents should be informed as soon as the doctor had pronounced and not before. The final piece of the house parent's art was to know their parents well and to be able to judge when to make exceptions to the general rules above so as to ensure their happiness and confidence.

For most of the 1990s I was blessed with Jim Malcolm as my deputy head. He was a Scot who had the ability to appear dour without being that in the least. This skill was a great asset in his dealing with both students and indeed staff; he did not appear to be someone to mess with and whilst he was straight to the point and crisp yet he was marvellously compassionate and knew instinctively when an arm round the shoulder was needed. He could deal with administration too without making a religion of it (all too common in schools) and never shirked the tedious or nasty bits. He was much respected by all our staff and by the students as a genuinely fair person. To add to these winning characteristics he could teach well and also sign on new students when I was away on holiday, for the parents and their offspring could sense that they were in the presence of an enthusiast who would deliver.

It was no surprise that when Jim left St Bede's he did so to take on the difficult task of running a school that was not in a successful period of its history and turned it around, doubling its numbers in a few years. It gained a fine reputation in East Anglia and he based its operations fairly and squarely on the model of St Bede's. One of the results of his efforts, before a very serious road accident and its aftermath forced him to retire early on grounds of his health, was that the staff at this school found that they had to work harder and offer their skills more widely than in the classroom. Inevitably a few poor performers left but the majority noticed that the morale was suddenly much higher and they were enjoying their jobs so much more. It has been gratifying to notice the spreading influence of the St Bede's model within the independent sector of education; one or two are direct copies whilst in many others a simple thought process has reached the same obvious conclusions.

Undoubtedly the staff at The Dicker worked very hard indeed but also, I believe, relished their work more than many in other schools because of the variety of involvement with the students that was required of them. As we have seen they were: teachers of subjects, yes, but also managers of their own extra-curricular programmes, which they had to devise and sell; tutors, and as such the all-important confidant and liaison officer for a number of individual students; responsible for administrative and disciplinary duties; preachers or performers in the school's chapel meetings; and contributors to the weekend programme with their own chosen offerings for the boarders. Not everyone looked forward to making a weekend contribution but even the most pessimistic were nearly always happy at the outcome, for the students appreciated their efforts and were at their most amenable and charming on these informal outings or unofficial sporting contests.

WEEKENDS

For boarders, weekends at school can be the most tedious and even unhappy times for those away from home. Not every student stayed at school each weekend for it was possible to elect to go out as long as the arrangements were clear and officially tied up by mid-week. But teenagers often wanted to be with their friends rather than at home, whilst those from overseas could not go home at all easily. The majority therefore did stay at school at weekends. From my own experience as a boarder I could remember that it was nice to have periods of time when there was no official organisation and personally, even as a manic games player, I really welcomed the occasional Saturday afternoons when there were no fixtures. Thus Saturday afternoon was not the main time for inter-school matches at The Dicker – the majority took place during the week instead.

It was apparent that morale amongst our boarding community was high because there was a chance each Saturday to do some independent, exciting growing-up, when the school transport and whole fleets of taxis took off for Eastbourne or the less exciting but practical shopping town of Hailsham. Sixth-formers were able to sign out for the evening too but the younger members of the school had to return for a meal at 5.30 p.m. Casual clothes could be worn but everyone had to be reasonably smart.

In fact once school had ended on any day casual clothes could be worn. Furthermore, it was possible to dress up as Coco the Clown if that was desired, although to do so meant remaining in one's room whilst so attired. Luckily no one saw the anarchic potential in such a move!

Sunday was a different type of day. The morning started at 9.45 after a lie-in. Then there was a choice of church or other religious services to go to or else the School Meeting to attend. Each student could choose which of these options to follow at the beginning of each term; the rule was that you had to stay with your choice for the duration of that term.

The Sunday Meeting was a thoughtful period in which a message would be put across in one way or another, which, it was hoped, would be helpful in enabling one to lead a more harmonious life. Social and ethical issues were raised and there was always an element of surprise. So a group might be invited from outside who Danced for Jesus; or The Samaritans might explain what they did; or one of the houses might put on a meaningful short play; or an imam would come to speak; or the vicar might make himself known; or a touring group of Namibian gospel singers might show up.

The longest School Meeting went on for one hour and 45 minutes; I remember congratulating the troops on their fortitude and good manners after the far from riveting speaker departed. The shortest was three minutes long, when the boys of Camberlot Hall put over a succinct but truly effective message; it has to be said it was a highly popular meeting, for it led to a much longer period of free time than normal!

Sunday then progressed to a leisurely and much enjoyed lunch, followed by the option of outings or organised events laid on by staff or another free afternoon. This was often spent getting some overdue work done or watching football or a film on the television or just socialising as one does in one's teenage years; hanging out, to give it its proper title.

The fact that Sunday mornings went well, and the reason that religious worship did not fall into the 'it's so boring' category, was a product of the school's policy whereby anyone of any faith would be able to follow that faith and their choice would be respected. Nor would the school ever indicate in any way that there was only one approach to God: there was no official line in this respect. Sundays also went well because of the work and devotion to the cause of John Berryman.

Sometime in 1982 I received a letter from a man in Polegate telling me that his son was returning from the Bahamas and wondering whether there might be a job for him. I replied that he would be welcome to come and see me when he got back. So John Berryman came and we talked; he seemed exactly the sort of teacher who would suit us. He joined the staff at the beginning of 1983, with a reference from his father! He is still on the staff as I write. Those were the days before inspectors rifled through every filing cabinet in the school and needed documentary proof of every reference. Some good teachers would never have got a job at all if references were *de rigueur*. The head of our most local comprehensive, for example, refused point-blank to provide any references to independent schools, so deeply rooted was his socialism and his devotion to class warfare!

References aside, what appealed to me about John was that he was a good all-rounder who was used to teaching a variety of subjects and that he was a Methodist lay preacher. He was clearly a man at ease with people of all races and creeds and our school needed as many staff as possible who were absolutely clear of any tendency to generalise along racial lines. He was also enjoyable to talk to about biblical matters and moral and ethical issues. He had spent some time at St Edmund Hall in Oxford but I did not hold this against him! We needed someone who would be open-minded and, in a way of speaking, completely neutral, to take over the direction of the school's spiritual and religious life.

From his arrival until well after we left, John organised the Sunday morning programme, ensuring that Anglicans and Catholics went to their appointed places, that those who wished to go to the Free Churches or, say, a Christian Science church or to any other bona fide place of worship were able to do so. He also organised the varied feast that was the School Meeting and during the week organised the rota whereby all members of staff took it in turns to present a weekly 'chapel' to the school.

John and I were agreed on one important thing, and that was that the 20 minutes spent in the village church each week were the most vital minutes of the week. However much it was possible to prize maths or science or English or history or art or football, these 20 minutes were devoted to the harmony of our lives and to our happiness and without these anything else was unlikely to come to much. The task of bringing other teachers along to lead our meetings was not an easy one and the fact that they did so was a testimony to John's great ability to persuade his colleagues to do things that they, or many of them, really did not want to do at all. In truth John was difficult to refuse. He was respected greatly by all the staff and the students because he was always ready to help anyone in difficulty. He was the champion of the underdog, and a listening counsellor to both old and young who had problems.

He certainly did not wield authority by the strength of his administrative skills; he often needed help to save himself at the last minute from his own 'hit or miss' admin methods. John liked to put it about that he was administratively inept, a good tactic even if it did contain an element of truth! Generally he got support, for what he was doing was obviously valuable and right for the boys and girls; people knew that John was not a person to say no to, if one desired a clear conscience. They also knew that he would do whatever it was himself and muddle through, if it came to that.

Hence the Sunday meetings always had an extra element of surprise: would the designated speaker turn up that day or would he arrive a week later, giving us a choice of two? Whatever happened, John (with, I suspect, his Caribbean training behind him) was shielded against imperfection and if necessary would step up himself as if that was the plan anyway. In many ways JB was just what the school was about: unpretentious, somewhat 'left' leaning, not frightened by the possibility of making mistakes, not in thrall to uniformity and above all able to find some humour in most circumstances. John truly loved every one of the students and it showed without the need for any proclamation.

DIFFICULT MATTERS

The subject of weekends, the detour about John Berryman excepted, leads naturally into the realm of difficult matters. Most difficulties caused by the students arose from events either at the weekend or at night, or when students went out with friends or to highly relaxed home regimes. If the phone rang at our home at any time after lunch on a Saturday there was an expectation of bad news. This wasn't always the case but the expectation was there nevertheless. Most weekends did not contain such a call but when one did come through, it had to be a serious matter if my services were required at once. Was it going to be drugs or sex or drinking? Was it unexplained absence? Or was it an incident that required my presence to establish the real seriousness of the offence in the mind of the offender, such as a violent outburst or bullying or serious rudeness to a member of staff?

There were straightforward ways of dealing with most offences which did not involve parents; as has been said, it was always worth holding back parental involvement as an encouragement not to repeat the offence. Thus if Glen Carr at the village shop, or any other shopkeeper come to that, detected some shoplifting, the culprit would be sent back to Glen or the shop concerned to apologise, hand back the goods, and pay for them but not receive them. If the goods had been eaten or otherwise rendered unreturnable but the offence accepted, then the rule was to apologise face-to-face to the shopkeeper and pay double!

The same policy of making an immediate apology applied to outbursts of rudeness to staff. I would insist that the rude one apologised at once to his or her victim and that within a short time limit I had a confirmation that the apology had been received and accepted; all done on the understanding that if a similar offence occurred then parents would be involved and at least a period at home to discuss matters with them would be guaranteed. I cannot recall anyone coming back for a second time to put my solemn promise to the test; maybe members of staff had mercy on them!

Dealing with bullying was always difficult. The secret lay in spending time explaining what bullying was; essentially, it was knowing that another person had a weakness and then knowingly taking advantage of that weakness. Most boys thought bullying was about physical oppression, and it could be, but were less aware that baiting someone verbally with the intent to make them 'lose it' was just as much bullying – as indeed was consistently calling someone a name knowing that that person was upset by it. Girls could also bully in most unpleasant ways by picking on a physical characteristic or mode of dress or whispering behind a victim's back. The key for me was to take the time to awaken the bully's imagination so that they could picture something similar happening to them and then to ask them if they thought it unkind. When the bully agreed that it was unkind, then they could be told that there was no place for unkindness in our community and that if it happened again then we would have to part company. A private apology could then be organised, for public exposure did nothing to help either party get over it.

In my days at boarding school it was smoking that caused alarm bells to ring; and possibly being found out of bounds was regarded as serious too. But smoking had become a category three offence by the late 20th century and my services were only required if the offence was blatant. Smoking within the school buildings was clearly blatant; in these circumstances offenders were given an immediate warning that suspension would follow another such episode. Otherwise any individual committing a fourth offence, parents having been warned after the third what to expect, received a suspension for a short period with a warning that a further offence could result in being asked to leave permanently. There was never any real need to be caught smoking for staff had better things to do than ransack the Sussex countryside trying to unearth smokers. Indeed in the latter part of the 20th century smoking was becoming something to grow out of in the eyes of an increasing number of young adults; more and more it seemed to them that to smoke appeared unintelligent, a bit stupid, in the light of all the scientific evidence relating to ill health. It was seen by many, but not all, older students as a rite of rebellious adolescent passage and they, the seniors, having grown up, had, in many cases, got past that stage!

Drink, I suppose, was category two. It was not possible to get truly, deep-down irate or particularly horrified about things that most healthy young people indulge or flirt with in that period of life when adolescent experimentation, allied to the need to keep up with the more daring of one's peers, coincides with a lack of experience but a surfeit of spontaneous 'bottle' – a doubtful choice of word perhaps in this context. The problem was that first-time drinkers often got seriously legless, and therefore a danger to themselves, before they realised what was happening. The alcohol was often bought at shops that failed to apply the law but equally often it came into school from Dad's cupboard; it didn't seem to do Dad much harm was the thinking perhaps.

The drink of choice was normally a fashionable one, well advertised by the glamorous and exceedingly handsome in cinemas, or it was vodka, discreet and odourless but not if taken half a bottle at a time over a 20-minute session. Part of the problem of drinking at school was that it had to be done quickly so as to avoid being caught. It was also advisable to finish the bottle off and throw it into some anonymous place for it was not easy to conceal evidence from teachers or other fellows who would most probably spread the word; this resulted from time to time in a bottle of Martini (the 1970s) or a bottle of Baileys (the 1990s) being shared between two 14-year-old (the most common age) girls, one of whom had passed out while the other produced a volcanic vomit whilst telling matron of her anxiety about her comatose friend. I came into the picture the next morning to tell them that they had not been a sophisticated, cool or elegant sight at all and that if it happened again they had my promise that they would be sent home. I cannot remember ever seeing a returnee, although I cannot be sure that all offenders remained teetotal. At the sixth-form Summer Ball, as they were about to leave the school for good and they were all over 18, they might even remind me of past incidents whilst offering to buy me a drink!

Boys were much the same in results, but the main period of experimentation often happened a year later than the girls and could carry on until the Leavers' Summer Ball; I well remember one such glamorous festive evening when, everyone having seemed to have gone home, Jim Malcolm and I came across a recumbent and incoherent figure beside the exit pathway. Eventually we managed to ascertain that he wanted to go home; luckily we knew where he lived, for apparently he did not! His driving home to Reigate being out of the question, we hoped that perhaps his mother might like to fetch him. She acquiesced when we explained, and, given the distance she had to travel, we estimated that we would have enough time to sober him up sufficiently for him to greet her rather than shock her.

This particular youth must have had an almighty hangover but miraculously he cycled into school the next morning (30 miles) for the final assembly. Spotting him in the audience, I asked everyone to give him a prolonged period of applause on account of his exceptional devotion to duty. Those who had been at the ball had big smiles on their faces! The rest just thought it was part of end-of-term stupidity. Perhaps, though, his vengeful mother had forced him out of bed and then the house!?

From the 1970s onwards drugs became an increasingly important issue. Any secondary school that proclaimed that it did not have a problem with drugs was undoubtedly, by the 1980s, living in a world of make-believe. One of the problems we faced in the early days was that most of us who were in charge had little or probably no awareness of drugs, most commonly cannabis or party amphetamines such as ecstasy. Additionally, those using these substances were not as obvious as those who had had several large vodkas on top of a strong cider. Indeed cannabis users might well appear uncommonly congenial and malleable. But the possession of such substances was illegal and so we had to take a very tough approach. Furthermore, the fact that anyone who was involved to any regular extent was, although often amiable, more or less totally useless in any serious part of their academic work and palpably failing to realise their potential in any field apart from the social, meant that we had a serious duty to be on our guard and to impose the sternest sanctions on those that indulged.

So we arranged for speakers to come to the school, to educate, to forewarn or even to frighten the student body. Staff went on training courses and we quickly became expert at observing the tell-tale signs. The school's policy, made known to all students, was based on two premises, spelt out very clearly by me and by the house staff: firstly, we had a duty to help them to lead productive lives, and secondly, we were not able to waive the law of the land. Thus it followed that anyone who was found in possession of drugs or who could be proved to have been in possession of them at school or to have brought drugs into the school was handed over to the police, who were very good at issuing theatrical cautions which deterred most offenders; additionally they were asked to leave the school. Those that were suspected of involvement but whose guilt could not be proved were put on a testing regime, whereby at any time a test could be arranged (testing packs were readily available on the market); those failing were liable to be asked to leave permanently.

By the 1990s some schools, including some of the leading independent schools, were beginning to push these matters under the carpet: suspensions and warnings and second and even third chances were given. The reason for this weakening was that if a school had to expel too many students, bad publicity would result. Perhaps they wondered where it would all stop and then what would the consequences be for the bottom line? We never bought into that view; it was quite clearly a bad example to shield young people from the consequences of illegal activity and we should not make ourselves 'accessories after the fact'. Also the consequences of drug-taking, as far as the culprits' future prospects were concerned, were clearly very serious indeed; certainly by the late 1990s scientific research was beginning to show clear links to serious mental health issues, ranging from paranoia and anxiety at the bottom end of the scale to schizophrenia at the top.

As it happened we did get some front-page national coverage when I had to send away four or five boys for possessing and using cannabis. One of our girls had a mother who either worked for or had strong links with the *Daily Express*. All newspapers delighted in revealing that a school where the fees were enormously high so that only the privileged could attend (the fees were normally bumped up considerably for the purposes of sensation) had had to expel a 'drugs ring'. The result, as always, was that to those of sound mind we were seen as being properly organised and taking a firm line. I had no difficulty in explaining our policies and the rationale behind them to the media when they inevitably called and we actually benefited on the whole from totally undesired publicity.

If drugs were category one, then so was sex. Although perfectly legal when it involved those over 16, at The Dicker it nevertheless resulted in the same consequences as drugs offences. If any student was found to be having full sexual relations with another student then they both had to leave at once. A school in which there were hundreds of healthy youths both handsome and beautiful with hormones racing around was a testing place in which to maintain celibacy. Yet there were only four or five occasions over 23 years when I had to apply the sanctions.

There are several explanations for this and not one of them provides a definitive answer. Angela's belief was that offenders were never, or hardly ever, caught. This was an upsetting conclusion for me. I thought it was more complicated than that. Firstly, it was possible to notice which boys and which girls had formed strong relationships and, thinking of the boarders who were our primary responsibility in these matters, we being *in loco parentis*, it was therefore possible for house staff to have a quiet word in the appropriate ear and keep more of an eye on the couple concerned. Secondly, it was always possible to go and stay with friends at the weekend, thereby shrewdly avoiding, under a more permissive regime, the draconian laws applicable at school. Thirdly, most of the relationships were truly beneficial to those concerned and existed because both were at school together and the parties did not desire to be 'sent off'.

In addition, being promiscuous at school caused real problems. It was difficult to keep things quiet and a reputation for being a sexual opportunist was not approved by most fellow inmates. 'One-night stands', even if conducted by day or in the evening, suffered from the fact that the other party was always there at breakfast the next day and in class, and day after day too. In talking to parents I felt confident in saying that the chances of having casual sex and the life-disrupting circumstances that could result were more likely at parties out of school than in school, and that day students were far more likely to be vulnerable than were boarders.

Undoubtedly Angela was right to some extent, for the staff could not patrol everywhere. The Sussex countryside was often welcoming, house staff had to sleep and school was not a prison: windows opened for one thing. Furthermore Angela was there with the doctor every day assisting, and when a girl asked if she could be seen in confidence, with Angela sent out, then she knew what the conversation was likely to include. This did not happen much, perhaps once a term, and presumably not every occasion was one when the 'morning after' pill was requested.

It was certainly requested at least once. The girl concerned, instead of finding a way to get to Hailsham to receive her prescription (if she had been caught out of school during lesson times she would have been grounded for a period), decided to ask her matron to get it for her. The matron felt that concealing such a matter would be unprofessional and put her job in danger. What a sadness to have to say goodbye to a delightful girl and a charming boy! Hard cases do make bad law, for if once any pair had been made an exception and told that they would have to leave if it happened again, then we would have been in chaos. All students would have believed that they were entitled to one go before the axe fell. It would have been extremely hard to sell such a policy to the parental body too.

The only flaw in the policy we followed on sexual relations was that it could be taken advantage of if a pair of students acted in collusion to facilitate their departure from the school. What can be done when into my study comes X and says that he has something very important to tell me. 'Carry on,' I say. 'Well, sir, I am really sorry to say that I have just had sex with Y.' Clearly I had to test this assertion thoroughly, but if I was unable to break him down his dubious confession had to stand, and the two of them had to leave that day. The fact that their GCSE exams started the next morning and neither had done much work was very likely a telling factor! Short-termism is not unknown in teenagers. If I had refused their 'request' to leave, again chaos could have ensued.

It was always incredibly sad when we had to say goodbye to students who had fallen foul of the rules. Strangely, and other heads will back this up, when at some event in the future we meet those who have been expelled they are very often the very best of company. Possibly this is because they were, and still are, risk-takers and therefore have had interesting and successful careers. Almost universally there is a desire to make peace and exchange some mutual respect and sorrow that things did not work out; perhaps because an act of stupidity or inopportune timing on the one hand had come up against an inability to waive the rules on the other. It is always a great relief that the past can be buried and relations focused on the present.

At St Bede's I was lucky that my senior staff were on the whole supportive of a policy that kept boys and girls in the school even if they were a persistent cause of disruption. It is too easy to lose patience and take the easy route of expulsion but that reveals a school's management as being weak, when its duty is to help young people and see them through difficult phases in their lives. Is the education of others adversely affected by the presence of such miscreants in their midst? Possibly, if there is serious wrongdoing. But generally education is strengthened by observing right and wrong and making a judgement, and made more entertaining by the antics of a few enterprising lawbreakers. Good educational leaders keep calm and stay aloof from the hue and cry.

It has to be said that maintaining a strong sense of law and order and a balanced response to breaking the rules did involve a remarkable degree of vigilance by staff. It was fortunate that there were enough of us who enjoyed the process of vigilance, our efforts being repaid by the satisfaction of arrests made as well as the excitement of the detective and pursuit processes. On the one hand it was necessary to up the risk factor for the students, for this discouraged the great majority from chancing the consequences and thus avoided rampant disorder. On the other hand parents were not paying fees for their sons or daughters to be breaking the law or wasting their lives away or both.

It was equally important for staff morale that they should be considered worthy opponents, respected because they could miraculously arrive and 'feel the collar' just as the best-laid plans were progressing really well or had actually reached fruition. It was exciting to move silently after dark armed with a wonderfully powerful torch and in thick woodland to unearth a camp full of drinkers. It took intelligence when it was suspected that some lazy lawbreaker was smoking in his shower cubicle to go and observe the outlets from the extractor fans and pounce. It took skill to notice that certain people were always absent at regular times and to organise a stalking party. It took energy to get up again at one a.m. to check that everyone was still in their beds and true devotion to keep at it after drawing a blank on several occasions. But as Derek Newton rightly pointed out, it was always when things were quiet and satisfactorily law-abiding that one could be sure that something untoward was going on. So it was inspired lateral thinking when, on discovering an empty bed, Derek decided to call the absentee's mobile phone; it was not an inspired reply on the absentee's part to answer it from an Eastbourne night club and to tell Derek that all was well as he was in his room, where Derek was standing!

So torches shone twice in 20 years on couples *in flagrante*; they shone on smokers and drinkers; but more often they shone on the backs of those making a run for it! Even then the possibility of being caught was a deterrent, thinning the ranks by removing the least daring or addicted. By far the most efficient torch-shiner was Raymond Mutimba from Uganda, who was Derek Newton's assistant at Stud House for several years. Raymond, an outstanding teacher who had had to flee from a repressive regime in his homeland, was naturally of a forensic turn of mind but outstandingly effective at night when the deep blackness of his skin was particularly valuable.

However vigilant we were my phone continued to ring at weekends, for teenagers never ceased to surprise. We appeared to be having a quiet weekend once when the phone rang and David Graham said that he had to go to pick up one of his boys from Brighton police station. The boy was under arrest. For some reason this 16-year-old had decided to take a replica pistol with him when he had signed out to go to the cinema with some friends. It was at the height of IRA terrorist activity and when this young man was in the cinema's loos with his friends he chose to show them the replica firearm, which had such an authentic appearance that another gentleman using the conveniences took public-spirited notice and duly informed the police. Sauntering out at the end of the film our hero was bundled to the ground by four large policemen, pinned there, handcuffed and removed to the local nick. He was dark-skinned, not at all Irish in appearance, but even in the time before the police lost the 'institutionally racist' tag it was a reasonable arrest. We brought him back to school a wiser person although without his pistol. As for us, we never ceased to be surprised!

Subtle, or not so subtle, enquiries were always made of those who returned from shopping trips: such as have you had a good time, what did you buy today, in other words normal parental stuff. Sometimes such vigilance paid off and 'let's have a look' was followed by 'oh, I'd better have these Stella Artois Extra Strength … and this small bottle of Smirnoff!' Camps were often discovered deep in the woods, on one occasion on an island in a large pond where a wartime structure remained in eerie silence, except when the revellers were there at weekends. What a pity that they left behind a photograph of the whole gang, posing with their beers and wine and fags in the actual den!

Neighbours were always asked to keep an eye open too. Teachers who were not associated with the weekend boarding community but lived in Eastbourne were asked to go and surreptitiously visit certain pubs, the pier and other well-known centres of illegal trade, and report back. It was always surprising to be told where you had been all Saturday afternoon by your amazingly skilful and invisible housemaster.

All these measures added up to produce a community that was in order but not oppressed; they provided humour and good stories on both sides, particularly in retrospect. It was part of what made teaching so much more entertaining than most other jobs, even if a successful coup didn't result in any sort of financial bonus.

MOMENTUM

From the early 1980s onwards a St Bede's Yearbook was produced. Each book recorded all the school's activities over the course of one academic year, featuring in photographic and word form everyone involved, from the students to those who worked for the school in every capacity. These yearbooks clearly illustrate how it had grown; depicting building sites, the increasing range of the school's involvement both nationally and locally, and the house and school photographs not only show the ever-increasing numbers but also the larger size of many students, as the sixth form expanded slightly disproportionately to the rest of the school.

The growth in sixth-form numbers was a result of the extraordinarily wide range of subjects on offer, which drew in students from other local schools and increased its attractiveness to students from outside the UK. In particular, German students came in numbers, not only to perfect their English but also to escape the strictures of the rather narrow curriculum they were obliged to follow in their own schools.

What the yearbooks of the middle to late 1990s show, above all, is the quite extraordinary vitality and ambition across all areas of school life. Rightly or wrongly, depending on a moral judgement, the school seemed to be pleased with itself (in a good sense) and that confidence resulted in it becoming noticed nationally and internationally. Consequently large numbers of prospective parents came to see us and, despite the chalets, signed on! The word was out, not only through our better marketing efforts but because our students were appearing with distinction in every sort of positive guise, well reported in the media.

Twice in five years there was wonderful coverage of our 'Twenty-Four Hours To Showtime' in the local radio and press. On a Friday at 7.30 in the evening Nicky Miles, head of drama, would announce that Saturday's production would be, say, *The Sound of Music*, or *The Wizard of Oz*, and the next evening at 7.30 the show was performed in a very large tent to an audience of hundreds. In that one day, actors and understudies learnt lines, orchestras learnt the music and rehearsed, props were made, costumes were created and a dress rehearsal took place. The whole process was followed throughout by local radio, who broadcast our appeals for certain props, and in they came. The enthusiasm and the size of the audiences were enhanced hugely by the fact that the whole thing was being done for local charities, chosen by the students.

No other school was doing things like this. Such events and the whole wonderful array of dramatic productions that Nicky Miles and her daughter Sarah produced each year (there was as many as 20 in some years) gave St Bede's a growing reputation for theatre in all its shapes and sizes. When the 'Shakespeare Tour' to preparatory schools was added in, it was not surprising that there was a growing number of candidates for our drama scholarships.

It is particularly rewarding to note that two of our most talented actors from this period have gone on to greater things as theatre directors – Michael Pigott, a writer and director of distinction in Sydney and Jamie Lloyd in London, where he has directed to great acclaim at the National Theatre and is regularly attached to productions at the Donmar Warehouse.

A string of outstanding musicians came through our scholarship programme in these years, attracted by the fact that we had in Andrew and Penny Barclay both charismatic leadership and technical excellence. When John Long and his jazz players and electronic music were added we had a wonderful range of opportunities for musicians. There was plenty of ambition too, for the annual Gala Concert gave the opportunity for singers to take part with professionals in some of the great choral works. *The Creation, Requiems* by Mozart and Faure, Mendelssohn's *Elijah* and Haydn's *Nelson Mass* come to mind. Chamber and orchestral concerts were regular events. The jazz band went out to various prep schools and did our reputation no harm at all. Our singers and instrumentalists even represented Sussex in America, performing in both the Lincoln Centre and Carnegie Hall. What an experience!

We could speak to good effect too. In May 1996 St Bede's reached the final of *The Observer*/English Speaking Union's National Schools Debating Competition, staged at St Paul's Girls' School in London.

That we had reached the final was because one of our teachers, John Tuson, had always enjoyed debating and done rather well at it as a boy at Lancing. He started to enter us for competitions and we did well locally but then started to do well further afield. In that year we saw off the local opposition, then St Paul's and Dulwich College, proceeding modestly on to the final. Deborah Quysner and Nigel Blinman made up our team. Their presentation was crisp, their speeches well researched, they were quick to pick up on opposition slips and, in Nigel's case particularly, capable of eliciting quite a lot of laughter from an audience. They did not win the final despite being the more eloquent team but were defeated by an academy from the West of Scotland whose team were undoubtedly fiercer and much ruder to their opponents.

I confess to having taken great pleasure in this event; in truth I still do. We tended to be regarded as a school that took anyone, however weak or strong academically (aren't you the school with all those students with special needs?) and yet our debating success proved that intellectually our best were as good as anyone else's best, and that a school existed to allow all to thrive, as they did with us. Academically throughout this period St Bede's was sending students to Oxford and Cambridge every year and our A-level results were right up there with schools that selected their students purely on academic merit.

In one area we undoubtedly excelled and that was in art. Examining boards regularly told us that we were their leading school; students received accolades as the best entries nationally in painting or design or ceramics. There was no better time to take prospective parents and students around the school than when there was an art exhibition on. They were just simply amazed at the talent and at the daring of the creations, for we had a trio of highly motivating artists on the staff. David Graham was head of art, Steve Jordan led the A-level painting and design classes, while Roger Whitmore specialised in ceramics: all were truly outstanding. When Roger Whitmore was succeeded by Anthony Hammond in 1999 ceramics moved even further ahead and in the next three years the only results from the many ceramicists at A-level were A grades – there was not even a single B!

Games players kept us firmly in the national gaze too at this time. As I have said, the fact that a boy or girl with real talent in an individual sport could devote themselves every day to that sport was of course a real help in furthering their ambitions. That they were looked after by very fine coaches was another positive factor. Tennis in particular went notably well, as it had done from our earliest days. Both boys' and girls' teams regularly appeared in the national finals after winning regional qualifying events.

I well remember watching a 15-year-old Jordan Freitas playing quietly, honestly and with impeccable good manners whilst beating in three sets a large, moaning, arguing, ball-whacking, racket-abusing, line-call-questioning 18-year-old, to win the critical match in a victory over Millfield in the last eight at Queenswood where the finals were played. St Bede's regularly featured amongst the top six schools nationally but could never get the better of the Lawn Tennis Association's elite training schools.

Our golfers rarely lost a school match and one went on to win the German junior championship and another to be a successful professional. Swimmers excelled; we had a full-time coach who also spent time with other local swimmers and who had been recommended to me by the ASA because of the excellent work he had done at their centre of excellence at Edinburgh. His training and the outstanding talent at his disposal meant that we consistently had students representing national teams and setting national times; at one time one of our former students, Nick Poole, who had broken a UK record for the 100-metre breaststroke as a junior, came back to join the coaching team.

The teams were becoming more widely noticed as well. During this period our senior soccer team won the County Cup and began to excel in the Sussex County Leagues. Under the leadership of Simon Gough, who arrived in 1992, our fixture list grew impressively so that by the second half of the 1990s we were playing regular matches against Charterhouse, Eton and all the main independent and state schools of the south, and successfully too. We were well on the way to becoming a leading light in Southern Independent Schools football, a progression which culminated, well after my time, in the winning of the FA National Schools' Football competition in 2008. Several St Bede's boys went on to become professional footballers. Dan

Harding, who played for the England Under 21 team, is still playing, now for Nottingham Forest.

Simon Gough, our head coach, was a great enthusiast and like all coaches hated losing. Rarely was a defeat not attributed to some sort of bad luck or the inexplicable actions of the referee. Simon came from a professional footballing background and when I played in the Staff versus School match, an annual event much enjoyed by a large crowd who enjoyed seeing their teachers made to look silly, it was surprising how much Simon G. knew about shirt-pulling and various other blindside activities: he was ribbed mercilessly about this by his fellow players. It cannot be said that it was a good example to the students but he did not mean any harm, it just came as second nature. When I was eventually removed from the playing team to become referee, I knew that it was safe to blow up for a foul every time Simon was involved at close quarters even if I could not see what had happened. All that said, Simon was a huge influence through his development of both football and cricket. He was responsible for very impressive fixture lists. He took an important part in the work of the Independent Schools Football Association and got our name around. Here, as in every area of our activities, things went from strength to strength where there was a 'maniac' (very great enthusiast) at the helm.

As a school, perhaps stemming from me as its head, we were not enthusiasts for a touch-line culture. Large gatherings of parents and other relatives on touch-lines was common amongst our opponents and often, at other schools, there were tea parties after each game for the assembled observers. The heads of such schools were always there too and developed a coterie of favourite parents whose lives appeared to be lived around the adulation of their offspring's prowess. It is one thing to encourage children to take part but quite another to encourage them to get things out of proportion, which inelegant and unconditional loud support or criticism from parental spectators certainly did. My view, as a games player, was that those fortunate enough to play got a lot of satisfaction from doing so and great delight from winning and that that should be enough of a reward. It was wrong to give them hero status as well, when, for example, one of the contraltos in a fine choir did not get or expect such praise. I myself kept away from touch-lines apart from the occasional game because, for one thing, I could not guarantee that I could keep quiet myself!

In squash, hockey, rugby, basketball, rounders and cricket our teams competed well and had some highly successful moments. In netball, thanks to some excellent coaching in this period, St Bede's were consistently amongst the top teams in the county. What a marvellous experience for young people to play in a team and what an important thing the teams did in publicising the school's name. It was particularly rewarding to notice that in general our teams went about things modestly and with good manners; there is nothing like over-ambitious expectations or pressure from above – be it institutional, parental, from the head, or from long unbeaten records – to ruin the way young people play and make their demeanour somewhat boorish and even embarrassingly silly.

Not every venture aimed at promoting the school's name in the public consciousness produced sparkling results. Long days were spent at independent schools' exhibitions, held in this or that centre or town hall; they were never inspiring places. All our competitors and their stands always seemed much better than ours. They had videos playing, always seemed to have queues waiting to book in, their stands were larger, and their representatives appeared far more charismatic. As we waited, backs stiffening from all that standing, we could ease our disquiet by telling ourselves that all the expense would seem infinitesimal if just one new student signed on in the end.

Still, it was a bit like sitting in an examination hall where everyone else seems more intelligent, writing away furiously; you only see this of course when you glance up, and, conversely, while you are busy writing, others might look up and you can appear ominously proficient to them. Apparently our competitors all thought our stand was eye-catching but only noticed our interested 'customers' when they had a lull themselves. The only real value of these days was to chat with one's rivals, picking their brains but making friends with them too; though it was useful to be able to chat up preparatory school heads too and invite them over to Upper Dicker for lunch.

These exhibitions were always held on Saturdays and the punters, weary from shopping, would drop their Sainsbury's bags and use the event as a point of relaxation during their weekend. Their children would race round the stands seeing if they could collect more leaflets, prospectuses and freebies than their friends or siblings, and one could imagine all this enthusiastically produced literature going straight into the recycling box once they got home. It was always a wonderful moment when the exhibition organisers said it was all right to start packing up and a very large gin seemed only an hour or so away!

The Sussex Partners in Education venture was more impressive in title than in results. In fact I have tried really hard to think of anything beneficial to St Bede's that resulted from this brave new project; only its grand launch is memorable. We had always had a good relationship with Roedean and in the late 1990s both schools had lively marketing directors who happened to get on well together. Between our two schools and Hastings College, a place of higher education that benefited from encouraging students from overseas to take up their courses, this joint venture was spirited up. The idea was that joint marketing would cut costs; all three organisations would push the merits of the other partners and take trips abroad under a joint banner.

This seemed a good idea and we were always willing to experiment at St Bede's, remaining open-minded until something was obviously a waste of time. I cannot actually recall one single student who came our way as a result of the partnership and I cannot remember any meetings of the members – perhaps Sally Wellings, our marketing director at the time, can. What I do remember though was the launch of the venture, which took place at the House of Commons at the invitation of a local MP. This memorable day enabled Michael and Trevor Wallis, our catering team, to put on an exhibition of their work at the House of Commons and they rose to the occasion with their customary skill and good humour; it was an excellent lunch. It also resulted in masses of publicity in the local press and made us appear very forward thinking, particularly to those who did not think much. As an exercise in getting publicity it was effective; as an exercise in raising morale in the school's kitchens it was first-rate; as an exercise in gaining more students for St Bede's – well!

MORE EFFECTIVE PARTNERSHIPS

From the mid-1980s, life grew tougher for those running preparatory schools. Various social factors were unhelpful. The custom of sending children, especially boys, to boarding school from an early age was becoming a thing of the past. What had been a particularly English fashion – having its roots not only in slowness of travel over distances but also in an imperial past in which it was often necessary to send children to the mother country for health reasons, as well as for education of a known quality – was dying out as transport improved and empire faded away. The belief that it was important to send young children away from the cities and their smog to the bracing air of the south coast was also a thing of the past, as Clean Air Acts and medicinal advances did their work.

All this had a particularly punishing effect on preparatory schools here in coastal Sussex. During the first 15 years of our time in Upper Dicker no less than five prep schools and five girls' schools that were based upon boarding closed their doors for good. The recession that began in 1988 did not really clear until 1992 and, as mentioned earlier, this slowed the growth of our own school, and was a crucial period for even the strongest and most resilient of prep schools. Fees never fail to rise, even in periods of recession. The teachers always got a pay rise, and, in periods such as the 1980s and early 1990s when inflation was running at a high rate, these rises could be substantial. As teachers' pay was by far the greatest item in any school's budget the fees rose as national prosperity failed to keep pace.

If it was possible to argue that it was better parenting to keep children at home at least until they reached adolescence, and there seemed little doubt that this really was the case for most young children, then one appeared a more enlightened parent. When this argument tallied with saving vast sums of money in school fees, then it was possible at the smartest dinner tables to appear as the very models of intelligent modern parents without the need to admit, heaven forbid it, that money was tight (often the true reason).

Thus boarders drained away from the traditional prep schools and by the early 1990s there were only two prep schools left in Sussex that could truly claim to be boarding schools. Damage was also done by two other factors. Firstly it was becoming apparent that paying fees and/or boarding before the age of 11 could be avoided: it was smart to be able to claim that the free local primary school was really excellent. Even if it was not really that good, it could be argued without losing face that it was better to reserve any significant financial outlay for the children's education for later, enabling local secondary schools to be avoided for the crucial part of schooling, when career-setting public examinations took place. Even if this was not necessarily prudent reasoning – for establishing the right patterns of study and appreciating its worth in the early years might have been a better investment – it was a common form of reasoning and the losers were the prep schools. Of course a large number of people still would not contemplate their children going anywhere else but to the same schools that they had attended. There were less and less of them though, as the trend towards social levelling developed apace throughout the 1970s, 1980s and 1990s. Furthermore, such people were gradually losing their position as leaders of opinion, except amongst their own narrowing circle.

As boarding declined as a British phenomenon, the value of English as a language was growing rapidly year after year as the world grew smaller and commerce, driven largely in this period by the Americans, became increasingly globalised. Given that English was also the language of computers and the worldwide web, it had inevitably become the 'world' language. Assisted by the fact that the UK was closer both geographically and culturally than the USA to Europe, and that the reputation of English education worldwide (the independent sector, that is, which was of course the only relevant sector for those coming from overseas) was superior at this time at secondary school level to that of America, there was increasing demand from foreign students for boarding places. Once again the preparatory schools did not gain from this trend as much as the senior schools, for parents from overseas, faced with saying goodbye to their beloved little ones, often baulked at the prospect but relented when these same little ones became less malleable teenagers. This attitude was common throughout the rest of the world apart from certain parts of the former

British Empire, particularly African countries, where boarding was still acceptable and commonplace from a young age.

Sending children later also saved parents a lot of money, for if English could be perfected in one, two, three or four years, it was obviously better financially than learning it in ten. If it is taken into account that most of the world had co-educational educational systems, then there were going to be a number of the more traditional single sex schools that were going to be less attractive to this growing and essential market. Thus St Bede's at The Dicker, with its open-minded attitude to those from all parts of the world and its particularly dynamic approach to the teaching of English as a second, third or fourth language, grew in numbers, especially boarding numbers, in a period when the national trend was for decline.

Fortunately, St Bede's Preparatory School was of the strong and resilient variety. It had a fine reputation locally and nationally and an inventive head in Peter Pyemont. Although it was not immune to the trends outlined above and the number of boarders dropped dramatically in the decade between 1985 and 1995, Peter kept at bay the worst of the financial problems that the loss of boarding fees could cause. He used any spare boarding capacity for his European Scheme, started in the 1990s, whereby regular numbers of students, from Germany in particular, hungry for the English language spent terms at St Bede's Preparatory School. This scheme, allied to a profitable Summer School, boosted income successfully. It did not however boost it to the same levels as had existed in the early 1980s when nearly half the school of about 400 were boarders.

Even at a school as strong as St Bede's Prep, it was hard to make a financial surplus and thus to improve facilities. The real problem was that a school set up for boarding had certain specific overheads and once these were in place and paid for, the larger fees paid by the boarding students were significant both for profit and cash flow. Even if the boarders were replaced by an equal or greater number of day students, the number of teachers required did not reduce, nor did the demand for increasingly state-of-the-art facilities. Furthermore the day parents were always there and they could compare facilities with other schools; they probably had a more materialistic view of a school than the parents of boarders, whose prime concern was the happiness of their children, something not overly affected by the physical nature of classrooms or the presence of wall-to-wall interactive whiteboards. Thus budgets set for one sort of school were not always appropriate when that school changed into another sort, especially when it had done so very quickly.

The schools that managed best in such circumstances were those that were able to take drastic action to convert to day-only schools and to set up a new fee structure and staffing levels that were right for a lesser level of income. This was not at all easy without risking a loss of confidence among parents as they observed staff redundancies, larger class sizes and the selling of now superfluous assets; something that rival establishments would be quick to point out to interested parents. Other schools starting from scratch in the new commercial climate would also prosper and there were examples in the area.

These were undoubtedly hard times for St Bede's Preparatory School and Peter Pyemont was actively looking for ways of improving its viability. In the 1990s he even entered into negotiations to see if there might be a prosperous future and synergy in St Bede's amalgamating with its arch-rival, St Andrew's, which had also seen a marked downturn in its financial results. Eventually these amalgamation plans came to nothing.

What had not escaped Peter's notice, however, was that at The Dicker, of which he was a governor, things were going from strength to strength; as the 1990s advanced, so did the profits we made. Therefore in 1996 the preparatory school governors asked whether our governors would consider taking the St Bede's School Trust Eastbourne into our Trust (St Bede's School Trust Sussex). It was obvious to us that this had to be done, for the top management of both schools would then be vested in the senior school and thus there would be a greater degree of certainty of boys and girls coming on to The Dicker from St Bede's Prep than had been the case in former years. And so finally in 1999 I found myself, on paper, the chief executive of a joint trust, looking after about 1,000 students ranging in age from 2 to 19. I say 'on paper', for it never occurred to me that the running of the prep school was my job; it was much better left to those who knew about such things and I made no move to interfere with anything at Eastbourne.

It was also important in my opinion that those who ran the prep school should produce an independent set of accounts and have the clear task of managing things so that the Eastbourne section was not a financial drain upon the very hard-won resources of The Dicker. For us at The Dicker there was still much that needed to be done to bring our facilities up to the standard enjoyed by the more prosperous of the long-established independent schools.

During the next five years, until my retirement in 2001, things went on according to this plan. My successor took a different view. He saw himself quite naturally as the head of both schools (he had known nothing else) and thus he took a close interest in matters at Eastbourne – some might say too close an interest. The result of this was that over a period of some five or six years about £5 million was spent on improving facilities at the prep school. Undoubtedly this was money well spent and it, of course, thoroughly justified Peter Pyemont's decision to ask for our help rather than that of his near neighbours. The investment in the prep school did not stop the advances that had to be made in Upper Dicker, but it did mean that there was no chance of such expenditure coming from earned income and so, having fought so hard to get out of the vast debts incurred in setting up the school, it now entered another period of significant indebtedness, albeit when interest rates were not at 17.5 per cent!

There is no doubt that once again, as a serious recession has taken hold, the old habits of watching the pennies, working hard as a team to make certain that the best deals are obtained and ensuring that administration is not allowed to grow at the expense of teaching staff, will be needed once again. But it has to be said that there was, by 2009, a school of nearly 1,400 students. Even if too many of them, for the financial as opposed to the social good, were day students, St Bede's at The Dicker is now a very large school with very great assets and more than a match for any recession.

ANOTHER AMALGAMATION

In 2000 another amalgamation took place that was nothing but a pleasure. Nicolai Gustavovich Legat had immigrated to London in 1922 from Russia. This renowned ballet dancer, ballet master and choreographer then set up a school of dance in Kensington. Amongst those he had trained or worked with were Nijinsky, Diaghilev and Anna Pavlova and, in England, Ninette de Valois, Margot Fonteyn and Anton Dolin. When he died in 1937 his wife, Nadine, a famous dancer in her own right, moved the famous ballet school to Rotherfield in East Sussex and it remained in East Sussex or Kent from then on.

After Rotherfield the Legat School was based for some time at Finchcocks, a country mansion at Goudhurst, and it was also attached for a number of years to Wadhurst College, a school for girls. As Wadhurst College had declined in numbers, it amalgamated with Micklefield School, Seaford, another fading girl's school, and the ballet school joined the combined venture. Gradually it became clear that the joint enterprise had failed entirely, but the Legat School was fortunately led at the time by two Wendys, neither of whom was likely to fade away or fail.

Wendy Vincent-Smith, a distinguished Fellow of the Royal Academy of Dance, had been a leading dancer and was a marvellous teacher. Wendy Hayes was the administrator of the Legat School. When it was obvious that time was soon going to be up at Wadhurst College and a year or two before it was bought as a school but sold as a prime development site for housing, the two Wendys arrived in my office and said that Christopher Pyemont, younger brother of Peter, had suggested they come to see me. I seem to remember that our first meeting was late in 1999. By September of the following year, 2000, we had built our first dance studio and the Legat became part of St Bede's. It was immediately apparent on the day of our first meeting that any operation led by Wendy Vincent-Smith was going to be very high-class indeed. She had wonderful presence and was clearly one of those highly sought-after 'maniacs' (in the sense of a totally committed enthusiast) who was not going to rest until she had achieved exactly what she expected.

The Legat School of Ballet had found a stable home at last in a very strong school that operated in a way that allowed its students to do what they needed to be doing, to excess if necessary. Just as golf or any other sport could be played every day, it was possible to create a programme within the St Bede's structure in which the development of talented dancers took absolute priority, with the rest of the academic day being fitted in around that. To us, what on earth was the point of having the chance to create a brilliant future in dance, which clearly is best done in one's youth, if the school then insisted that geography and science lessons took priority?

For young people to have the chance of reaching the heights in sport or dance, exceptional programmes must be arranged for them. If the dream of reaching those heights is unrealistic, within a few years that will become quite apparent, and then you are never too old to undertake standard academic studies. Anyone running a school with such potential in its ranks must let it have full rein and risk the fact that the school's academic results will perhaps be lowered a little and the precision of the day's timetable become a little ragged. Why should the chance of a wonderful career be blighted by such boringly ordinary matters and fearful leadership? In any case, those seeking the highest standards in dance, sport, music or theatre will almost certainly make sure they do their academic work to a high standard too, finding ways to get round the missing of lessons here and there. Too many leaders in schools, and teachers too, fail to realise that missing a few lessons rarely makes any difference to a student whose morale is high and who is committed and happy.

It was a lucky day when we gave a home to the Legat School, for into our midst came some wonderfully talented and committed young people who set a great example to their contemporaries. They not only produced brilliant shows in their own right but gave an additional touch of the highest quality to musicals and other theatrical productions and often performed as a complement to our concerts.

An extraordinary number of our dancers have gone on to join the most distinguished schools of dance and thus St Bede's at The Dicker gets the credit for ensuring that a distinctly non-profitable part of the school is allowed to thrive and maintain the wonderful traditions of

Nicolai Gustavovich Legat, as carried on with great distinction in my time by Wendy Vincent-Smith. Perhaps the Charity Commission should be reminded how many poor but highly talented dancers are supported by the school, thus helping to satisfy the 'public benefit' criterion – as if bringing in millions of pounds from countries all over the world, and saving the state many more millions by educating the children of those who have usually paid taxes to support its schools, is somehow no 'public benefit' in itself!

WHO CHECKS THE CHECKER?

As the 1990s drew to a close and the new millennium opened up before us, we, like all those running schools, became aware that we were being watched ever more closely, and being watched moreover by organisations that were 'official' and therefore a bit frightening. I suppose that they were only frightening if one got frightened but a lot of people were indeed sore afraid. The main problem was that the news of new organisations set up to check up on us came out in advance, engendering a sense of panic based on rumour and dire predictions of the 'you won't be able to do that any more' type. There are always those who delight in telling you about the problems lying ahead, particularly if you are successful. Some seem to delight in seeing enterprise punished. One product of this fear of what is to come, especially if no one really knows what 'it' is, is that a lot of time can be wasted in preparing for 'its' arrival. Perhaps even more importantly, morale can be easily damaged by having to do lots of things that seem like a complete waste of time and which, because of their bureaucratic nature, are soul-destroyingly boring to those who just enjoy teaching and want to get on with that interesting job.

We are arriving in the age of the Health and Safety Executive. We are at that stage in progress when Social Services are ordered by the government – frightened perhaps by rare happenings in, let us say, a children's home – to extend their duties to inspecting all schools that have boarders, however successful they are and however well-policed by their own need for a first-class reputation. Despite the fact that most of those working in the Social Services knew absolutely nothing about the culture of boarding schools and probably resented the additional burdens placed upon them, they were still expected to perform this scrutinising role. There were of course those amongst them who relished the prospect of entering the supposed bastions of privilege in the hope of discrediting us in some way and creating a sneering headline in a sympathetic tabloid.

We are arriving at a time when the most alert of entrepreneurs began to offer services that would take the burden of complying with forthcoming legislation away from us, even though no one really knew what that burden might be; a profit could be earned from communal fear. For example: we will do your risk assessments; we will write your health and safety policy. We will take over your kitchens so that they accord with this or that directive on public health and are environmentally sound. We will inspect all your electrical appliances and give you an annual certificate – even though there is no telling that said appliances will not develop faults the next day, as so often happens as soon as my car is serviced!

Then there is Ofsted with all its attendant acronyms and its small and large inspections and spot checks. The poor performance of some state schools means that all are to be persecuted and of course the independent schools cannot be seen to be 'getting away with it' even though their paying parents would soon vote with their feet if standards were allowed to fall. Then there is a whole body of paid officials that are part of the Independent Schools' Associations who, fearful for their schools' future in uncertain political times and possibly for their cosy retirement jobs, want to be seen to be able to out-Ofsted Ofsted. They set up their own inspectorates, which then charge a fortune for coming and doing with six people in four days what could be achieved by two good people in one day. If only they produced reports that were of value to the head, rather than telling him what he already knew! It would, for example, be helpful if a report revealed clearly that Mr X seemed rather ineffective (probably not a word that could be used as it would be deemed too judgemental); then the head, who already knew this, could further the time-consuming, student-failing, tortuous process by re-educating or removing Mr X. Alas, almost certainly Mr X, anticipating the inspection, which would have been announced months or even years in advance, would have arranged to have marked his books for once and also cooked up his one and only lively lesson of the term for the crucial day.

Apart from the vast range of health and safety issues, covering everything from our construction operations to the laboratories, workshops and classrooms, to the kitchens, to our lake, ponds and trees, to everywhere we walked, or where someone might walk, or in fact anyone might do anything, we had to devise written Bullying Policies as well. It was not good enough just to have such a policy; we had to write it all down. We set about detailing our Inclusivity Policies too and producing exhaustive student and staff handbooks. Hardly anyone ever looked at any of these documents except inspectors; they were there to prove that, believe it or not, we actually were thinking and trying to run things properly.

Luckily for the financial well-being of the school, I was not given to fear and would not be rushed into taking expensive measures to combat an unknown foe. The best approach was to do nothing at all until the officials arrived. Very often we were doing everything just right anyway but if we were not, these wise and powerful figures would tell us what we needed to do, help us to do it and give us a time limit by which we must comply. All this advice came free and straight from the horse's mouth, as it were. Normally, a shrewd amount of paperwork to show a policy, or a coat of paint to render a part of the kitchens compliant, could easily be done, without months of anticipatory stress and in the sure knowledge that it would certainly be passed by the inspectors. A committee or two that produced minutes and met every term to reconsider all possible risks, showing that we were on the ball, usually kept everyone happy.

But what a vast army of unproductive bureaucrats and hangers-on was created. All too often we met inspectors who knew less than we did by far and whose ideas of good practice were at best debatable. Perhaps our practice was better and they had not thought of it! The vast profits to be made from producing notices that warned of this and warned of that, at £70 or more a go, must have been wonderful. Where was the Big Society when we needed it? Too late, for we are now so far in acceptance of endless state nannying and interference that everyone thinks it ordinary. Any preaching against it is dismissed as the opinion of a back-woodsman, possibly even of a crank. It was, of course, the insurance companies who indirectly policed the whole array of legislation, by threatening not to pay out unless every policy was in place and written down. School governors were worried into compliance and the condoning of much expense because they feared for their own personal liability.

My own feeling, probably a riskily independent one, was that there was not enough courage being shown. Of course it was necessary to manage any enterprise with a shrewd eye to hazards and to point out the dangers to employees, the public at large and the students. But the law has always existed to give this protection and if it can be shown that harm has come to someone as a result of another's negligence, then the courts will punish the negligent individual or organisation by awarding both damages and costs. It would have been helpful if a few school cases had got to court, to show that most of us were responsible and not negligent, and that the way we managed our schools was intelligent. We did not need an army of officials to check that we were reasonable people. Luckily, whatever I thought personally, there were wonderfully patient people like Derek Newton around to write any number of policy documents, once someone told us what the minimum requirements of such a document were.

As things stand, my successors have to work in an environment in which these government and civil service-inspired practices are not reducing. They are the product of people who are employed to summon up this or that 'initiative', or to draft this or that 'code of practice', and to foist them on those who are already showing some initiative and are most definitely in practice. When Lord Melbourne was Prime Minister, he made it clear that government in his opinion was not there to interfere in the lives of the governed – he called the practice of so doing 'botheration'. It is. Having met a lot of the practitioners of botheration, and not always been impressed by their thoughtfulness or worthiness for power, I wonder who checks up on them? Who, I wonder, checks the checker and the checker's checker, and so on and so on? It could, in a world just slightly madder, go on and on until we each have our own personal inspector! Luckily there is a wealth of darkish humour in all this or it could be extremely worrying.

As a postscript, it already has become worrying, for we now hear that hundreds of schools pronounced 'outstanding' by the good people of the Office for Standards in Education were not classed as outstanding as far as teaching was concerned! Teaching, what's that? I have visited at least one school where the policies were all in order, issues of governance were beautifully displayed, everyone had had a Criminal Records Bureau check, and there were continuous, well-evidenced, risk assessments – but no one was much good at teaching! As long ago as 1920, H.G. Wells wrote, on noticing the increased interference from men in departments, 'in the future when history is written there will be much about clerks and nothing about conquerors'. In education, for conquerors read teachers.

THE MILLENNIUM AND OTHER ANNIVERSARIES

Fortunately there are less sombre things to dwell upon. Any excuse for a really good party was always taken at The Dicker. Horatio Bottomley had set a very high standard in this respect and there was something about the house and gardens that perpetuated his spirit. In any case, so hard did we all work in those early days that it was imperative to let one's hair down as often as possible. Not only was the spirit there and some beautiful settings but also Angela was able to make our parties look really special. She had a wonderful way with colour and design and was always able to bring people along with her. Thus the kitchen staff raised their game to unimaginable heights and everyone else joined in willingly for they knew that they were involved in something really good. Very often they would be there themselves to enjoy the party too. It was important that all who worked in the school, from the head to the part-time cleaner, felt that they were part of the success. Outside firms were never involved in our events for we could have a better party at far less cost by doing it all 'in house'.

The celebration of 20 years at The Dicker, coinciding as it did with the school's 21st birthday, was a marvellous event. The year was 1999 and the school roll had already grown to be over 550, of which over 300 were boarders. The financial surplus for the year that had just ended in July 1999 was a few pounds short of £1 million and every space was filled for the next year; in fact, as was prudent, we had as usual overbooked by about 20 boarders. The weather was fine and on the first day of the summer holidays everyone was in the right mood. The guests included a fine turn-out of former students, including most of the original 22, plus former members of staff, all those who currently worked for the school in any capacity with their wives, husbands and partners, our governors, friends of the school and members of the village community. Numbering well over 350 in all, we ate, drank and danced in and around an enormous marquee in the picturesque setting by the lake. The food was splendidly produced by Michael Wallis and his team, the tent was wonderfully decorated florally by Angela, and the band that played for some uninhibited dancing was led by Trevor Wallis, Michael's brother, also a talented cook as well as the leader of a well-known local band.

The most memorable of all our parties were those held annually at Christmas-time and the barbeques that finished each school year. These took place as soon as the students had departed for their holidays. No dignitaries were present and so the celebrations were subject to little restraint, as everyone knew that they had worked extremely hard and deserved to relax and play just as hard. These parties benefited hugely from having the whole workforce there – they were not just for teachers as in many schools. It greatly amused the cleaning and kitchen staff to see the head and the senior teachers dishing up the food and acting as the waiters. It did the junior members of the grounds and maintenance teams good to show off their superiority on the dance floor, or perhaps to be surprised that teachers of history could be unbelievably 'hip'! What was almost inevitable was that one of the young general assistants from the kitchens would get hopelessly inebriated and would need guarding until it was possible for the return home to be made with some dignity! They were, after all, the same age as the students.

Whatever the cost in health terms the following morning, these events were just wonderful for morale and productive of many conversations between the different parts of the team that hardly had a chance to meet in the heat of the action of term-time. It reminded me of my early days in teaching at the Dragon School, where the leaders were always ready to take it if the chance for a good party emerged: the atmosphere there was just wonderful for us younger members of staff, as we were definitely a part of things. At St Bede's, for the teachers, and certainly for me, it was essentially therapeutic to be able to behave 'badly' for a spell after having to behave so well for the weeks and weeks of term!

NOT SO IMPRESSIVE

In 1997 we were inspected with a view to election to the Head Masters' Conference. In the field of independent education it was widely believed that the schools that were HMC were the elite. The HMC was a club that set standards for its members and had a central office that organised training and induction processes for heads who were new to the role; it also jealously guarded its reputation. The annual conferences, lavishly organised in five-star venues, gained much press coverage of the speeches made by the current chairman and an array of distinguished guest speakers. Within the narrow ranks of independent schools, mention of the HMC meant something and to be in its membership one sensed added to the aura surrounding the school in the eyes of its heads and governors. That the vast majority of the country and most parents had never heard of HMC did not diminish its standing to its members and most certainly it was a sort of kite-mark that proved that a school was an effective and respectable organisation – or at least that it had been at some point. As time passed, the HMC did take steps to ensure that its member schools maintained the best standards and organised regular inspections of them to try to ensure this.

In 1996 some of our governors thought that we had reached the point where we ought to join the HMC. I agreed to investigate this even though I was very happy with our membership of the Society of Headmasters of Independent Schools, as it was then called, before it became Headmasters and Headmistresses. This organisation, SHMIS, was less self-important than HMC. A number of HMC heads were also SHMIS members and found it more helpful to them. To add to your confusion, SHMIS is now known as the Society of Heads. I am not sure whether it calls itself SH or SOH, hopefully not either!

I did some careful research before talking directly to HMC. I discovered that we were larger in numbers than some 40 of the approximately 200 HMC schools. I discovered also that we appeared ahead of at least 30 of them in the annual A-level league tables and that our sixth form was larger than at least 40 of these esteemed centres of excellence. On talking to the Secretary of HMC, a delightful man named Roger Griffiths, who had been head of Hurstpierpoint College in his day and knew of us, it became clear that we met the membership criteria. Mr Griffiths, who came to spend a day with us as a preliminary inspection, thought we ought to apply.

I reported back to the governors and they asked me to go ahead. From my point of view, the attraction of being a school admitted to membership faster than any other from the date of foundation counted for something, although the prospect of being in a rather self-regarding club, which might try to influence the way we did things, was a concern. An inspection date was duly announced for 1997. The cost of this inspection seemed ridiculously high to me but such was our self-confidence at this time and so greatly had we been encouraged to apply that we paid up willingly – but having been examined, we discovered that to certain others we were not that impressive.

In short, our application was refused. Although we were politely invited to apply again later, such an outcome was pretty annoying. It would have been really annoying if it had mattered all that much, but in truth it was a minor dent to our pride. Possibly that was a good thing, for it caused us to make a brief examination of some of our policies but not to change them! We had wasted a lot of time and some money on the application and inspection, and we were still ahead of many of the HMC members in the light of their own criteria. There was a bit of a post mortem but in truth it did not last long and our 'failure' made absolutely no difference to the school, which continued to grow in numbers and reputation in the eyes of parents, most of whom had never heard of HMC, unless they had been to such a school in their youth. I had been to one myself but it made no difference to my time there or to my sense of its importance as an organisation.

But why had we failed to impress? The simple answer is that we came as a bit of a shock to the inspectors. We just did not do certain things the way they were used to seeing them done. When the next body of HMC inspectors came, 10 or was it 11 years later, the school was hailed as just what they wanted and a 'breath of fresh air', for by that time the same practices that had worried the earlier group were seen as enlightened.

What were the aspects that worried the 1997 inspectors? Put broadly, those that did not conform to the rigid pattern in which these retired or highly experienced heads of institutions that had been in existence for centuries had conducted their own schools. Why was it not compulsory for every student to follow science courses to GCSE? Why were some boys and girls not following foreign language courses to GCSE? Why were games not compulsory? Why was there no chaplain? Why were church services not compulsory for all on Sundays? Most of the inspectors came from long-established day schools and from schools that were distinguished because they got very good results, largely because they were selective by examination.

There was simply no getting past them; their minds were, if not closed, certainly not open enough to understand us at the time. I felt this strongly as soon as the somewhat austere and besuited figures entered The Dicker: our very name already exuded more fun than was good for anyone. Surely everyone must study physics and chemistry to be properly educated: do you not think you are letting them down, they asked. We explained that we had amongst us young people with serious difficulties in the most basic applications of maths and that we were teaching them patiently in groups of three or four, or even individually, to give them the confidence to advance towards GCSE when they were aged 18. When we asked whether it was better to allow these young people to study subjects in which they had a chance of success, rather than to waste their time with physics and chemistry in which they were absolutely certain to fail, they just dismissed us as eccentric liberals.

Similarly with modern languages; a young person whose brain registered virtually zero on the 'coding' component of an IQ test, and who was thus so extremely dyslexic that the acts of reading and writing English needed small group or one-to-one teaching by qualified experts, was clearly not going to thrive when it came to French or Spanish or German or Italian or Russian or any other foreign language we taught. Apparently we were letting them down too. Why not have a good laugh at their expense as they flounder?!

These inspectors' views had been formed in an age when dyslexia was another word for laziness. When we asked them whether it was possible to lead a perfectly successful life without knowing chemistry or understanding French, they brushed the questions aside. When we pointed out that many of our students were multilingual anyway and that it was a waste of their time to study languages that were their native tongues, we still failed to fit the perceived pattern of an HMC school.

One of the team asserted in the report that the school had no spiritual life and that even though there was a member of staff in Holy Orders, he did not run the spiritual side of the school. Clearly, 'spiritual life', for these particular leaders, should have a set pattern too. We certainly had had a form of spiritual life at the school I attended as a boy, and doubtless at the schools where these inspectors grew up and later taught. Indeed the school I attended was a church foundation and the connection between church and school was at the heart of 19th century education. The schools that made up the HMC were generally old established schools, many of which still had those religious links.

At the time, state schools still had to provide an act of worship at the start of each day and it was to be a Christian act on the whole. The fact that all our staff had to take part as leaders in the weekly meetings in the local church and that our students knew that the spiritual side of life was too precious to put into the hands of just one version of the truth, for this was explained to them very carefully, was not 'spiritual' in this inspector's eyes. There were boys and girls of all religions in the school and they all attended the meetings in the church but we did not have one chaplain putting forward a daily message from one point of view. This cut no ice with the inspector.

In our community, all religions were to be respected. As I have explained, the boarders could either attend a church of their and their family's choice on a Sunday or failing that went to a School Meeting where matters of the spirit and ethical considerations were top of an enlightened agenda: but again this was not considered suitably spiritual. The plain fact was that as far as the inspectors were concerned, unless there were hymns, preferably from *Hymns Ancient and Modern*, and bible readings and a chaplain, there simply was no spiritual life. Oh dear! We were certainly not going to undertake to change to what in our view would be a less spiritual approach.

Why should there be compulsory games? There were plenty of other ways of keeping fit. Any student who wanted to play games every day could do so and was respected along with everyone else. In truth, the inspectors had to produce their academic criticisms for without them their verdict would have been invalid in the eyes of their own organisation.

However I have always believed that the HMC were just not ready for us in 1997. We would probably have accepted without any quarrel a report that said that there were too many portable buildings and a miscellaneous assemblage of rather crowded boarding accommodation; we could not help it that lots of boys and girls wanted to join the school and that there was a prudent way to accommodate them without endangering the school's financial stability. We would have understood any suggestion that we needed to improve the ratio of showers to students in certain areas of our boarding accommodation and that our current provision might have brought the HMC into disrepute. We could even have accepted an explanation that certain neighbouring HMC schools had cast doubts about our suitability to join their august body in their debates on new member applications. But to accept the criticisms of our curriculum or our spiritual life or our logical approach to games was just not possible: to do so would have let certain boys and girls down very badly indeed.

My sources tell me that when it came to the final decision as to whether St Bede's at The Dicker was suitable for HMC membership, it could well have been the reservations expressed by the heads of two schools not far distant from us that influenced HMC to refuse our application. I could understand their concern, as we were advancing very fast!

In any case, the inspectors who came in 2008 thought our approach an enlightened one and the school is now in membership of HMC and, I am led to believe, did achieve that status in a shorter time from foundation than any other member establishment. I just hope that those who run the school now are well aware that any club will tend to develop its own 'hymn sheet', literally and metaphorically. The tendency to be approved because the school is like the rest and not truly independent will undoubtedly be a temptation, and one to be resisted at all costs. The temptation to be lured into singing too closely from that hymn sheet would most certainly damage the school, which in this context is the boys and girls and staff who are there right now, this very day. Their particular needs and talents must be looked after and encouraged, and then looked after and encouraged again, and again. These young people do not exist primarily to glorify the impersonal 'school' or its leadership. The school will always be a great school if this is its obsession and will never be out of date.

A TOUGH FIVE-SET MATCH

Showing around prospective parents in my latter years was in many ways far easier but in others just as exciting as it had always been. The unexpected could still catch you out: the sixth former fast asleep in the middle of lessons, not in the classroom but tucked up in his now rather smart study-bedroom (incidentally, we had started making our own furniture in the Chicken House and it looked modern and relatively stylish); the sudden overpowering smell of tobacco in a room, far more noticeable to visitors now that hardly anyone smoked except the young; diabolically flooded and foul-smelling bathrooms in the boys' houses (if only people had more daughters); occasional snatches of disorder in a classroom or, worse, a mighty outburst of wrath that seemed to go on and on, quite therapeutic for one or two colleagues but not encouraging to putative parents and nervous children.

However, The Dicker offered many more impressive new facilities to take their minds off such things and the view up to the Long Man at Wilmington was still entrancing – as long as it was not during break, when I could not help but notice a steady procession of boys and girls walking across the field towards the Long Man with a purpose I could not reveal to the visitors even if I had been asked. This mysterious journeying towards no discernible goal was a phenomenon normally associated with Marlboro – but not the school or market town in Wiltshire!

The whole campus now encompassed over 100 acres, so obviously these tours did not cover everywhere. Overall, though, despite occasional adrenalin-boosting moments, there was much to feel easy about and even a little proud. Above all the prevailing atmosphere was one that evoked friendship and a lack of stress. The young people we met talked easily and smiled. Their great variety, reflected in the individualistic but respectful way in which they dressed, reflected what was best in Britain: tolerance, enjoyment of difference and not needing to look over one's shoulder in fear. The students appeared confident in their own abilities, knowing that these were recognised and valued by me and, more importantly, by their contemporaries.

It was exciting for our visitors to be surprised, perhaps by the beautiful and un-science-blocky laboratories, or by the Kennels, or by the brightly coloured chalets that had echoes of the earliest Butlin's, a hint of retro chic even, or by the individualised prefabricated classrooms. It was even better to come across breath-taking ceramics or paintings; passion-filled physical theatre in a drama studio; a professionally designed dance studio with music and movement to match; the sound of a string quartet of great quality; a stress-free yoga session; or a national champion practising his archery. It could be just as surprising for prospective parents to see the Conservatory in the distance with its horticultural richness, or to hear that there were pigs and sheep just through the woods, reared by our agricultural students and marketed as part of their courses.

They could also see the more ordinary side of school life that took place in classrooms, where small classes enjoyed being taught by those who really enjoyed their jobs, not least because they could contribute so much outside the classroom as well. There were over 150 extra-curricular activities going on each week in the years around the millennium and nearly 40 different subjects were taught, enabling all but a very few persistent adolescent resisters to feel wanted and appreciated for their own skills.

This approach greatly reduced the potentially stultifying effect of constant comparison. After all, who could begin to compare the merits of a champion archer with those of a boy involved in the Maths Olympiad? I know some who would try to, including those who can declare with Delphic authority that there are some superior and difficult subjects and some that are easy and inferior. It surprises me that such pundits are not able to live our lives for us as well as their own. It is worth noting once again at this point that the majority of students at St Bede's followed an entirely orthodox curriculum.

As I write in 2012, the current education minister, determined as he is to improve national standards, does seem at times to believe that all schools should be like the one that he went to, where 'standards' were 'high'. When will 'grammarschoolitis' and the need to judge things solely on academic results cease to re-emerge, with its paralysing results for so many who are not able to profit from that sort of curriculum?

I know what sort of school I would rather grow up in and be willing to work in and I am encouraged to think that there are many who share my beliefs; witness the fact that more and more students have come through our school's doors. I hope fervently that Bede's (to give the school its new title, for its sanctity was lost in a re-branding exercise in 2011) will continue to be judged on how it improves the life of each of its students, both in the breadth of their understanding of others and of personal fulfilment, throughout the years to come. It will probably need bravery to resist the pressure of the apparent certainties and comfort for the insecure that the educational establishment would seem to offer; likewise it will be difficult to brush aside inevitable attempts to make unflattering comparisons. Not flinching in the face of opposition of whatever kind will undoubtedly cheer the important people in any school, the whole community in other words.

What we have in St Bede's is a school of charm and eccentricity, of scholarly achievement and very robust sporting excellence, of victory over handicaps and deeper understanding of others, of freedom of expression and law-abiding respect, of brilliant colours and designs and vivid movement and speech, amongst so many other things too numerous to mention but no less important. It is obvious that it must be kept that way; I am sure that it will. What sort of 'results' do we want, after all?

To get to the stage where a school existed that had undoubtedly taken root and was strong enough to withstand economic downturns, the whims of bank managers or fleeting movements of social opinion and dinner-party gossip was a hugely rewarding feeling. The process, for Angela and me, had felt like a close, hard-fought, five-set tennis match. Simultaneously it was highly satisfying, great fun and also a great relief to know that we had won.

My contract took me to the age of 60 and when the governors asked me whether I would like to carry on for another five years, or perhaps another three, we discussed things carefully at home and decided that my contract would be fulfilled but not extended. There were other activities, particularly Angela's future as an artist, which ought to be followed particularly whilst we were still relatively youthful. But most important was the sure knowledge that I had to leave at some time and that at the end of a hard-fought five-setter it would be foolish to say 'shall we make it the best of seven?'!

What is more, when we were empowered by the governors to find my successor, or rather to come up with a shortlist of three for their consideration, we knew that even if we made a mess of this task, the school could not fail to march on. In 2001 The Dicker was on a roll and there were going to be inevitable increases in numbers for at least the next three years whoever was in charge. It is important to leave when an enterprise is safe and its future assured, so that is what we did. There were plenty of people who could fulfil my role most capably; whether there were many who could fulfil Angela's was more open to question.

What a tough match it had been: it felt like 9-7 in the fifth!

THEY DID WANT TO COME TO OUR SCHOOL

There have been a number of clues in this story as to why St Bede's at The Dicker succeeded and became almost certainly the leading foundation in independent education of this generation (a generation being considered a period of 30 to 40 years). Anthony Seldon might not have known why anyone would want to come to our school but after a few years of thought I think I know: I probably knew when I took his phone call. Why did the school succeed? There is never just one answer to such a question. All that can be done is to point out a number of factors that had been favourable to St Bede's, weigh them in importance, and perhaps come to the conclusion that they were all part of the story.

There can be no doubt that we started the school at an opportune time. The moment for co-education in British schools had come. Closer links with continental Europe, which came about in the 1970s, brought the British into contact with continental schooling and this was predominantly co-educational. Additionally, the advent of comprehensive schools and advances in the general understanding of equality of opportunity between the sexes made the traditional structure of British education, with its single-sex approach, seem very old-fashioned.

Within the independent sector some of the schools that increasingly caught the eye had gone co-ed or started as co-ed establishments. Bedales, Millfield, Gordonstoun and a rejuvenated Oakham spring to mind at senior level and these had gained support from those, including the Royal family, who helped direct public attitudes; if it is good enough for them it must be good enough for us went the reasoning. At prep school level, co-educational schools such as Windlesham House and our own St Bede's were clearly thriving, and their parents spread the word. By the late 1970s it was just a little 'trendy' to opt for co-education and it does not take long for a trend to become a norm: within 20 years of St Bede's Senior School's foundation it *was* the norm.

The popularity of St Bede's at The Dicker had little to do with examination results; it was to do with the greater width of opportunity that a mixed school offered and a more natural progression to a balanced life, both in secondary education and life thereafter. As the Victorian, somewhat repressive, attitudes of so many of the founders of British education and the dominance of social patterns dictated by warfare and the armed services faded away, a fundamental change in outlook dawned. It is not fanciful to detect in the late 1970s and early 1980s a moving away from military influence; for example, precise details of how jackets should be buttoned, not only to show smartness but also to designate rank at school, now seemed remarkably petty and quaint. Although some schools persisted in the view that bringing in girls would weaken the fabric of tradition and the dominance of rugby football or some other religion, and although the armed forces themselves continued for some time to resist the full integration of women, nevertheless the social changes that came about were, by this time, inevitable.

That our school was able to take advantage of the trend towards co-education was made much easier by the fact that we were starting from scratch. All the pressures that made other schools in the independent sector hold back were absent. There were no traditions standing in our way. There were no powerful Old Boys' or Old Girls' organisations casting a watchful and sceptical eye over our affairs. There was no Founder's Charter or the like to get around in legal terms. There was no need to re-arrange anything with the Charity Commission. There was no predominantly male or female staffroom to resist change. There was no need to remodel facilities and accommodation to enable boys or girls to fit in; the governors of the established schools were bound to baulk at such a large expense when they considered things to be satisfactory as they were. The paralysing fear of the unknown also weighed very heavily on these established schools; meanwhile St Bede's at The Dicker got away to an unopposed start as the only co-educational senior school in Sussex except for the Rudolf Steiner Schools.

As I have already been mentioned, the demise of grammar schools in Sussex and the suspicion in which the comprehensives were held in the late 1970s and 1980s were other helpful factors that made Peter Pyemont's decision to launch the school particularly prescient.

There were other huge advantages in being able to start without any baggage from the past. For example, we had no need to mollify a teaching staff who had always done things in a particular way and who therefore resisted change – in our case, there was no change. We were also able to employ teachers who had the enthusiasm for a new venture. We were able to ask them to work in ways that the schools they came from had not; they were expected to take part in every aspect of the school's programme, not just in the classroom. They relished the opportunity to offer their pet enthusiasms to the students and the students liked the freedom of choice just as much.

All our teachers really enjoyed being part of a small but growing team and doing things differently but with belief. They liked being leaders in their particular areas of expertise and setting up their own courses and resources. They liked the fact that in return for this full commitment, which ran into the weekends too, they were from the very start at The Dicker paid above standard teaching salaries. I can confidently say that compared to the teachers in every other school that I have observed or been associated with, our teachers' commitment was fully engaged and their talents fully exploited. As the school grew, this became a source of pride to the staff and clearly helped to weed out the very few who did not subscribe to the school's ethos; they tended to leave of their own accord, probably thinking we were mad!

Starting from scratch involves a lot of making it up as one goes along. It is quite useless to over-plan as may well have become apparent from this narrative. How many students will arrive and what will they be like? Will any arrive at all? How many rooms will we need and how much furniture? What staff will be needed?

Luckily the governors were helpful in practical ways but left the business to us and did not interfere. What a blessing this was, for the last thing we needed was someone trying to second-guess all our decisions. What a blessing, too, that they did not want to make the school a replica of the ones they had been to themselves; nor did they have stereotypical ideas about how the administrative set-up should work. Those governors, who were with us for a very long time, the group so stable from the early 1990s, were just remarkable, and the school was fortunate that they were there. We were able to keep the administrative team down to a very small size for years, meaning that our meagre resources could be spent directly on the needs of our students. In practice this meant that for many of the earliest years, Angela and I carried out most of the tasks that would have come within a bursar's remit, and the subsequent savings helped us to get by – just! It is quite amazing how much money organisations waste by doing things in what is the accepted style, or by wasting time, money and effort on planning for the unknown. Let's see what happens and then work really fast to meet the issues raised and the consequent deadlines; that was the St Bede's style.

We were fortunate that our students arrived at the age of 13 and so we were a school for teenagers. This helped in all sorts of ways. It was particularly advantageous to the boarders not to have to be governed by rules that took into account the added caution that dealing with younger children involved. The full attention of the teaching staff was focused on this older age group and there is no doubt that the whole approach to teaching them does not fit well with the fussier, more 'mumsy' and 'dadsy' style that can be appropriate for the years before adolescence. The students liked to be treated as if they were adults even though many of them took a long time to justify this; to appear to trust their adult good sense whilst keeping a very sharp eye on what they were up to is the key to leading this age group.

We had been fortunate too that finance arrived just in time on so many occasions when we appeared to be in danger of going under. But, in reality, all the reasons for our success I have mentioned, though important as background issues, were not, even in their combined force, the main reason why the school succeeded. What I had said to Dr Anthony Seldon in 1999 was the key to it all: we looked after the students. We looked after them with a real intensity and in their interests and not those of 'the school', or to fit to a pattern laid down by government, or indeed any part of the educational establishment. St Bede's at The Dicker was a radical school in the true sense of that word: we analysed the fundamental needs of each student and tried our best to address them in the interests of his or her long-term success and happiness.

We were not prepared to accommodate any prejudice that was not going to work to a student's advantage, wherever it came from, even from parents, whom we would normally manage to work round to a useful way of thinking. Thus when Father said that young Ben had to do GCSE French because that was an essential part of a 'good' education, such as he had had himself, we would gently point out that young Ben was dyslexic (he had probably inherited the condition from his father; we did not mention that) and needed time first to overcome his difficulties in English. If he would like us to give Ben a course in speaking French (presumably the purpose of any study) that involved no toiling with the written word or grammar, we would willingly do so. Father duly came round!

Thus it can be said that in a real sense it was the boys and girls who came to the school who determined how it would develop and whether it would succeed or fail. As the years passed it became clearer and clearer that, even when we reached a stage of popularity when it would have been possible to bring in some form of academic selectivity, it would have been entirely wrong to do so. It was simply much more fun, much more of a challenge, not to be selective, and, as I have said before, it was a much better preparation for life after school to be used to the company of all sorts of people. After all, let me ask once more, what was the purpose of going to school? It was, quite simply, to leave; and if, on leaving, one's confidence was high and one had to that point fulfilled one's potential, one had definitely been to a good school.

Although we did not manage to succeed with quite all our students, there were surprisingly few who did not realise that this school was on their side. Certainly in our early days there were enough villains about to keep us fully on our toes and detention sessions on Saturday afternoons (a thoroughly unpopular time to be grounded) were populated by the same characters week after week; they considered it a price worth paying for a life of law-breaking and the excitement of trying to avoid capture. They either 'turned the corner' or were moved on.

There were one or two who tried to move themselves on literally, and I recall with both some alarm and some amusement the day in June 1981 when we awoke to find that two delightful girls, Jane and Deborah, had departed in the night. It was the night before they were due to start their O-level exams and they could not face them; their parents lived on the other side of the world and so were unable to give them courage or reassurance. The good thing was that after trudging across the Sussex Downs and along various roads they finished up at Seaford police station, from whence they were collected and reappeared to face the examiners.

The very best bits of this adventure were in the comprehensive note the girls had left behind when they ran away: 'Please tell Mr Daly' (young and personable PE teacher) 'that we don't blame *him* and give him our love. Tell our parents that we will be all right; tell Louise her jeans are in the cupboard by the window; let Abigail know that she can keep the bracelet I gave her and say bye and we love you to all our friends except Julie ...' (Presumably an ex-friend at the time!) A year or two ago an attractive young lady waved at me from a hairdressing salon and to my amazement she beckoned me in. I was even more amazed when she said she was Jane the absconder, that she owned the salon and was married with two children! We had a very good laugh about the incident and she wondered where Mr Daly was now! I hope she won't tell her own children the story when they are 16.

St Bede's emerged over its first two decades as a truly 'comprehensive' school, in the best educational sense. Also it moved naturally with the times. Its curriculum was not dictated by the past but by the realities of the world of the late 20th and early 21st centuries. Our IT provision was far in advance of most other schools; we were the first school to bring artists into residence so that our students could witness highly talented professionals at work; we were probably alone in running seven distinct science courses so that any individual's enthusiasms or particular skills – or lack of them – could be more accurately served. We were the only school I knew that was willing to offer any other language if it was desired and if it would be useful to the individual concerned (it was important that certain languages were not seen as more valuable than others and our highly multinational community helped that thought). We were the first independent school of our area to make an impact in the Young Enterprise challenge and, connected with this, we moved into the world of vocational courses such as NVQs, GNVQs, BTECs and City & Guilds, when many of the so-called educational leaders were writing them off as worthless and undemanding. Our religious studies courses were rightly popular because they included a world view well before that became more standard practice. The whole General Studies programme was aimed at enabling all our diverse students to lead happy and well ordered lives after they left the relative safety of school rather than simply trying to get another exam pass out of it.

Quite simply, the school refused to get stuck in any sort of rut and indeed, as it was set up, it could not do so, for there was a completely different body of students every five years. Just by concentrating intently on who these young people were and what they needed, the school was forced to move with the times. It required considerable bravery on occasions to run against the trends as set out by the media, the educational establishment, the department of education and the loudest voices at many a dinner party table in what was a conservative part of the world. Of course we did feel fearful at times but any nerves were vanquished by a fear of failure, which would have been much worse. Failure would have been to know that we had let our students down. Failure would not be failing to reach a lofty place in the exam league tables, but the lack of a clear conscience that our students had succeeded as far as their abilities and our assistance would allow. Obviously there was going to be a degree of failure at some level for it is simply not possible to achieve perfection, but we got as close as was possible through open-minded and flexible thought and action.

Fortunately, as I said, we were served by a wonderfully supportive, but splendidly unobtrusive (except when there was the need for clear professional or commercial advice or positively helpful and decisive action) board of governors. David Baker and his decisive introduction of his bank manager, Jack Hawkins and the generous gift of facilities and personnel from his company, Mervyn Griffiths and his timely financial intervention have all been mentioned. On another, perhaps humbler level, there was John Brewer, chairman of a leading painting and decorating supplies firm, a cherished governor until his untimely death, and a very dear friend. I recall, still with excitement, the day he gave me the use of a Brewer's lorry to go to Grantham, to pick up all the shelving and other library paraphernalia from a closing bookshop in that town. It felt good driving that lorry and eating a good breakfast at a plastic table outside a steaming caravan in a lay-by on the A1. It was really thrilling seeing all the equipment packed in, particularly as the journey saved the school thousands of pounds. The owner of the bookshop pointed out Margaret Thatcher's father's grocery store too! It pleases me even now to see that the shelving still graces the library. Our governors were indeed generous with both time and practical help.

Luckily we had a wonderfully varied body of teachers who on the whole fell in with the team plan, or at least appeared to do so. Those who wanted a school that had less of the 'alternative' about it tended to leave. The marvellous thing about our teaching team was that they constantly surprised us; they liked the way in which ideas that they came up with would be taken seriously. They had the sense, so important in this profession, or to describe it more carefully, 'way of life', that they were in charge of their own contribution to the whole and so were in many important ways almost 'self-employed', the essence of team work. They were varied not only in their talents but in their values; it was for example pleasurable to me that in a school that was as liberal as ours there was a thriving, and entirely voluntary, Army Cadet Force, because one respected member of the teaching team wanted there to be such a thing and an important number of boys and girls agreed. Amongst the staff there was a great balance between the male and the female, and between the older and experienced and the young and faster-moving. There was a valuable racial and cultural mix in the staff common room and great mutual respect. It upsets me that I cannot in this account mention them all; without them it would all have been academic! I hope they enjoyed some of the fun.

IN SUMMARY

The last section has tried to explain why a major independent school came to exist against the odds. We might have been lucky but equally we were never distracted from our task. When I look back on the process, I can recall 23 years of the most acute concentration day after day. Was it selling, was it personnel management, was it teaching (those Latin lessons were often the most enjoyable hours of my week), was it enforcing the rules, was it building, was it financial responsibility and the danger of going under, was it celebrating the great achievements of the students, was it simply partying, was it holidaying with equal intensity, was it making them laugh or failing to do so, was it making speeches or talking to assemblies, was it enjoying the company of the students as the very best antidote to a day when it all seemed to have gone wrong? The answer is it was all of it. Looking back, observing the continued growth of the school, I pray that it will remain as open-minded and un-skewed as the students deserve. I do also, it must be admitted, feel a certain sense of pride.

I feel pleased that all those who worked for the school, and not just the teachers, felt that they were important elements of the team as a whole and whose efforts were noticed on a daily basis. Our parties were great celebrations and involved all of us, from every part of the school. I feel really proud that we did our own building work; the results, humble or less so, were achievements for our team, possibly against the odds, but not really when you consider what skilful people we had. We also had the courage to start – after all, building is only completing one small act after another, in the right order!

I am happy that our school was notable for its inclusivity, something which came naturally and was not dictated by the official doctrines of the state. I am truly proud of our programmes for those for whom English was not their first language and even more so of our treatment of those with dyslexia or other acute learning difficulties; the inspirational leadership of Graham Jaggers and Linda Gilham in this field, and the acceptance of all the staff of their responsibilities in respect of these students, placed the school in the forefront in these areas without detracting anything from the education of the most academically gifted, who became sensitive to this body of fellow high achievers.

I am also proud of the vibrant internationalism of the community and the width of relationships and understanding that this fostered amongst the young. Perhaps most of all I am pleased that we rose from being very small and insignificant without running down anyone or any institution along the way, and without any tendency to self-satisfaction or looking down upon others; this is thankfully a very un-snobbish school.

Finally, I believe that the young people at The Dicker really did begin to grasp the idea that everyone they met would probably be better than them at perhaps ten things, or even more, which was a reason for great joy and confidence: for as you met them, so they met you and, if they talked to you or observed you, they would realise that you were better than them at certain things too. What a source of liberation, what a potentially great contribution to the harmony of life and what a simple idea – simple! That's where this account started.

When we retired, Angela and I were treated to a wonderful party to see us on our way. Gathered together were nearly all the people who had helped us on the journey; governors, staff from all periods of the school's life, students – from those in our very first year to those in our last – and those who worked so hard for the cause from every area of our operation, cleaning, driving, gardening, building, you name it. There too were countless well-wishers whose support had buoyed us up mightily over the years. Not only was there a first-class meal and plenty of refreshment but also some witty speakers. We were honoured that our old friend Griff Rhys Jones came down to say a few words, thus ensuring that the celebration ended with much laughter and rightly so: for if the things that are most important in life and occupy so much of one's time do not make one smile and laugh, what hope is there?

APPENDIX 1

THE ORIGINAL 23
The boys and girls who formed the first entry to the school
in September 1978

Sarah Barsby	Jason Coleman	Edmund Creed
Ronald Duckworth	Daoud El Khalifa	Lyndon Elmes
Cindy Ford	Jean-Marc Gellatly	Reza Horn
Husain Jaffa	Roy Johnson	Adelita Khoury
Paul Kleinman	Daniel Lester	Nelson Melo
Amin Mitha	Aldo Notarianni	Maria Panico
Deborah Ransome	Simon Risby	Adrian Smith
Fariba Yarrmohamadi	Hossein Zamani-Tork	

APPENDIX 2

PROPERTIES PURCHASED AND DEVELOPMENTS

1977
November: initial enquiry regarding The Dicker; letter from Peter Pyemont to Mrs Oldham

1979
28 February: The Dicker purchased (£140,000). It accommodates after conversion boys' and girls' boarding, dining room, kitchens, library, five classrooms, staff common room, medical room and changing rooms for day students. There is a science laboratory and a further classroom in the stables and a multi-use floodlit play area the size of two tennis courts constructed behind Stables and in front of Aviary.

1980
January: First agreement to rent rooms at Dicker Stud
April: Acquisition of cedar-clad laboratory building from Parkside School; this included initially the Cottage Classrooms and laboratories for physics and chemistry. (Free) Removed in 2000 to make way for Perrin Building
August: Acquisition of Pickard land and buildings including Crossways Cottages, Tack House, Kennels and all land to right of main entrance gate to corner of Stables and land to rear of Tack House as far as boundary with Clifton Farm, including the concrete road. (£70,000)
August/September: Prefabricated dormitory accommodation from Presco Buildings installed for Dorms and subsequently Dorter boarding houses. (£210,000 including £110,000 foundations!) Existing boys' boarding accommodation in The Dicker becomes part of girls' boarding house.

1981

January to March: Crossways Cottages converted to Crossways Cottage and remains Head's house.

March/April: Kennels converted to maintenance workshop.

April: Tack House re-roofed and converted to CDT workshop and stores. External staircase to first floor of Tack House installed and art classrooms and stores made there.

July: Aviary converted to music practice rooms.

August: Camberlot Hall purchased (£160,000). Portacabin changing-room for Camberlot boys installed by main entrance. Cedar-clad sectional building acquired (£250): this was initially two additional cottage classrooms and subsequently became a second biology laboratory. Changes made to The Dicker: the two billiard-room classrooms become a girls' dormitory. Propane gas storage tanks installed beside concrete road near Aviary.

October: 22 acres of farm fields purchased (£31,000) from Mrs Philpot of Parkwood Farm; these fields are opposite the Stud House and adjacent to the village primary school (Park Mead) and now include football pitches and golf practice holes.

1982

March: Drainage of new Stud playing fields.

June/July/August: Five Dorter chalets built to rear of Dorms house.

Student recreational common room for boarders (subsequently from 1983 this became first drama studio/lecture room/room for Sunday Meetings). Orchard classrooms (O1 and O2) built at same time with storage link to recreation room.

Staff common room moves from The Dicker main house to a conversion of part of lodge/unfinished indoor swimming pool (now offices opposite the present staff common room entrance).

Second-hand sectional building purchased (£150). Assembled to rear of Tack House and became maintenance workshop (subsequently second art room and then moved to behind old gym as a further extension of art department when 'new' art department building erected in 1996.

Village hall field rented for first time.

1983

March: Dicker Stud purchased (£140,000). Plans submitted for conversion of stable yard to boarding accommodation.

Camberlot Hall on the market but withdrawn in July as boarding numbers were too high to permit sale.

July-August: Three new tennis courts constructed on land behind lake. Further conversion of Aviary to additional music rooms. Conversion of Stables at Dicker Stud to sixth-form study bedrooms begins.

October: Purchase of small field adjacent to main Stud playing fields (site for many years of cricket nets and horse pasture) from Mr Emery (£4250).

1984

Riding arena (ménage) to east of Stud House (site of subsequent car park and now new boarding house) completed.

Conversion of stable yard at Dicker Stud to sixth-form accommodation for boys of Stud House and girls of Crossways House (Dicker main house renamed Crossways).

New building for changing rooms and lavatory facilities built behind stable block on main school site.

Completion of conversion of Aviary for music department.

Creation of flat for housemistress in Crossways House (formerly Mrs Bottomley's bedroom, boys' dormitory, staff common room and now offices).

Agreement for school's use of village cricket ground commences.

1985

First request for masterplan of school's development and a Section 52 Agreement from Wealden Council.

Maintenance and grounds and gardens departments moved to Chicken House at Dicker Stud.

1986

Discussions regarding potential purchase of Ben Wise's scrap yard in Camberlot Road on-going.

Proposal to sell Camberlot Hall surfaces again: put on market for £300,000.

Negotiations re exchange of land with Mr O'Driscoll begin (land adjacent to Dicker Stud property, on which multi-purpose sports hall and riding stables now partially stand).

1987

Section 52 Agreement (now called a Section 106 Agreement) with Wealden Council completed allowing substantial development of school's land for educational purposes.

Granary building at Dicker Stud converted to housemaster's accommodation.

Shared equity purchase with T. Murphy of bungalow known as Fairlands in Coldharbour Road, Upper Dicker.

Kennels at The Dicker changed in use to pottery.

Kitchens extended and new washing-up facility installed.

Twelve new classrooms opened: nine are fabricated in Chicken House and erected in former orchard to rear of Tack House continuing the development of O1 and O2 along the concrete road, and three are Portacabins and conversion of Kennels.

1988

Plans for additional boarding house next to Stud House granted planning approval but not pursued.

Proposed sale of Camberlot Hall to Mr Cullen falls through and Camberlot Hall taken off market once more.

Shared equity schemes involving Shalome (now deputy head's house) and Numbers One and Two Coopers Cottages (properties in village) commenced.
Exchange and partial purchase of land with Mr O'Driscoll completed. (See above)
First drama studio created.
Aviary extended by addition of a second floor to provide additional space for music department.
Fifth science laboratory created.
Plans for new library and staff common room drawn up.
Indoor archery range created in Chicken House.

1989
Work on building to house new library, staff common room and sixth-form common room and additional office space and classrooms commences.
Number Six Stud Cottages purchased (£90,000). Used for staff and student overflow.

1990
Number Four Stud Cottages purchased (£70,000).
Building of new library proceeds.
Site hut to rear of Tack House becomes additional art room (now moved to rear of old gym).
Numbers Four and Six Stud Cottages let out as teaching staff accommodation, as were Numbers One and Two Coopers Cottages (now wholly owned by school).

1991
Village shop, including Providence House, purchased (£240,000).
Number Three Stud cottages purchased (£65,000).
New sixth-form common room section of library building opened.

1992
January: new staff common room section of library building opened.
Day students' house extended into former staff common room.
Three further tennis courts built in area behind lake.
Crossways House flat extended into old library.
April: New library opened for use but officially opened in July by Lord Lieutenant of East Sussex.
Golf practice course made.
Plans for new 25-metre swimming pool, squash courts and fitness centre on land at Dicker Stud submitted and approved.

1993
Field next to Dicker Stud (now site of astroturf and school cricket ground) purchased (£20,000).
Providence House (village shop house) converted to staff accommodation.

Number One Stud Cottages and adjoining plot (now two staff houses) purchased (£120,000).
Cedars (now offices on corner opposite Stud Cottages) purchased (£105,000). Initially used as housing and rented to Herbie Wodehouse, the estates bursar.
Fairlands and Numbers One and Two Coopers Cottages placed on market.

1994
Swimming pool completed, initially as outdoor pool with temporary changing rooms.
Day House (now finance offices) extended by addition of a second floor and of additional space to rear.
Number One Coopers Cottages sold. Fairlands sold.
Steel frame for covering and completing swimming pool, squash courts and fitness suite erected.

1995
Number Two Coopers Cottages sold.
Swimming pool covered.
Two new Dorter house chalets built.
Five new (prefabricated in Chicken House) classrooms built down extended concrete road.
Granary at Stud House extended.

1996
New two-storey art building erected by the Old Gym (notable for felt roof purporting to be red tiles!).
All six Stud Cottages now purchased with the acquisition of Numbers Two and Five (£75,000 and £80,000 respectively).
Fairfield (now Dorms House staff house) purchased (£179,000).
Plans submitted to turn the six Stud Cottages into a boarding house; this to be the New Dorms and to release the original prefabricated Dorms to be teaching rooms, a girls' day house and some boarding accommodation for Dorter girls.

1997
New home economics (now food technology) department created, by extending building behind Stables at Dicker site.
School kitchens extended into former home economics room.
Swimming pool, squash courts and fitness gymnasia completed and furnished.
Stud Cottages converted into new Dorms House for 65 boys and opened in September (costs £700,000 including costs of cottages, land and furnishing – a testimony to doing our own building!).
Plans for new riding stables and ménage made.
Plans for new science laboratory building (on play area between Aviary and Stable block) made. Plan to move play area to riding ménage next to Stud House made.

1998
Building of two staff houses on garden of Number One Stud Cottages completed.
Planning consents received for new science building and full sized astroturf pitch.

1999
New stables for riding school and new ménage completed.
All-weather astroturf pitch constructed.
New building for archery and school shop on site of old Dicker Stud barns and part of Fairfield garden being constructed.
Malvern House (former vicarage next to village cricket ground) purchased (£400,000).
New laboratories and information technology rooms being built.

2000
Archery and school shop building completed.
New building for grounds and gardens staff and equipment built to east of swimming pool.
New science, information technology and lecture room building completed.
Fifty acres of land from Stud Fields to River Cuckmere at Michelham Bridge purchased from Michael Piper (mainly let to Parkwood Farm but also now paddocks for riding school horses).
Front quad by main entrance being cleared of all cedar-clad laboratories and teaching rooms.
New netball courts being constructed by archery/school shop building (these have now disappeared under new boarding houses).

2001
Building of new classrooms, two houses for day boys, and food technology teaching rooms on land to right of main entrance (now known as Perrin Building) is in progress. Perrin Building opened 2002.
New workshop for technology to rear of stable block (S Rooms) created.
Purchase of Wise Motors site, with planning permission for ten houses completed (£650,000).
Two houses next to Wise Motors land, known as Amaryllis and Mrs Northey's, both purchased to increase the size of Wise Motors/Cedars site, with a view to further potential development. These houses used for staff and student overflow accommodation (£220,000).

APPENDIX 3

HOUSES AND HOUSE STAFF

BOARDING HOUSES

21 DARLEY ROAD
1978-79   Stephen Barnes

THE DICKER (boys and girls)
1979-80   Roger Perrin

ROOS HOUSE
1980-81   Johann Roos

DORMS HOUSE
1981-82   Roger Moses
1982-84   Dennis Gibson
1984-85   Nigel Addison
1985-89   David Miles
1989-96   David Graham
1996-99   Andrew Short
1999-2000   Philip Trenaman
2000-   Simon Gough

CAMBERLOT HALL
1981-83   Derek Newton
1983-85   Douglas Pye
1983-87   Walter Dudley
1987-90   Cedric Wildblood
1990-93   Stephen Pollard
1993-98   Mark Rimmington
1998-   Nigel Hatton

CROSSWAYS HOUSE
1980-81   Gillian Northey
1981-82   Phoebe Gibson
1983-85   Gay Bolton
1985-88:   Jo Gialanze
1988-90   Angela Pollard
1990-95   Lillianne Hadley-Coates
1995-98   Oonagh Colton
1998-2001   Penny Barclay

STUD HOUSE
1983-   Derek Newton

DORTER HOUSE
1984-87   Peter Whitby
1987-   Lou Belhriti

DAY HOUSES

DICKER HOUSE
1979-80   Roger Perrin
1980-83   Bruce Jefferson
1983-84   Nigel Addison
1984-87   Michael Taylor
1987-88   Michael Taylor
            and John Berryman
1988-89   Dicker House divided
            into two houses for
            one year:
Downs House   Keith Gibson
Weald House   Terry Murphy
1989-1992   Andrew Barclay
1992-94   Stephen Waters
1994-95   Sally Wellings
1995-97   Lillianne Hadley-Coates

1997 Dicker House split into Dicker
Girls and Dicker Boys

DICKER GIRLS
1997-2001   Sally Wellings

DICKER BOYS
1997-99   Philip Trenaman
1999-   Giles Perrin

Dicker Boys has from 2001 been
sub-divided into Dicker Deis and
Dicker Knights

APPENDIX 4

SCHOOL GOVERNORS

1978-1980 - FOUNDING BOARD
D.F. Martin-Jenkins (Chair),
J.E. Hawkins, T.G.L. Ford, Professor
M.W. Thompson, D.O. Baker,
A.C.S. Hawkins, P. Pyemont

1980-81
JOINED: A.C. Gottleib, J.B. Winter,
Rt Rev. Peter Ball (Bishop of Lewes),
R.D. Peverett
LEFT: J.E. Hawkins (deceased),
D.F. Martin-Jenkins (resigned and
made President)

At beginning of school year 1980-81
J.E. Hawkins became Chair and after
his death D.O. Baker was elected Chair.

1981-82
JOINED: J.R. Brewer
LEFT: T.G.L. Ford (resigned)

1982-83
JOINED: Lady Cara Hampden
LEFT: Professor M.W. Thompson
(resigned), Rt Rev. Peter Ball

1983-84:
JOINED: Mrs S.E. Mackenzie
LEFT: A.C.S. Hawkins (resigned),
J.B. Winter (resigned)

1984-85
JOINED: P.D. Herbert
LEFT: P.D. Herbert

1985-86
No changes

1986-87
JOINED: Hon. Rosemary Legh (later
Lady Newton), A. Mays-Smith,
J.A. Sellick
LEFT: R.D. Peverett (resigned).

1987-88
LEFT: Mrs S.E. Mackenzie (resigned).

Governors at beginning of the 1988-89
school year, ten years after the school's
foundation were:
D.O. Baker (Chair),
Lady Hampden (Deputy Chair),
P. Pyemont, A.C. Gottleib,
Hon. Rosemary Legh, J.R. Brewer,
A. Mays-Smith, J.A. Sellick

1988-89
JOINED: Mrs J. Cameron

1989-99
No changes

1990-91
JOINED: D. Summers
LEFT: Lady Hampden (resigned)

Hon. Rosemary Legh is elected
Deputy Chair.

1991-96
No changes

1996-97
LEFT: J.R. Brewer (deceased)

1997-99
No changes

1999
Amalgamation with St Bede's School
Trust, Eastbourne

JOINED: A.L. Meier, K. Edwards,
M. Griffiths, Mrs J. Lucas and
T. Martin-Jenkins

2001
JOINED: D. Troy

APPENDIX 5

CLERKS TO THE GOVERNORS

1978-85	S.E. Penhallow
1985-89	W. Pritchard
1987-95	Mrs N. Rayment
1995-	Mrs Patricia Russell

APPENDIX 6

BURSARS/FINANCE OFFICERS

1978-80	Lieutenant Colonel O.P. Keef
1980-82	Wing Commander J. Granville-White
1983-84	Lieutenant Colonel R. Smith
1984-92	Dennis Butler
1992-	Mrs Patricia Russell

APPENDIX 7

CATERING MANAGERS

1979-81	Brian Ayres
1982-85	Grand Metropolitan Services
1985-88	Brian McClellan-Dunn
1988-	Michael Wallis

MAINTENANCE/BUILDING MANAGERS

1979-81	Peter Howard
1982-93	Eric Rogers
1993-95	Dennis Bradford
1995-	Shaun Pantry

HEAD GROUNDSMEN

1979-81	Peter Spiers
1981-84	Peter Walters
1984-86	Bill Manley
1986-88	Brian Wauchope
1988-91	No head groundsman
1991-	Leigh Bennett

ARCHITECTS

1980-83	Tony Brand
1983-84	John Innerdale
1984-2001	Richard Hudson

APPENDIX 8

MAXIMUM STUDENT NUMBERS IN YEAR
(boarders shown in brackets)

1978-79	23 (15)	1990-91	340 (249)
1979-80	78 (43)	1991-92	352 (262)
1980-81	160 (98)	1992-93	355 (261)
1981-82	221 (167)	1993-94	392 (269)
1982-83	227 (183)	1994-95	414 (273)
1983-84	261 (211)	1995-96	458 (279)
1984-85	308 (248)	1996-97	481 (302)
1985-86	299 (244)	1997-98	501 (295)
1986-87	320 (239)	1998-99	542 (306)
1987-88	341 (248)	1999-2000	559 (307)
1988-89	325 (245)	2000-01	579 (310)
1989-90	333 (264)	Sept 2001	612 (315)

APPENDIX 9

ANNUAL FINANCIAL RESULTS
(deficits shown in brackets)

1978-79	attached to prep school	1990-91	£80,397
1979-80	(£2325)	1991-92	£305,255
1980-81	£50,615	1992-93	£429,637
1981-82	£62,265	1993-94	£585,692
1982-83	£69,302	1994-95	£587,685
1983-84	£23,261	1995-96	£862,000
1984-85	£102,819	1996-97	£862,356
1985-86	£49,280	1997-98	£757,870
1986-87	£89,442	1998-99	£957,851
1987-88	(£892)	1999-2000	£1,118,000
1988-89	(£48,472)	2000-01	£977,481
1989-90	£4,664		

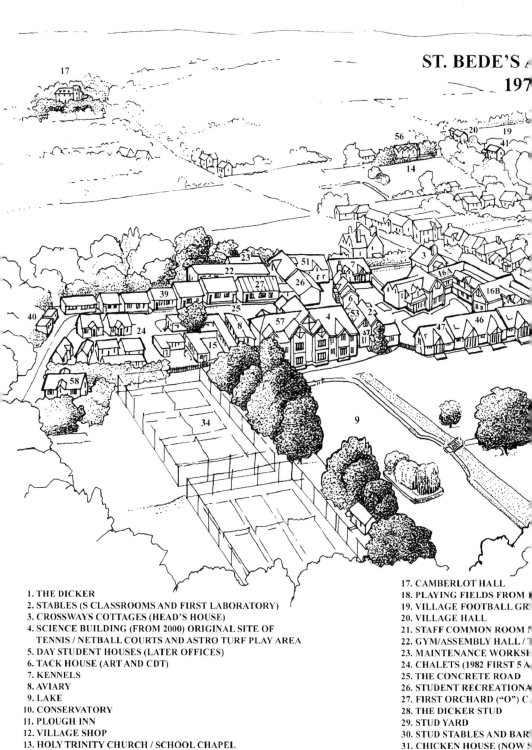

1. THE DICKER
2. STABLES (S CLASSROOMS AND FIRST LABORATORY)
3. CROSSWAYS COTTAGES (HEAD'S HOUSE)
4. SCIENCE BUILDING (FROM 2000) ORIGINAL SITE OF
   TENNIS / NETBALL COURTS AND ASTRO TURF PLAY AREA
5. DAY STUDENT HOUSES (LATER OFFICES)
6. TACK HOUSE (ART AND CDT)
7. KENNELS
8. AVIARY
9. LAKE
10. CONSERVATORY
11. PLOUGH INN
12. VILLAGE SHOP
13. HOLY TRINITY CHURCH / SCHOOL CHAPEL
14. VILLAGE CRICKET GROUND
15. PRESCO BUILDINGS: DORMS HOUSE 1980 – 1997, DORTER HOUSE 1984 …
16A. PERRIN BUILDING SITE OF ORIGINAL SECOND HAND PREFABRICATED
      CLASSROOMS AND LABORATORIES
16B. N ("NEW') BLOCK: MORE PREFABRICATED CLASSROOMS.
      CAMBERLOT PORTACABIN

17. CAMBERLOT HALL
18. PLAYING FIELDS FROM
19. VILLAGE FOOTBALL GR
20. VILLAGE HALL
21. STAFF COMMON ROOM
22. GYM/ASSEMBLY HALL / T
23. MAINTENANCE WORKSH
24. CHALETS (1982 FIRST 5 A
25. THE CONCRETE ROAD
26. STUDENT RECREATIONA
27. FIRST ORCHARD ("O") C,
28. THE DICKER STUD
29. STUD YARD
30. STUD STABLES AND BAR
31. CHICKEN HOUSE (NOW S
32. STUD FIELD (NOW CAR F
33. CROSS COUNTRY RIDIN(
34. TENNIS COURTS (1983); B
35. RIDING MÉNAGE 1984 (2(
36. CRICKET NETS AND HOF
37. CHANGING ROOMS